# The American Crisis Series
# Books on the Civil War Era

*Steven E. Woodworth, Associate Professor of History,*
*Texas Christian University*
Series Editor

James L. Abrahamson. *The Men of Secession and Civil War, 1859–1861.*

Robert G. Tanner. *Retreat to Victory? Confederate Strategy Reconsidered.*

Stephen Davis. *Atlanta Will Fall: Sherman, Joe Johnston, and the Yankee Heavy Battalions.*

Paul Ashdown and Edward Caudill. *The Mosby Myth: A Confederate Hero in Life and Legend.*

Spencer C. Tucker. *A Short History of the Civil War at Sea.*

Richard Bruce Winders. *Crisis in the Southwest: The United States, Mexico, and the Struggle over Texas.*

Ethan S. Rafuse. *A Single Grand Victory: The First Campaign and Battle of Manassas.*

John G. Selby. *Virginians at War: The Civil War Experiences of Seven Young Confederates.*

Edward K. Spann. *Gotham at War: New York City, 1860–1865.*

Anne J. Bailey. *War and Ruin: William T. Sherman and the Savannah Campaign.*

Gary Dillard Joiner. *One Damn Blunder from Beginning to End: The Red River Campaign of 1864.*

Steven E. Woodworth. *Beneath a Northern Sky: A Short History of the Gettysburg Campaign.*

John C. Waugh. *On the Brink of Civil War: The Compromise of 1850 and How It Changed the Course of American History.*

Eric H. Walther. *The Shattering of the Union: America in the 1850s.*

Mark Thornton and Robert B. Ekelund Jr. *Tariffs, Blockades, and Inflation: The Economics of the Civil War.*

Paul Ashdown and Edward Caudill. *The Myth of Nathan Bedford Forrest.*

Michael B. Ballard. *U. S. Grant: The Making of a General, 1861–1863.*

David Coffey. *Sheridan's Lieutenants: Phil Sheridan, His Generals, and the Final Year off the Civil War.*

# SHERIDAN'S LIEUTENANTS

# SHERIDAN'S LIEUTENANTS

## PHIL SHERIDAN, HIS GENERALS, AND THE FINAL YEAR OF THE CIVIL WAR

### DAVID COFFEY

ROWMAN AND LITTLEFIELD PUBLISHERS, INC.

*Lanham • Boulder • New York • Toronto • Oxford*

CPL

ROWMAN & LITTLEFIELD PUBLISHERS, INC.

Published in the United States of America
by Rowman & Littlefield Publishers, Inc.
A wholly owned subsidiary of The Rowman & Littlefield Publishing Group, Inc.
4501 Forbes Boulevard, Suite 200, Lanham, MD 20706
www.rowmanlittlefield.com

P.O. Box 317, Oxford OX2 9RU, UK

Distributed by NATIONAL BOOK NETWORK

British Library Cataloguing in Publication Information Available

**Library of Congress Cataloging-in-Publication Data**


Coffey, David, 1960–
 Sheridan's lieutenants : Phil Sheridan, his generals, and the final year of the Civil War /
David Coffey.
  p. cm.
Includes bibliographical references and index.
ISBN 0-7425-4306-4 (cloth : alk. paper)
 1. Sheridan, Philip Henry, 1831–1888—Military leadership.  2. Sheridan, Philip Henry,
1831–1888—Friends and associates.  3. United States. Army—Biography.
4. Generals—United States—Biography.  5. Command of troops—Case studies.
6. United States—History—Civil War, 1861–1865—Campaigns.  I. Title.  II. Series:
The American crisis series; no. 18.

E467.1.S54 C65 2005
973.7′3′092 B 22

                                                                              2004002490
Printed in the United States of America

For Katie Lee Adkins

And Always—In Memory of My Parents

# Contents

# Illustrations

# Maps

Maps by mapsmith, etc . . . Fort Worth, Texas (817) 370-8972

# Preface

*E*ver since the Civil War ended, historians and other interested observers have argued the finer points of victory and defeat, usually focusing on battles won and lost. Yet never has there been a true consensus when it comes to selecting *the* decisive event. Certainly Gettysburg receives much attention in this regard, but what about Vicksburg or Chattanooga? A case can be made for a good many battles from Fort Donelson to Nashville. On the other hand, one might argue that the Civil War produced no single decisive battle. Indeed, many of the war's most important, even decisive, events took place far removed from the fighting—in the government offices of Washington and Richmond, where mortal men made life and death decisions. Before battles could be fought, leaders had to be selected, and it was this process—the choice of leaders—perhaps more than any other single aspect of the war, that proved truly decisive.

Without a doubt, both the Union and the Confederacy suffered from poor or unfortunate choices in command personnel, and both sides profited from wise or fortuitous selections. The subjective nature of such appointments complicated matters. Presidents Abraham Lincoln and Jefferson Davis, along with their advisers, made command appointments based on perceived or demonstrated ability, political considerations, and personal loyalties, and they could be swayed by the machinations of the various candidates or by individual prejudices, petty vendettas, and outrageous egos. The importance of these decisions, though, is often lost to the more stirring events of the battlefield. But the two cannot be separated. The selection of Civil War leaders truly defined the war and has provided myriad what-ifs ever since.

For example, Robert E. Lee was not President Davis's first choice to command Confederate forces in Northern Virginia; Joseph E. Johnston was. And had Johnston not been wounded at Seven Pines in the spring of 1862, the war most definitely would have progressed differently. Davis, confronted with Lee's audacious genius, had the good sense to retain him once Johnston recovered from his wounds. Conversely, Davis's loyalty to friends such as Braxton Bragg and Leonidas Polk proved costly if not devastating for the Confederacy. On the

Union side, Lincoln, compelled by the realities of making war in a democracy, appointed numerous politicians (and officers with mighty political backing) to high commands. One can only imagine what benefits the Union might have realized had the lofty positions occupied by Benjamin Butler, John C. Frémont, or Nathaniel P. Banks been filled with proven soldiers. Again, the course of the war likely would have been much different.

Frequently, Lincoln and Davis, both very much hands-on commanders in chief, had the opportunity to reverse initial decisions, and both men learned from earlier mistakes. Still, they found it necessary to tamper repeatedly with the leadership of their major armies in the field. Troubled by the Army of the Potomac's lack of success, Lincoln employed six different commanders (including the brief tenure of John Pope and his short-lived Army of Virginia) until George Gordon Meade won his unlikely debut at Gettysburg. In search of the winning combination, an exasperated Lincoln relieved the popular but underachieving George McClellan twice, for which he received much criticism. Davis faced a most similar situation with Joe Johnston, whom he quite justifiably pulled from command and replaced with John Bell Hood during the Atlanta Campaign of 1864—a decision popular Civil War writer Bruce Catton nonetheless rated "probably the single largest mistake either government made during the war." Johnston, more so than McClellan, managed to perpetuate the myth of his military ability to the extent that he emerged from the war highly esteemed by Southerners but having done little to earn such standing. Sometimes the presidents could not win for losing.[1]

Complicating decisions for the presidents and their advisers, at least early in the war, was the fact that they had little to go on, and much of what they had in the way of information did not always help. Lincoln and Davis could consider such attributes as a West Point education, Mexican War experience, regular army service, and political connections. Davis, a West Point man and proud Mexican War veteran himself, put great stock in such experience and also valued personal friendship to perhaps an unhealthy degree. Historians have long considered a West Point education and Mexican War experience important ingredients for Civil War success. But, in truth, neither guaranteed it. In fact, by the outbreak of the Civil War, only a few active officers had commanded a full regiment; fewer still had commanded anything larger. Surviving division commanders from the Mexican War—Gideon Pillow and Sterling Price—offered plenty of proof that Mexican War experience did not a great officer make. A West Point education was no guarantee of martial competence either. And one's standing in the regular army meant next to nothing when it came to commanding a large force in a conventional battle. Most officers had acquired the bulk of their military experience on the frontier, fighting Indians. Many high-ranking officers had filled staff positions for much of their careers, yet they had access to decision makers or could rely on the army's seniority system when courting a Civil War command. Lincoln found his options limited by the resignations of dozens of prominent officers following the secessions of their respective states. This helps, somewhat, to explain how Irvin McDowell, a career staff officer with no real combat experience, came to command the Federal army in the First Battle of Bull Run.

At the bottom line was the sad truth that America was not prepared to fight a major war. Not a single man in America—North or South—was prepared realistically to command a regular infantry division, much less a corps or an army. Even such vaunted veterans as Lee and Albert Sidney Johnston had comparatively little experience in command. The Civil War, of course, would be for Americans a war like none other. It was unimaginable. So, previous experience might help, but it was no guarantee of success. Youthful enthusiasm and raw physical courage, in this eventuality, became just as valuable. The charge for Lincoln and Davis, then, became not to rely on experience and education but to cultivate leadership talent within the crucible of war—to find or create leaders for this completely new challenge. In this way the Civil War brought a number of unlikely heroes to the forefront, nonprofessionals like Joshua Lawrence Chamberlain, John Brown Gordon, Wade Hampton, Nelson A. Miles, and Nathan Bedford Forrest to name but a few. High attrition throughout the war ensured that there would be plenty of opportunities to find new leaders.

None of this fully explains the rise of Ulysses S. Grant, and with him those of William T. Sherman and Philip H. Sheridan—the great triumvirate of Union victory. Some men are simply good at war; others thrive in combination with dynamic collaborators, military and political. These men bore out these truths. And no one could have imagined it. The Civil War gave Grant a last opportunity to salvage his life, and he made the most of it with a series of Western Theater victories that kept the Federal war effort viable while it foundered in the East. But Lincoln deserves credit for fueling the Grant war machine with the two most significant, if not decisive, moves of the war. The first was to retain Grant after his embarrassing loss-turned-victory at Shiloh, when the president responded to calls for Grant's head, "I can't spare this man; he fights." The second great move on Lincoln's part was to bring Grant, fresh off a stunning victory at Chattanooga, to Washington, where he received promotion to the newly authorized rank of lieutenant general and overall command of the armies of the United States.[2]

Grant made the third and fourth most important personnel dispositions of the war when he pegged his loyal friend Sherman to command in the West and summoned little Philip Sheridan to lead the cavalry of the Army of the Potomac. Grant made other momentous decisions during the final year of the war, but once he turned loose Sherman and Sheridan the war assumed a new attitude, and the Federal armies both East and West applied the irresistible force the Union needed to finish the Confederacy.

Just as Lincoln protected and cultivated Grant, Grant protected and cultivated Sherman and Sheridan, not always to the good of the cause. Once in charge of their own armies, Sherman and Sheridan began to cultivate their own cadre of special subordinates, upon whom they would rely to carry the Union to ultimate triumph.

This, then, is the story of Sheridan and his chief subordinates, his favorites, during the final year of the war. Among Sheridan's lieutenants one could find many similarities—audacity, physical courage, inventiveness, and inexplicable talent. Sheridan, an excellent judge of talent, made it a healthy habit to surround himself with men who could deliver glory and victory. He found men who, like himself, had risen through the ranks on merit, from out of nowhere, men who would fight with the relentlessness that he expected. Although these men shared certain traits, they were very much individuals. Together, they directed the most potent fighting force during the war's final year and went on to influence the army into the twentieth century; individually, they amassed remarkable service records while becoming some of the most significant soldiers in American history.

During the final year of the Civil War, thirty-three-year-old Phil Sheridan emerged from relative obscurity (and a potentially career-ending fiasco at Chickamauga) to become Grant's chief instrument of destruction in Virginia. He led the troops who defeated and killed fabled Rebel cavalryman James Ewell Brown "Jeb" Stuart; he directed the Union effort to clear the all-important Shenandoah Valley of Confederates and then presided over its destruction; he and his hard-charging troopers led the final pursuit of Lee's army. And it was Sheridan's command that cornered Lee at Appomattox. At war's end, Sheridan, now a major general in the regular army, stood third only to Grant and Sherman in public esteem and military stature; he had started the war as a lieutenant.

Of course, he did not accomplish all of this by himself. Along the way dozens of fine officers and thousands of men fought and died for Sheridan and the Union. He inherited a fine instrument in the Cavalry Corps, Army of the Potomac, which had already begun to humble Stuart's revered Rebel horsemen by the time Sheridan arrived in Virginia. The cavalry included a solid core of veteran campaigners—David McMurtrie Gregg, Alfred T. A. Torbert, Henry Davies Jr., John Irvin Gregg, Thomas Devin, George Chapman, and John McIntosh—and a wealth of young brilliance in George Armstrong Custer, Wesley Merritt, and James Harrison Wilson. Sheridan could attribute much of his eventual success to these determined horsemen and their intrepid troopers. When the war moved again to the Shenandoah Valley, Sheridan relied on a host of gifted infantry commanders, many of whom were Sheridan's senior in age and military service, including Horatio Wright, David Russell, George Washington Getty, James Ricketts, William Emory, and Cuvier Grover. From the infantry emerged such bright stars as George Crook, young Emory Upton, and even younger Ranald Slidell Mackenzie, and two future presidents, Rutherford B. Hayes and William McKinley. These men, most of whom toiled in obscurity, contributed mightily to Sheridan's meteoric rise to national prominence and, more important, to the Federal victory in the Civil War.

Little Phil, though, found in the flamboyant twenty-four-year-old Custer and the quietly outstanding twenty-eight-year-old Merritt men who matched his own drive and who could carry out his plans in grand style. When Sheridan took charge of the Middle Military Division, with responsibility for neutralizing the Shenandoah, he added to his assets the talents of his former West Point classmate Crook, who at thirty-six was the old man of Sheridan's favored lieutenants. There in the valley, Sheridan became a national hero in October 1864, with his ride from Winchester to the battlefield at Cedar Creek to turn an embarrassing defeat into a dazzling victory (although in truth his subordinates had the situation well in hand by the time Sheridan arrived). There, too, he discovered yet another brilliant young leader in twenty-four-year-old Ranald Mackenzie, just two years out of the academy and already five times wounded when he rallied his regiment to share in the final assault that won the day at Cedar Creek. These four, particularly, along with their chief, not only played major roles in the closing stages of the Civil War but went on, as Indian fighters and agents of expansion, to become some of the most prolific warriors in American history.

Few soldiers have had a greater impact on American military history over such a long period of time than did Phil Sheridan. He played an undeniably pivotal role in the closing stages of the Civil War, which brought him into the upper echelon of the army's command structure. For twenty years, as a regional commander and as commanding general, he was the chief prosecutor of the Indian Wars in the West. Among the five most prominent instruments of that prosecution, four—Crook, Custer, Mackenzie, and Merritt (Nelson Miles being the fifth)—owed their postwar careers, in large measure, to service under Sheridan in 1864 and 1865. And Sheridan's impact continued after his death in 1888. In 1890 his Civil War chief of staff James Forsyth commanded the 7th Cavalry in the regrettable Battle of Wounded Knee, and in 1898, Wesley Merritt led the ground troops that took Manila during the Spanish-American War. It is, therefore, useful to examine the genesis of the martial brotherhood that dominated the American military establishment for almost forty years.

# Acknowledgments

$\mathcal{T}$he inspiration to write about Phil Sheridan and his lieutenants during the last year of the Civil War came from my long-term fascination with the U.S. Army of the post–Civil War era. Growing up in Texas, I became enamored of the frontier army, and I possessed a lively curiousity about George Armstrong Custer—more I think for his long hair than for his martial prowess (it was the 1960s after all). As an adult I spent hours driving from old fort to old fort and battle site to battle site with my dad. My interests came to include the Buffalo Soldiers of the 9th and 10th Cavalries and the man most identified with the frontier army in Texas—Ranald Slidell Mackenzie. Mackenzie's was a great and tragic story that had languished in obscurity while, it seemed, a new book on Custer came out every year. Mackenzie's elite 4th Cavalry never got the attention that Custer's dysfunctional 7th Cavalry received, but the folks who wrote about the era—Ernest Wallace and Robert Utley among them—understood. My interest in Mackenzie led me to George Crook and Wesley Merritt and Ben Grierson and Nelson Miles. These men all had something in common: they came to prominence during the Civil War. Custer, Mackenzie, Crook, and Merritt had the additional connection of serving under Phil Sheridan in the final year of the Civil War. But, except for Custer, little scholarly attention has been devoted to these officers.

When I went to graduate school at Texas Christian University, I wanted to write a biography of Ranald Mackenzie. In fact, my first seminar paper covered Mackenzie's Civil War career. I'll always be thankful for that seminar, even though my plans crumbled that same year when Michael Pierce published his excellent treatment of the enigmatic soldier. But the desire to explore the Civil War as the genesis of the modern army, particularly as it pertained to those officers who fought with Sheridan, remained very much alive. When my friend Steven E. Woodworth contacted me about contributing a volume to his new American Crisis series, I jumped at the chance to tell the story of Sheridan's lieutenants. Unfortunately, my jump got squashed under a ton of other commitments and unexpected setbacks. Matthew Hershey, my original editor, graciously extended my deadline time and again. Steve and Matt have my deepest appreciation for giving me a chance to do this book.

My research on this subject began a long time back and included work in the National Archives, the Library of Congress, and the U.S. Army Military History Institute (USAMHI), Carlisle Barracks, Pennsylvania. Thanks to the great staffs of these wonderful institutions, especially to Richard Sommers of the USAMHI, who long ago took the time to talk with me about the research prospects of this topic and offered excellent advice in the process.

Many thanks to my friends and colleagues in the Department of History and Philosophy at the University of Tennessee at Martin (UTM), especially administrative secretary Susan Waterfield for all she does to make my life easier and former chair Marvin Downing. Thanks also to Steve Rogers and the excellent staff of UTM's Paul Meek Library, and to Dean Jerald Ogg of the College of Humanities and Fine Arts for his support. UTM students and friends Patrick Nesbit, Melanie Rea, Tony Warmath, and Donnie Winningham provided valuable assistance.

My deepest gratitude goes out to a number of colleagues and friends for their assistance, support, encouragement, or inspiration: Brandon Polk, Joe and Alice Specht, Marty and Pat Cipolla, Sally Utech, Jake Moore, Daniel Price, Tom and Carrie Mays, Stephanie Paris, Richard and Semone Deibert, Greg and Renee Scheinbart, Kathleen Bruton, Gene and Tracy Smith (Tracy produced the fine maps that accompany this narrative), and Catherine Grove.

I truly appreciate my far-flung family—siblings, cousins, nieces and nephews, uncles, and Aunt Jane, official and unofficial—for all the support and encouragement they have given me over the years. I wish especially to thank my brother Kevin; his wife, Tracie; the kids, Callum, Holly, and Rory; and my new pals in Stromness, Orkney, Scotland, for their recent hospitality. Many Orcadians are interested in the American West and particularly in George Armstrong Custer, whom some claim as their own. Thanks to Colin "Pucka" Kirkpatrick for explaining the Custer-Orkney connection over several pints in the Stromness Hotel pub. I could not help identify Custer with Orkney, but I vowed to explore the possibilities.

I dedicate this book to Katie Lee Adkins of Fort Worth, Texas, a fine woman who worked for my grandparents and then for my parents over five decades. I passed much of my childhood in her care, and it was time well spent. I am a better person for knowing her; and for that and years of friendship I am truly thankful.

Years after their deaths my parents continue to inspire me. I am ever grateful for the opportunities they provided, their wisdom, and their example, and for the wonderful way they lived their lives, which made my life all the more rich.

# Introduction: "Little Phil"

*I*n March 1864, Americans on both sides of the conflict braced for a fourth spring of bloodletting in this most uncivil of wars. Back in 1861 few people North or South thought the war would last long; now many wondered if it ever would end. Despite major victories at Gettysburg, Vicksburg, and Chattanooga the previous year, Federal forces had failed to deliver the final blow, and Confederate troops showed no inclination to give up. Certainly, the Union victories of 1863 devastated the hard-pressed Confederacy, virtually eliminating the chance of foreign intervention or an outright military victory. But as long as Southern armies remained in the field the war would continue. The dearly won triumphs also failed to quiet unrest in the North as momentum continued to build for a negotiated peace.

It was inconvenient for the Federal war effort that 1864 was an election year. Northern Democrats, soon to back ousted Major General George B. McClellan, angled for a settlement that would end the carnage—a settlement that promised to leave President Abraham Lincoln's goal of restoring the Union unfulfilled. Lincoln, who believed his days as president were numbered, resolved to do everything in his power to win the war during the time he had left or, in the worst case, work with the incoming president to see the job completed.

To achieve ultimate victory within the time remaining, Lincoln needed a military commander who shared his vision and also possessed the ability to win battles in the field. Throughout the war, Lincoln had placed his faith and the armies of the United States in the hands of dozens of men—McClellan, John Pope, Ambrose Burnside, Joseph Hooker, Henry Halleck, Don Carlos Buell, and William S. Rosecrans to name but a few—all of whom he found wanting in drive and, most important, in success. Even George Meade, who commanded at Gettysburg, had ultimately disappointed. By the end of 1863, Lincoln knew of only one man who had delivered consistently the kind of performance the president needed so desperately to see—Ulysses S. Grant.

Of all the improbable rises to military prominence during the Civil War, U. S. Grant's was among the more astonishing. So it seemed. But Grant, who

*General Ulysses S. Grant. Courtesy of the National Archives*

failed at most everything he attempted in civilian life, excelled at war. He rose from obscurity early in the conflict by capturing Confederate Fort Donelson and opening the South to invasion. He escaped disaster at Shiloh only to rebound and win a momentous victory, after which accusations of incompetence and alcoholism threatened to derail his career. Lincoln, though, in the spring of 1862, saw something in Grant that he found lacking in his other generals—he would fight. Grant showed exceptional determination and resourcefulness in conquering the Mississippi River bastion of Vicksburg, which split the Confederacy, and went on to take the vital railroad center of Chattanooga, Tennessee, in one of the most amazing battles of the war. If the Union possessed a savior, it was surely Grant.

On February 26, 1864, with Grant clearly in mind, the U.S. Senate passed an act to revive the rank of lieutenant general, last held by George Washington. Lincoln signed the act three days later, and on March 1, he nominated Grant, whom the Senate quickly confirmed at the new grade. The always understated Grant traveled to Washington to receive his commission at a subdued White House ceremony. On March 10 he assumed overall command of the armies of the United States. It was Grant's war now, and he immediately set in motion his plan to win it.[1]

Even as overall commander, Grant had no desire to lead from a desk in Washington. In fact, he intended to remain with the Western armies, with which he had won his new position, and leave the recently victorious but much-maligned Army of the Potomac under Major General Meade. After assessing the situation in Virginia, however, Grant decided that he should conduct the war from the high-profile Eastern Theater. He planned to retain Meade as titular commander of the Army of the Potomac, but Grant would be calling the shots once the army moved against the damaged but still deadly Confederate Army of Northern Virginia and its now-legendary General Robert E. Lee. Finally, the war's two most successful generals would duel it out over the saturated fields of Virginia. To fill his place in the West, Grant turned to his friend and longtime subordinate Major General William T. Sherman. While Grant directed the campaign against Lee, Sherman would march against the Confederate Army of Tennessee under the popular but timid General Joseph E. Johnston in Georgia. Meade and Sherman, as well as the other Federal field commanders, were to pursue relentlessly the destruction of Rebel armies rather than geographical objectives. Cities, even the capital at Richmond, could be captured in due time, but as long as the stubborn Southern forces held out, the rebellion would continue.

Grant made other command alterations but mostly left things in place for the time being. Still, he came to Virginia with one specific change in mind. "In one of my early interviews with the President," Grant recalled, "I expressed my dissatisfaction with the little that had been accomplished by the cavalry so far in the war, and the belief that it was capable of accomplishing much more than it had done if under a thorough leader." He wanted "the very best man in the army for that command." Major General Henry Halleck, recently deposed as general in chief and now serving as chief of staff, was present, and offered, "How would Sheridan do?" To which Grant replied, "The very man I want." Apparently, Sheridan was not Grant's first choice, but the mention of the fiery young general struck a note; the decision was made. On March 23, Sheridan, who commanded an infantry division in Tennessee, received orders to report to Washington.[2]

If Grant's rise to national prominence was improbable, that of Philip Henry Sheridan was downright incredible. Five feet five inches tall, bandy-legged, with what was often described as a bullet-shaped head covered with coarse, closely cropped black hair, the son of Irish immigrants presented less than an impressive appearance. His military career prior to the Civil War had been mediocre at best; he was still a second lieutenant the month before Rebel guns fired on Fort Sumter. But the war brought opportunities for men of action, and Sheridan, like Grant, was such a man, all appearances notwithstanding.

The actual date and place of Sheridan's birth went unrecorded. In his *Memoirs*, he claimed to have been born on March 6, 1831, at Albany, New York, although he gave conflicting dates and places throughout his life. His birth could have occurred anywhere between Ireland and Somerset, Ohio, during his parents' long migration. Somerset, where his family eventually settled, became his home. Sheridan experienced a typical small-town upbringing, receiving some education and toiling in a general store to help support the family. Capable, hard working, and honest, he showed promise as a businessman. But the war with Mexico, which began in 1846, brought heady days for young Sheridan. Although too young to enter the fray, he recalled, "the stirring events of the times so much impressed and absorbed me that my sole wish was to become a soldier, and my highest aspiration to go to West Point as a Cadet from my Congressional district." He soon got his wish through a fortunate set of circumstances and in 1848 received an appointment to the U.S. Military Academy.[3]

At West Point, Sheridan struggled with academics, but it was his temper that almost ended his cadet career. He became anything but the stereotypical West Point cadet. Not only was he physically unattractive and of small stature but he also could be combative and profane. And he was unquestionably Irish, which posed a major social and political handicap at that time. In 1851 an altercation with a fellow cadet cost Sheridan a lengthy suspension and prevented him from graduating with his class of 1852, which included his friend and future subordinate George Crook. Once he returned to the academy, Sheridan entered the rather stellar class of 1853, joining studious John M. Schofield, elegant James B. McPherson, who finished at the top of the class, and tall, handsome John Bell Hood. All would lead armies during the Civil War, but doubtless no one projected such a future for "Little Phil." During his final year, Sheridan accumulated almost enough demerits to derail his career again, but he managed to graduate a respectable thirty-fourth in the 1853 class of fifty-two.[4]

Sheridan entered the regular army as a brevet second lieutenant. His class standing mandated an infantry assignment and, as a young officer in an impossibly undermanned service, he endured the hazards of frontier duty at isolated posts such as Fort Duncan on the Rio Grande in Texas and Fort Reading in the Pacific Northwest. He saw action against hostile Indians but mostly suffered the boredom and privation of army life. Advancement in the pre–Civil War army was virtually nonexistent, the pay poor, and the job often thankless. Even as the United States deteriorated under sectional strife, and Indians across the Trans-Mississippi West desperately contested white encroachment, the army remained small, overburdened, and stretched far too thin, and the young officers who remained in the service awaited promotion that seemingly never came. In March 1861, Sheridan was still a second lieutenant. But in April, Southern troops at Charleston, South Carolina, opened fire on defiant Fort Sumter in Charleston Harbor, initiating the long-feared, regrettably inevitable Civil War.

The war brought demands that the old army could never meet, but it provided welcomed opportunities for military advancement for regular officers. America's traditional aversion to a large standing army argued against an expansion of the regular force, so the Federal government created a separate organization to prosecute the war—U.S. Volunteers. The Volunteers required experienced leaders, although initially most of these positions went to nonprofessionals and political appointees. Too, the defection of many prominent Southern officers created some choice openings in the regulars. Sheridan finally saw his career path open a bit, receiving promotion to first lieutenant in March 1861 and to captain in May, yet he remained mired in the lower echelons of the regular ranks as many of his brother officers moved into command positions on both sides of the conflict. Moreover, as fighting erupted in the East, Sheridan stood post in the Northwest, far removed from the action.

In September 1861, Captain Sheridan was ordered to join the new 13th U.S. Infantry at Jefferson Barracks in Missouri. Still at his regular rank, he served ably as chief quartermaster and commissary for the Army of the Southwest, attracting the wrath of fellow officers for his by-the-book management of affairs. Detailed to Major General Henry Halleck's staff during that officer's glacially slow advance on Corinth, Mississippi, which followed the Federal rebound victory at Shiloh, Sheridan continued his supporting role while cherishing a field command.

His industry and zeal did not go unnoticed. State governors needed experienced officers to command Volunteer regiments, and while many considered professionals ill suited to command green volunteers, some looked to the regular ranks to fill command slots, a practice the Federal government facilitated by granting leaves to selected officers. In May 1862, Sheridan entered the Volunteer ranks when the governor of Michigan pegged him for command of the 2nd Michigan Cavalry. For the next four months, Sheridan campaigned in northern Mississippi, acquiring an excellent reputation and a fine black charger he named for the site of a recent engagement—Rienzi. Sheridan's actions in northern Mississippi also brought him to the attention of fellow Ohioan William Tecumseh Sherman and, more important, U. S. Grant, who assumed command of Federal forces in Mississippi when Halleck was called to administrative duty in Washington. In Sherman, Grant, and Halleck, Sheridan found powerful advocates, but for the next thirteen months he would toil far away from their appreciative attention.

That September, Sheridan's command was dispatched to Kentucky to support Federal forces then attempting to turn back an ambitious two-pronged Confederate drive into that state. Upon reaching Louisville, Sheridan learned that his promotion to brigadier general of U.S. Volunteers, requested by his superiors for months, had been approved, to date from July 1. He commanded an infantry division in the indecisive battle at Perryville, Kentucky, in October, and less than two months later, in the wintry slaughter on Stones River near Murfreesboro, Tennessee, he and the division performed superbly. In April 1863 his promotion to major general of Volunteers (to rank from December 31) came through. In less than a year, Sheridan had risen from quartermaster captain to major general, and he was only getting started.

The new year brought little activity; even as the spring fighting season opened, Sheridan and the rest of the Army of the Cumberland, now led by Major General William S. Rosecrans, remained essentially idle in Middle Tennessee. To the south, Grant's Herculean campaign to capture Vicksburg, the last important Rebel bastion on the Mississippi, neared fruition, while back East, Confederate General Lee dealt another crushing defeat to the Federals at Chancellorsville and soon turned his army northward, toward Pennsylvania. Despite heated admonishments from Washington, cautious Rosecrans refused to move until ready. Finally, in late June 1863, with Sheridan's division leading the way, Rosecrans launched a campaign of maneuver that in one week and with remarkably little bloodshed drove General Braxton Bragg's Army of Tennessee out of its Tullahoma stronghold and back on the vital railroad center of Chattanooga. The effort went mostly unnoticed and unappreciated, obscured by the news on July 4 of the dual Federal victories at Vicksburg and Gettysburg.

Attention now turned to Tennessee, where again Rosecrans balked, reluctant to expose his army in the rugged mountains of the region, and again Washington prodded. But patient maneuver had paid off once and would do so again. During the first week of September the Army of the Cumberland converged on Chattanooga in overwhelming force. Bragg yielded the city without a fight, slipping into the fastness of northern Georgia. Sheridan had taken a leading role in one of the most successful campaigns of the war. Despite the late start, the Cumberlanders had driven the Confederacy's primary Western army out of Tennessee, secured Nashville and Chattanooga, and had done so with astonishingly few casualties. But for a war in which casualty figures provided the measure of success, Rosecrans's failure to destroy Bragg's army rendered hollow all that his soldiers had accomplished. The general, therefore, resolved to bring Bragg to battle.

Rosecrans sent his army into Georgia after Bragg, who, along with Confederate leaders in Virginia, conspired to turn on the Federal pursuers with decisive force. Sensing the opportunity to crush a major Federal army, Richmond dispatched most of Lieutenant General James Longstreet's Corps of the Army of Northern Virginia by rail to Georgia to bolster Bragg's forces. The showdown came among the dense thickets along Chickamauga Creek on September 19, with neither side quite prepared for the confused, horribly bloody battle that resulted. The next day, as the Confederate reinforcements from Virginia hit the field, the Federal position quickly grew unmanageable. At this most inopportune moment, Rosecrans lost control of his nerve and his army. An order to shift troops from the Federal right to the more threatened left and center opened a gap on the right just as the Confederates under Sheridan's West Point classmate Major General John Bell Hood attacked, piercing the line. Left isolated by the untimely shift, Sheridan's division broke, joining Rosecrans and much of the army in retreat. Sheridan managed to rally his shattered division in time to join the stubborn defense mounted by Major General George H. Thomas that saved the Army of the Cumberland from total destruction. Thomas's stand at Chickamauga also might have saved Sheridan's career.

The battered Army of the Cumberland withdrew into Chattanooga, pursued lethargically and eventually besieged by Bragg's equally battered Confederates. Although the Federals held the important city, they soon found themselves cut off from supplies, and food grew scarce with winter coming on. Washington ordered reinforcements to the beleaguered army, and in October, Lincoln named Grant commander of the newly organized Military Division of the Mississippi, giving him charge of the situation at Chattanooga. For Rosecrans and two of his corps commanders the war was all but over. For Sheridan it was just beginning.

*General Philip H. Sheridan. Courtesy of the National Archives*

Grant arrived at Chattanooga in late October. Quickly, the besieged Federals opened a supply line into the city, and presently, heavy reinforcements—two infantry corps from the Army of the Potomac under Major General Joseph Hooker with most of Grant's old Army of the Tennessee under Sherman—filed in. Grant also replaced the demoralized Rosecrans with Thomas. All the while the Confederate situation deteriorated. Freezing and hungry, the Rebels lost the fighting advantage won so dearly at Chickamauga, and morale among officers and men plummeted. Widespread resentment of Bragg's leadership threatened mutiny. To make matters worse, Bragg had dispatched Longstreet and his men on a fruitless mission to liberate Knoxville, further thinning the line around Chattanooga. By late November the besieged were in much better shape than were the besiegers.

On November 23, Grant's conglomerate force prepared to drive the Confederates from heights above the city. Under the commander's approving gaze, Sheridan's division and that of Brigadier General T. J. Wood easily drove the Rebels from their advanced position on Orchard Knob, preparatory to an advance against Bragg's center on Missionary Ridge. The following day, Hooker directed an incredible assault on Bragg's right that swept the defenders from supposedly invulnerable Lookout Mountain in the so-called Battle above the

Clouds. On November 25, Sherman's attempt to turn the Confederate left on Missionary Ridge met fierce resistance and bogged down. Hooker's advance on the right was slowed as well. Attention turned to Thomas's Army of the Cumberland in the center. Hoping that an attack on the center would free up the flanks, Grant ordered the Cumberlanders to take the first line of Confederate rifle pits on Missionary Ridge.

To cries of "Remember Chickamauga," the blue line pressed forward with bayonets fixed. Sheridan on horseback led his division with grim determination. Under steady fire, the Federal advance gained the rifle pits, but the men found themselves exposed to a hailstorm of lead from Rebel positions above. As officers sent messages back and forth and pondered the next move, the soldiers took matters into their own hands—they kept moving up the ridge. Sheridan had not ordered the advance; no general had, but to his great good fortune he did not stop it. The Cumberlanders climbed relentlessly up the ridge. Faulty Confederate dispositions now came into play, preventing the kind of heavy volley fire that could buckle the Union assault. Many defenders held their fire for fear of hitting their own retiring soldiers, and Rebel gunners could not depress their artillery tubes enough to make a difference. An anxious Grant, watching events unfold with Thomas on Orchard Knob, angrily demanded to know who ordered the continued advance. Thomas, rather embarrassed, admitted that he had not, nor had the corps commander, Major General Gordon Granger. Grant assured Thomas that if this unauthorized attack failed, someone—likely Thomas himself—would pay.

Of course, no one had issued the order, but Sheridan and his men took full advantage of the moment, driving amazingly to the crest of the ridge and through the Confederate line. With the center pierced, Bragg's position collapsed, putting the ill-used Army of Tennessee to flight. Sheridan's division offered a vigorous pursuit, but darkness and a brilliant Southern rear-guard action allowed Bragg to bring off much of his army, which again sought safety in northern Georgia.

For the Army of the Cumberland the stunning turn of events did much to erase the stain of Chickamauga. For Sheridan the impromptu charge up Missionary Ridge, taking place as it did before Grant's eyes, yielded huge rewards. He received the lion's share of glory from Missionary Ridge. Grant's simmering low regard for the deliberate Thomas and his equally deliberate but hard-fighting army meant that any praise for that fine officer and the Cumberlanders would be subdued. Sheridan, though, attracted Grant's unqualified commendation: "To Sheridan's prompt action the Army of the Cumberland, and the nation, are indebted for the bulk of the capture of prisoners, artillery, and small arms that day. Except for his prompt pursuit, so much in this way would not have been accomplished."[5]

Once a man made an impression on Grant, positive or negative, it most likely stuck. With few exceptions, the general's initial opinion of a given officer held. He praised and protected his favorites such as Sherman and James B. McPherson, men who proved loyal and trustworthy if not always successful in battle. He remembered a slight or an insult or a botched assignment as easily as he recalled a fine battlefield performance. In some cases, as with Thomas, Grant's attitude appeared arbitrary or personal. Perhaps he viewed Thomas as a potential rival. Grant clearly showed preferential treatment to his former Army of the Tennessee while displaying a low-level disdain for the Army of the Cumberland. Simply contributing to Grant's success, therefore, was no guarantee of reward. Grant, to the extent of his awareness, held Sheridan in high regard prior to Chattanooga. But such could be said of many officers. In Sheridan's performance there Grant found something special: he found a warrior, a winner, and he would not forget the little general when he looked to bring a new intensity to the war in Virginia.

As he basked in the glow of victory on Missionary Ridge, Phil Sheridan stood to play a decisive role in the closing stages of the Civil War—a role not even in his wildest dreams might he have imagined.

# ⤝ 1 ⤞
# "The New Command"

*W*hen Major General Philip Henry Sheridan arrived in Washington on April 4, 1864, he made a decidedly uninspiring first impression. Lieutenant Colonel Horace Porter of Grant's staff described a man "worn down almost to a shadow by hard work and exposure in the field." According to Porter, Sheridan "weighed only a hundred and fifteen pounds, and as his height was but five feet six inches, he looked anything but formidable as a candidate for cavalry leader." But here indeed was the man whom Grant had summoned from Tennessee to command the Cavalry Corps of the Union's most high-profile fighting force—the Army of the Potomac.[1]

Sheridan made the requisite rounds about the capital. Since Grant had already taken the field, he visited his other important advocate, General Halleck at the War Department. "Old Brains" outlined Sheridan's new duties and filled him in on the military situation in Virginia before introducing him to dark-tempered Secretary of War Edwin Stanton, who left the young general unsure of what if any impression he had made. Halleck took him next to President Lincoln. "Mr. Lincoln received me very cordially," Sheridan recalled, "offering both hands, and saying that he hoped I would fulfill the expectations of General Grant in the new command I was about to undertake."

The meeting went well by Sheridan's reckoning; even Lincoln's playful but rather tasteless repetition of the tired indictment, "Who ever saw a dead cavalryman," failed to dampen the experience. Later that long day, Sheridan received his official appointment. The next morning he met briefly with Grant before traveling to General Meade's headquarters at Brandy Station, Virginia. After providing Sheridan with the details of his new command, Meade told him where he could find the Cavalry Corps.[2]

The situation into which Sheridan was thrust promised no shortage of acrimony if not outright hostility. To make room for the new commander, Grant had ordered the unceremonious reassignment of relatively effective but

1

troublesome Major General Alfred Pleasonton. News that the largely unknown Sheridan had been called from the West triggered much nervous speculation and no small measure of resentment among the officers and troopers of the Cavalry Corps. First, he was an outsider; second, for all they knew he was an infantry officer, and finally, he came as yet another savior from the Western armies, sent to show the Easterners how to win. For most of the war the soldiers in the Army of the Potomac had suffered reverse after reverse only to be blasted with news of brilliant victories in Tennessee and Mississippi. And there remained the sour taste left from the tragicomic failure of the first Western savior—the bombastic John Pope—who came East promising to bring that winning magic to Virginia only to be embarrassed by Lee in the Second Battle of Bull Run. Now came Grant and with him Sheridan. The men of the Cavalry Corps had ample fuel to feed the fire of discontent.

However, Grant was not Pope, and Sheridan came not as a boastful would-be savior but as a proven campaigner with a job to do. Without pomp or proclamation he took command. Any anxiety among the offers quickly dissipated when Sheridan retained most of Pleasonton's staff. For the Cavalry Corps, Sheridan's arrival signaled not only a change in leadership but also a bold new direction.[3]

The command Sheridan inherited was, in reality, far better off than Grant or Lincoln had led him to believe. Under Pleasonton and a potent mixture of veteran stalwarts and aggressive young officers, the Cavalry Corps had begun to turn the tide of war against flamboyant Major General J. E. B. Stuart and the redoubtable Rebel horsemen of Robert E. Lee's Army of Northern Virginia.

Back in June 1863 at Brandy Station, Pleasonton's corps had slugged it out with Stuart's in the largest true cavalry battle of the war. Although Stuart held the field, the Federals had given him all he could handle and in the process confirmed that Lee's army was indeed moving northward. The rough treatment he received at Brandy Station, in part, compelled Stuart to seek vindication in another spectacular ride around the Union army. He had after all made his reputation with such a raid in 1862. But this time the unintended result was to render Lee blind to Union dispositions as his Confederate army marched into Pennsylvania. Brandy Station also infused the much-maligned Potomac cavalry with a new sense of confidence; it had, as it turned out, awakened a sleeping monster. Then, on July 1, Brigadier General John Buford's outnumbered cavalry command held back Lee's infantry long enough for the Federals to gain and hold the good ground during the first day's fighting at Gettysburg. And on the third day of that storied battle, Brigadier General David McMurtrie Gregg's troopers whipped the late-arriving Stuart in heavy fighting that ended Confederate cavalry dominance in the East.

*General James Ewell Brown "Jeb" Stuart. Courtesy of the National Archives*

In all fairness, therefore, the Cavalry Corps' turnaround predated Sheridan's arrival.[4]

For the balance of 1863, as the two armies maneuvered for advantage, the cavalry on both sides saw hard service. But no longer did the mention of Jeb Stuart strike fear in the hearts of Yankee troopers, not that the Rebel horsemen had lost any of their fighting spirit. The South simply no longer could replace lost men and horses, and almost three years into this horrible war many of its most gifted leaders had been lost to death or wounds. Things were little better for the men in blue, despite their recent success. By the time active campaigning ceased in December, the Cavalry Corps had worn out its horses and equipment.

Although the Union could more readily fill its needs, unscrupulous contractors and horse buyers had made millions at Federal expense since the beginning of the war. Recruiting failed to keep pace with needs, and training for cavalry replacements hardly prepared new troopers for the task at hand.

The U.S. War Department attempted to alleviate these problems with the creation of the Cavalry Bureau in July 1863, but as yet another agency in the sprawling Federal bureaucracy, it managed to achieve little. Charged with the procurement of replacement mounts and weapons and the organization and training of recruits, the Cavalry Bureau ran up against the entrenched interests of the Quartermaster Department, the Ordnance Bureau, and various commanders in the field. Under Major General George Stoneman and Brigadier General Kenner Garrard the bureau languished in inactivity. In January 1864 ambitious twenty-six-year-old Brigadier General James Harrison Wilson, formerly of Grant's staff, assumed direction of the bureau. Wilson made progress, improving the quality of cavalry horses purchased and adopting the proven Spencer repeating carbine as the standard firearm for the branch. Horses remained a concern as demands on the mounted arm increased, and the Spencers never made it to many regiments, but Wilson's efforts brought some sense of relief.[5]

Despite the progress achieved by the Cavalry Corps in 1863, an ill-advised raid in late February 1864 threatened to reverse the positive trend and likely contributed to Grant's and Lincoln's negative opinions. Headline-seeking Third Division commander Brigadier General Judson Kilpatrick, known in the army as "Kill Cavalry" for his aggressive fighting and his glaring disregard for high casualties accumulated in pursuit of glory, hatched a plan to rescue Federal prisoners from Richmond prisons. The plan won approval based on the assumption that Richmond was lightly guarded and on reports of deplorable conditions in the Confederate prisons. Kilpatrick allowed another ambitious officer, twenty-one-year-old Colonel Ulric Dahlgren, son of Union Rear Admiral John Dahlgren, to lead one of the rescue columns. Launched on February 28, the raid quickly fell apart after managing some mischief. It resulted in 350 casualties, including the death of young Dahlgren, more than 1,000 horses captured or ruined, and the loss of much equipment. The debacle flamed fresh in many minds when Lincoln summoned Grant from Tennessee to take charge of Union forces.[6]

When Sheridan assumed command of the Cavalry Corps, he took charge of more than 13,000 officers and men in three divisions and a brigade of horse artillery. Most of the officers were by now proven campaigners, and many were younger than Sheridan's thirty-three years. Although Sheridan retained much of Pleasonton's staff, some new arrangements had to be made. Kilpatrick was out, exiled to the West, and to fill his place Grant pulled James Wilson from the Cavalry Bureau to command the Third Division. Sadly, the highly regarded John Buford, in many minds the best cavalry officer in the army, had succumbed to typhoid fever the previous December, necessitating a new commander for the First Division. For reasons never explained, Brigadier General Alfred T. A. Torbert, previously a brigade commander in the VI Army Corps with no cavalry experience, took charge of the division. Extremely competent Brigadier General Wesley Merritt, who commanded in Buford's absence, reverted to his regular position as head of the Reserve Brigade. Entering his new command, therefore, Sheridan had only one experienced cavalry officer in division command—David McMurtrie Gregg, who led the Second Division. But all three division commanders were professional soldiers and West Pointers: Gregg and Torbert had finished two years behind Sheridan, in the class of 1855, while young Wilson belonged to the fine class of 1860, which also included Merritt. Like Sheridan, Wilson and Torbert would have to learn on the job, and soon enough they would prove more than competent.[7]

Undoubtedly brilliant, Wilson had graduated near the top of his West Point class and briefly performed engineering duties in the Pacific Northwest. With the outbreak of war, talented engineers were in great demand. Wilson first applied his gifts along the Atlantic coast and participated in the expeditions against Port Royal and Fort Pulaski. He also possessed a knack for being in the right place at the right time—serving on Major General George B. McClellan's staff during the 1862 Maryland Campaign before joining Grant's advance on Vicksburg as a staff engineer with the temporary rank of lieutenant colonel. Promoted to brigadier general in October 1863, he served at Chattanooga. In February, with Grant's hearty endorsement, Wilson took charge of the Cavalry Bureau. A proven organizer and administrator, he had not held a troop command prior to his appointment to lead the Third Division. Theodore Lyman of General Meade's staff described Wilson as "a slight person of a light complexion and with a rather pinched face." Despite his many talents, Wilson never quite fit in the closely knit Cavalry Corps.[8]

The muttonchopped Torbert, a Delaware-born professional, spent his prewar years on station in Florida and the Southwest. A first lieutenant in the 5th U.S. Infantry in 1861, he apparently garnered a nomination for a position in the Confederate army but remained loyal to the Union. His first war service was to organize volunteers in New Jersey. In September he became colonel of the 1st New Jersey Infantry, which he led during the Peninsular Campaign in the spring of 1862 and in the Second Bull Run Campaign that summer. He commanded

*General Alfred Torbert. Courtesy of the National Archives*

*General David M. Gregg. Courtesy of the National Archives*

*General James H. Wilson. Courtesy of the Library of Congress*

the First Brigade, First Division, VI Army Corps, at South Mountain, where he received a wound; Antietam; Fredericksburg; Chancellorsville; and Gettysburg; and in the fall campaigns of 1863. His promotion to brigadier general came in November 1862. Although a competent and well-regarded infantry commander, Torbert nonetheless presented a surprising choice to head Buford's old First Division.

The lone holdover among the division chiefs, Gregg had been posted to the 1st Dragoons upon his graduation from West Point and was on duty in California when the war began. A captain in the 6th U.S. Cavalry in January 1862, he entered the Volunteer organization as colonel of the 8th Pennsylvania Cavalry, seeing action on the Virginia Peninsula and in the Seven Days' Battles. Promoted to brigadier general of Volunteers in November 1862, he led a brigade at Fredericksburg and a division during actions associated with the Chancellorsville Campaign. His division, with the rest of the Cavalry Corps, saw heavy fighting at Brandy Station and in the other clashes that preceded the Battle of Gettysburg. During the chaotic third day of fighting at Gettysburg, troopers under Gregg's direction, including Brigadier General George A. Custer's Michigan Brigade, drove Stuart's once-supreme cavalry from the field. By April 1864, with the death of Buford and the reassignment of Pleasonton, he had become the rock of the Cavalry Corps. Quiet, unassuming, and popular within the corps, the luxuriantly bearded Gregg continued to render fine service as the demands of war increased.

A roster of seasoned brigade and regiment commanders more than compensated for the relative inexperience at the division level. In fact, before Wilson and Torbert joined the command, three of the corps' four general officers present (the fourth being Gregg)—Brigadier Generals Wesley Merritt, George Armstrong Custer, and Henry E. Davies, destined for fame as Sheridan's "Boy Generals"—headed brigades.

Clean-shaven Wesley Merritt, twenty-eight when the campaigns of 1864 began, was the oldest of the three and by virtue of seniority the ranking brigade commander. Born in New York and raised in Illinois, he was an 1860 graduate of the U.S. Military Academy who began his career with the legendary 2nd Dragoons, serving under the equally legendary Colonel Philip St. George Cooke and Captain John Buford in Utah. With the outbreak of the Civil War, Merritt marched with his regiment, the part that remained loyal to the Union, overland to Washington, D.C., arriving in October 1861. Much like Sheridan, Merritt held a series of staff assignments during his early war experience, working as an aide to Cooke, who commanded the Cavalry Reserve, Army of the Potomac. He saw steady promotion, becoming captain, 2nd U.S. Cavalry (during an 1861 reorganization of the regular army the 2nd Dragoons became the 2nd Cavalry) in April 1862. He served during the Peninsular Campaign that spring and distinguished himself in the Federal defeat at Gaines' Mill in June. Cooke's fall from grace soon thereafter placed Merritt's career in limbo. He languished in staff assignments around Washington, missing altogether the carnage at Antietam and Fredericksburg.[9]

Changes within the Army of the Potomac during the spring of 1863 brought new prospects. Major General Joseph Hooker assumed command of the army and instituted a welcomed reorganization that included the creation of the Cavalry Corps under General Stoneman. In April 1863, Captain Merritt joined Stoneman's staff as mustering and ordnance officer. During the Chancellorsville Campaign in May, Merritt led a small detachment on a successful raid of destruction. In the wake of Lee's stunning Confederate victory at Chancellorsville, Stoneman took leave and was replaced by Pleasonton. Merritt retained his staff position briefly under Pleasonton, who knew the young officer from their days in the Dragoons.

Pleasonton developed a great fondness for Merritt and two other young staffers—Custer and Captain Elon Farnsworth. But Merritt soon left the staff to take command of his own regiment, the 2nd U.S. Cavalry in the Reserve Brigade.

Still a captain, Merritt led the regiment in the giant cavalry battle at Brandy Station and won praise for a bold charge that nearly cost him his life. In furious close fighting he suffered a saber blow to the head, a light wound as it turned out and the only one of his long and active career. During the two weeks that ended with the July 1 clash at Gettysburg, Merritt and his horsemen dueled frequently with Confederate cavalry as the war moved northward. Pleasonton had lobbied vigorously to reorganize his force. He needed more men and wanted to fill various command slots with aggressive young officers. More men came with the addition of a third division under Judson Kilpatrick. To fill vacant commands, he repeated an earlier request for the immediate promotion of Captains Merritt, Custer, and Farnsworth. General Meade, who had at this untimely juncture replaced Hooker at the head of the army, delivered the promotions quickly. On June 29 the three young officers received appointments as brigadier generals of U.S. Volunteers.

For Merritt particularly, his long staff service and close associations with Cooke, Buford, and Pleasonton prepared him well for his new role. Known for his intelligence and administrative ability, he rapidly became one of the most well-rounded and efficient general officers in the army. These qualities and his recent audacious performance at Brandy Station made him the ideal commander for the Reserve Brigade—the "Old Guard" of the Cavalry Corps, an organization dominated by regular units.

Merritt and the Reserve Brigade, detached from the main body, did not participate in Buford's brilliant action on July 1 at Gettysburg, but saw heavy fighting on the third day, dueling with Confederate infantry on the Union left, where, during a disastrous assault ordered by Kilpatrick, Merritt's fellow new brigadier Elon Farnsworth was killed. Over the next two weeks the Federal cavalry experienced almost constant duty, fighting numerous actions with Lee's retreating army. After a period of rest and refitting, which did little to improve the condition of the run-down cavalry, the Reserve Brigade took the field again during the Bristoe Campaign. In October, Merritt's mentor, John Buford, exhausted and ailing from years of arduous service, left the army to recuperate. In his absence, Merritt commanded the First Division during the inconsequential Mine Run Campaign. Buford never returned to duty, and Merritt commanded the division until Torbert's appointment in April 1864.

Merritt offered much more than a temporary replacement for the much-lamented Buford. He assumed his mentor's essential role as the stabilizing force within the corps. Like Buford, he was modest, capable, and dignified. He coolly rose to the challenge of battle and inspired confidence. And more than most commanders, he looked after his men and his mounts. Merritt lacked Custer's dash and shunned fancy uniforms, but he easily equaled his comrade in action and far exceeded him as a complete cavalry leader. While others gained fame, Merritt became Sheridan's most trusted subordinate.

Unlike Wesley Merritt, who conducted his business without fanfare, George Armstrong Custer was a star waiting for the opportunity to shine, and the Civil War gave him the stage. Born in Ohio, the cradle of Union war heroes, on December 5, 1839, Custer spent much of his youth with relatives in Michigan, a state with which he would forever be linked. Had he not made such a splash as a cavalry commander, Custer might well have earned renown for his remarkable tenure at West Point, where he rarely let military decorum interfere with his fun. He accumulated nearly enough demerits to cause his expulsion but managed to graduate dead last in his class of 1861, a year behind Merritt and Wilson, a year ahead of future comrade Ranald Mackenzie. By then the war was on, and Custer reported for duty in Virginia as a second lieutenant in the 2nd U.S. Cavalry (soon redesignated the 5th Cavalry in reorganization). Like Merritt, he fell into staff duty, but Custer quickly established his daredevil reputation by seeking danger whenever the opportunity arose, providing early evidence of what came to be known as "Custer's luck." After a series of daring performances during the Peninsular Campaign, he caught the attention of Army of the Potomac commander Major General George B. McClellan, who offered the fearless subaltern a position on his staff with the temporary rank of captain. Custer served the underachieving "Little Mac" until that officer's ouster following the Battle of Antietam.[10]

As was his way, Custer landed on his feet when General Pleasonton offered him a place on his division staff in the spring of 1863. He soon distinguished himself during the defining battle at Brandy Station and again at Aldie, but as a trusted staff officer he, like Sheridan, Merritt, Wilson, and Mackenzie, found his path to a line command blocked. Custer shouldered the additional impediment of being too closely associated with the failed McClellan. Yet the recent reversal of military fortune at Brandy Station gave the reform-minded Pleasonton new currency that paid big dividends for Custer and his brethren Merritt and Farnsworth. Promoted directly from captain to brigadier general of Volunteers on June 29, 1863, the garishly attired Custer, at twenty-three, became one of the youngest general officers on either side of the conflict. He assumed command of the Second Brigade of the newly organized Third Division. This was the Michigan or Wolverine Brigade, composed entirely of regiments from Custer's part-time home state. Less than a week into his new assignment, Custer led his Wolverines in an intense cavalry engagement with Stuart's troopers during the final day's fighting at Gettysburg, personally spearheading a ferocious charge that drove the Rebels from the field. Custer and the Michigan Brigade followed their successful debut with conspicuous performances in the many rear-guard actions that attended Lee's withdrawal to Virginia and continued to prove their worth in the otherwise ineffectual campaigns that fall.

Not surprisingly, Custer emerged the darling of the Northern press, attention he relished and openly courted. In manner and appearance he represented the polar opposite of Merritt, whose simple dress conveyed his understated persona. For the role of cavalry commander, Custer adopted a black velvet jacket and trousers accented with lavish complements of gold braid and stars, high cavalry boots, a wide-brimmed black hat, and a bright red necktie. His reddish-blond ringlets, droopy mustache, and nifty imperial below his lip inspired much admiration. Had he not backed his rather outlandish costume with uncanny timing and absolute fearlessness in battle he might well have been laughed from the army. Even his Michiganders looked upon their new leader with skepticism until they saw him in battle. He was outright inspiring.

Something of an anomaly among the leaders of the Cavalry Corps, dapper Henry Davies came from a civilian background. But unlike his more celebrated colleagues in the Cavalry Corps, all of his war service had been with troops in the field. Born in New York City on July 2, 1836, he compiled an impressive academic record, attending Harvard, Williams, and Columbia. He graduated from Columbia in 1857 and studied law, opening a practice in New York. With the outbreak of hostilities, Davies joined the 5th New York Infantry as a captain and saw action in the first land battle of the war at Big Bethel. Transferring as major to the 2nd New York Cavalry in August 1861, he spent most of the next year on duty in northern Virginia, participating in the Second Bull Run Campaign and commanding the regiment at Fredericksburg and during the

Chancellorsville Campaign. Promoted to colonel in June 1863, Davies fought at Brandy Station and Aldie during the advance into Pennsylvania, but missed the action at Gettysburg, being posted in Maryland. He assumed command of the First Brigade, Third Division, Cavalry Corps, following Gettysburg and received his appointment to brigadier general of Volunteers in September 1863. With the rest of the corps, he and his brigade participated in the fall campaigns in northern Virginia. Thin and erect with a large mustache and imperial, Davies possessed a fine martial appearance. Intelligent and capable, by the time Sheridan took charge of the corps, he ranked among its most experienced officers in terms of Civil War field service.

The other brigade commanders conformed to no set mold, but all proved capable. Colonel Thomas Devin, a New York house painter, and like Sheridan a first-generation Irish American, found his way into the war as a militia officer. Entering the fray as a captain of the 1st New York Cavalry, he assumed command of the new 6th New York Cavalry in November 1861. He led the regiment during the Maryland Campaign and took charge of a cavalry brigade at Fredericksburg. After fighting at Chancellorsville and Brandy Station, he and his brigade of Buford's First Division played a major role in holding back Lee's infantry during the initial clash at Gettysburg. After heavy duty in the fall campaigns of 1863, Devin participated in the failed Kilpatrick-Dahlgren Raid the following February. Well-liked and respected, Devin was, at forty-two, older than most of the officers of the corps. He commanded the Second Brigade in Torbert's First Division. Although certainly deserving, he had been overlooked for division commands that went to outsiders, but he would get his chance.

Colonel John Irvin Gregg, a distant relative of David Gregg, served as a regular in the Mexican War, after which he returned to private life. With the onset of the Civil War, he rejoined the regular establishment as a captain in the new 3rd U.S. Cavalry (later redesignated the 6th Cavalry). After early action on the peninsula, he entered the Volunteer establishment as colonel of the 16th Pennsylvania Cavalry, with which he earned a brevet at Kelly's Ford in March 1863. He then took charge of a cavalry brigade, leading it at Brandy Station, Aldie, and Gettysburg, and in the fall campaigns of 1863. In April 1864 he commanded the Second Brigade of David Gregg's Second Division.

Bespectacled Colonel George Henry Chapman, a Massachusetts-born Hoosier, led the First Brigade of the First Division upon Sheridan's arrival. Born in 1832, he entered the Navy as a midshipman in 1847 but left the service to publish a Republican newspaper in Indiana. He also studied law and passed the bar before becoming a clerk in the U.S. House of Representatives. In November 1861 he entered the war as a major in the 3rd Indiana Cavalry, rising to colonel in March 1863. In the process he saw much action during the battles of Second Bull Run, Antietam, and Fredericksburg. He led his regiment at Chancellorsville, at Brandy Station, and in Buford's stand at Gettysburg. In September 1863 he assumed brigade command and fought well during the fall campaigns. Like the other nonprofessionals in the corps, he earned his position based on merit, and he would continue to justify his place once the bloody work commenced in May 1864.

As the long-anticipated spring campaigning season approached, Colonel John B. McIntosh commanded the cavalry division of the XXII Corps, defending Washington, but he rightfully belonged with the Cavalry Corps, Army of the Potomac. The temporary assignment came as the result of a fall from his horse the previous October, which had required an unwanted recuperation. Born in 1929, McIntosh served as a midshipman during the war with Mexico, after which he became a New Jersey businessman. In June 1861, apparently in response to his brother's joining the Confederate service (James McIntosh became a brigadier general and was killed at Pea Ridge in 1862), he received a commission as a rather old second lieutenant in the storied 2nd U.S. Cavalry (which became the 5th Cavalry in reorganization). He fought in this regular unit on the Peninsula and during the Seven Days' Battles, winning promotion to first lieutenant. After action in the Maryland Campaign, he entered the Volunteer establishment as colonel of the 3rd Pennsylvania Cavalry, commanding a cavalry brigade in the Army of the Potomac at Kelly's Ford, Chancellorsville, and Gettysburg before injury sidetracked his career. But by May 1864 the full-bearded McIntosh resumed his place in the Cavalry Corps as commander of the First Brigade, Third Division.

Writing years after the war, Theophilus Rodenbough, a captain commanding the 2nd U.S. Cavalry in Merritt's Reserve Brigade in May 1864, described the impressive slate of division and brigade commanders of the Cavalry Corps:

> Sheridan's lieutenants were well chosen. Torbert had already distinguished himself as an infantry commander; Gregg had come from the regular cavalry and possessed the confidence of the whole corps for good judgment and coolness; Wilson, promoted from the corps of engineers, was very quick and impetuous; Merritt was a pupil of the Cooke-Buford school, with cavalry virtues well proportioned, and to him was given the Reserve Brigade of regulars—the Old Guard. Custer was the meteoric *sabreur*; McIntosh, the last of a fighting race; Devin, the "Old War Horse"; Davies, polished, genial, gallant; Chapman, the student-like; Irvin Gregg, the steadfast.[11]

He said it all. This was as fine a collection of talent and experience as could be found in any corps in either army.

The events surrounding Sheridan's appointment to command the Cavalry Corps, namely the banishment of Kilpatrick and the appointments of Torbert and Wilson to head the First and Third Divisions respectively, necessitated a reorganization of the corps prior to the commencement of spring campaigning. Custer and Davies, who commanded Third Division brigades, were senior in grade to Wilson and therefore could not be expected to serve under the new commander. Davies, therefore, moved to Gregg's Second Division as head of the First Brigade. His former command, the First Brigade, Third Division, went eventually to McIntosh. Custer, identified as he was with his Wolverines, saw his entire brigade reassigned to Torbert's First Division, trading places with Chapman's brigade.[12]

So as Grant prepared to unleash the mighty human and material resources of the Union, Sheridan's Cavalry Corps boasted plenty of talent and aggressiveness but would be taking the field as a substantially altered fighting force. The new order of battle reflected the spring's many changes. Torbert's stellar First Division included Custer's First Brigade, Devin's Second Brigade, and Merritt's inappropriately designated Reserve Brigade. David Gregg's Second Division lacked the marquee names of the First Division but remained solid, with Davies and Irvin Gregg commanding the First and Second Brigades, respectively. If the corps possessed a question mark it had to be the untested Wilson's Third Division, but the experience present in McIntosh's First Brigade and Chapman's Second Brigade more than compensated for its division commander's lack of exposure.

Any worries over the corps' organization paled in comparison to Sheridan's concerns about how General Meade employed the cavalry. The constant demands of picket duty—guarding the army's flanks and rear and its substantial supply trains—further exhausted already worn cavalry mounts. With heavy fighting expected to commence soon, Sheridan feared that the corps' horses would be used up at a time when they needed to be strong. Clearly, Sheridan and his immediate commander, George Meade, fundamentally differed in their views on the proper use of the Cavalry Corps. According to Sheridan, Meade, despite the role mounted elements played in his signal victory at Gettysburg, saw the cavalry in a supporting role to the infantry, much like artillery. Sheridan wanted to concentrate the cavalry as a semiautonomous force to fight the Confederate cavalry. To Meade's concern that a concentrated cavalry force would leave his infantry vulnerable, Sheridan recalled, "I told him that if he would let me use the cavalry as I contemplated . . . it was my belief that I could make it so lively for the enemy's cavalry that, so far as attacks from it were concerned, the flanks and rear of the Army of the Potomac would require little or no defense." Meade was unmoved, but the first of many such confrontations between the acerbic army commander and Sheridan did result in a sharp reduction of picket duty, which prior to the forthcoming campaign meant two weeks of beneficial rest for overused mounts.[13]

The rest for horses and men came in handy indeed. Since 1861, Federal armies had moved into northern Virginia with the express purpose of putting down the rebellion by destroying the Confederacy's military forces and taking its capital at Richmond. Each invasion brought a large battle, and each time the Federals had been turned back empty-handed. With the advent of Grant as the supreme Union military commander, things changed. Grant intended to reverse the pattern at all costs. He understood the undeniable truths of this sad war—that the North had the men and materiel to crush the rebellion, that he had the numbers on his side, that the South had run out of men, and that no European savior waited on the horizon. He also understood that Northern support for the war waned. Grant needed quick action, quick victories, before time ran out for Lincoln and his quest to restore the Union. He needed only to apply the irresistible force he had at his disposal, relentlessly, on all fronts, regardless of the gaudy casualty figures that undoubtedly would flash across the headlines of the nation's newspapers.

For its breadth, Grant's plan was remarkably simple. Federal armies from the Trans-Mississippi to Virginia were to attack and keep attacking until the Southern Confederacy collapsed. His personal goal demanded nothing less than the destruction of Lee's Army of Northern Virginia; his instrument would be Meade's Army of the Potomac. Sheridan's Cavalry Corps had a part to play, but the nature of that part remained to be determined. Sheridan clearly envisioned a starring role for the cavalry, but as the curtain opened on the long-anticipated campaign he found his horsemen cast as supporting players.

# ≥ 2 ≤

# "Many Gallant Officers and Men"

$\mathcal{I}$f anyone, after witnessing the slaughters at Antietam, Fredericksburg, or Gettysburg in the East or Shiloh, Stones River, or Chickamauga in the West, believed they had seen the worst of it, the campaigns that kicked off in May 1864 quickly put an end to such foolishness. In accordance with Grant's grand design, Federal military departments from coast to coast prepared for action. The new commander ordered garrisons reduced, commands consolidated, and lines of communication streamlined, all to concentrate the bulk of available soldiers at the points of attack, with the main armies, and to ensure that for once all the armies of the Union worked in concert toward a single objective.

In the Trans-Mississippi, Major General Nathaniel Banks was to abandon his unwanted and ultimately unsuccessful Red River Campaign, a Washington-spawned operation to conquer Texas and discourage any cooperation between the Confederacy and Maximilian's French-backed empire in Mexico. Leaving the effort in Louisiana, Arkansas, and Texas to Major General Frederick Steele, Banks was then to launch a long-contemplated drive against Mobile. Grant further ordered 10,000 troops diverted from operations against Charleston to augment Major General Benjamin Butler's Army of the James for a move up the Virginia Peninsula against Richmond. Forces under Major Generals Franz Sigel and E. O. C. Ord and Brigadier General George Crook were to operate in the Shenandoah Valley and Southwestern Virginia to disrupt Confederate food supplies and prevent the various Rebel forces in the region from reinforcing the major armies in Northern Virginia and Georgia. The destruction of the two major Confederate armies fell to Grant and Sherman.

To Sherman, who directed three Federal armies—Thomas's large Army of the Cumberland, the Army of the Tennessee, and the Army of the Ohio, commanded respectively by Sheridan's old classmates James McPherson and John Schofield—at Chattanooga, Grant assigned General Joseph E. Johnston's Confederate Army of Tennessee, Braxton Bragg's old command, which manned defensive positions near Dalton, Georgia. Grant wrote, "You I propose to move against Johnston's army, to break it up and get into the interior of the enemy's country as far as you can, inflicting all the damage you can against their war resources." For his part, Grant informed his friend, "I will stay with the Army of the Potomac . . . and operate directly against Lee's army wherever it may be found." That meant a new push into Northern Virginia, where the venerable warrior and his remarkable legions waited behind the Rapidan River amid the forbidding tangle of woods known appropriately as the Wilderness.[1]

By applying overwhelming pressure to all points of Confederate resistance simultaneously, Grant hoped to deny his opponents the use of their interior lines, which they had manipulated so effectively, and to cut off already dwindling food supplies. Unwritten but clearly implied in Grant's charge to Sherman and his other field commanders was the importance of making the war so unbearable for already hard-pressed Southern citizens that they ceased to support the rebellion. In this unsavory regard, and in the pursuit of the overall objective, Sheridan and his troopers would prove quite effective.

During the days leading up to the campaign's general commencement, Sheridan's men patrolled the front along the Rapidan River, scouting fords, watchful of Confederate movements. Sheridan found this sort of duty frustrating, but for the moment his hands were tied. And just as well. The Army of the Potomac would be moving into the dreaded Wilderness—a dense forest with thick undergrowth—where it had met disaster the year before under Hooker during the Battle of Chancellorsville. The Wilderness offered scant prospect for the kind of large independent cavalry action that Sheridan envisioned. Still, the mounted arm had a job to do.

What came to be known as the Overland Campaign began roughly on schedule after midnight on May 4 when Colonel George Chapman's Second Brigade of James Wilson's Third Cavalry Division crossed the Rapidan at Germanna Ford and moved into the Wilderness, opening the way for Major General Gouverneur K. Warren's V Corps. Meanwhile, David Gregg's Second Division crossed several miles downriver at Ely's Ford, ahead of Major General Winfield Scott Hancock's II Corps. To Torbert's First Division went the thankless task of guarding the army's 4,000 wagons and ambulances and their teams, a duty best performed, in Sheridan's opinion, by infantry. Unpleasant though such work might have been, in this used-up environment it was essential to keep supplies of food and forage, not to mention ammunition, close to the army. Even with the great attention accorded the trains, during the confused and fast-moving campaign that followed, men and animals alike frequently would have to get by on short rations.[2]

Grant and Meade determined to break free of the deadly woods before Lee's army could react to their presence. But Lee, with only two of his three

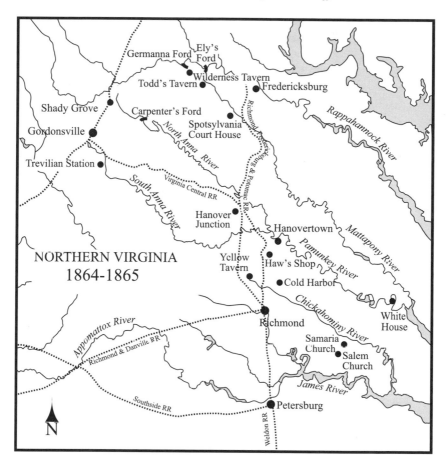

NORTHERN VIRGINIA
1864-1865

infantry corps on hand, chose instead to contest the Federal advance with his available force and wait for James Longstreet's veterans and Jeb Stuart's cavalry to arrive. Even with his full force at his disposal, Lee would be outnumbered by almost two to one. These, however, had been the odds at Chancellorsville, and he had triumphed there, brilliantly. A year before, the Wilderness evened the odds, negating the Federal advantages as the heavy blue columns bogged down in the impenetrable thicket, and artillery and cavalry had been rendered ineffectual. Lee counted on a repeat performance.

On May 5, as more than 110,000 men of the Army of the Potomac moved deeper into the Wilderness, Lee's infantry struck. For two days the two armies slugged it out in a nightmare stalemate, made all the more hellish as firestorms enveloped dozens of wounded men, with neither side gaining a clear advantage. Just as the Confederates appeared to be on the brink of collapse,

Longstreet's Corps pitched in, and when this furious counterattack threatened to spoil Grant's debut in Virginia, Union numbers held sway. Sheridan's troopers, by design, had no real impact on the battle.[3]

Wilson's division, the least experienced and the only one not tied to the trains, had a rough time during the first day's fighting. Charged with covering the advancing infantry on the Federal right, Wilson found his division scattered and well ahead of supporting infantry. Chapman's Second Brigade was driven back in disorder from its advanced position by oncoming Confederate infantry and had to be rescued by elements of the Second Division. Lieutenant Colonel John Hammond and 500 men of the 5th New York Cavalry from Wilson's First Brigade caught the initial impact of a much larger force of Rebel infantry advancing on Parker's Store. Fighting dismounted and employing their rapid-firing Spencers to great effect, Hammond's men gave ground grudgingly before retiring. By day's end the entire Cavalry Corps had concentrated on the Federal left near Chancellorsville.

On May 6 as the infantry fought ferociously in the burning forest, the Cavalry Corps skirmished heavily with Stuart's forces in the vicinity of Todd's Tavern, south of Chancellorsville on the fringe of the Wilderness. Custer's and Devin's brigades of the First Division carried the bulk of the fighting, mostly dismounted, against Confederate Major General Fitzhugh Lee's Division, which, according to Custer, was "driven from the field in great disorder," leaving its dead and wounded to the Federals. In the overall scheme of things, the cavalry action on the sixth, although quite successful, had a detrimental impact on the Federal effort. The intensity of the fighting on the Union's left led Hancock, whose II Corps' flank the cavalry protected, to believe that his flank had been turned. This prompted Meade to rein in the troopers, forcing them to yield the important crossroads at Todd's Tavern. Sheridan, already miffed at his role, had no choice but to comply. "I obeyed this order," he reported, "and the enemy took possession of the Furnaces, Todd's Tavern, and Piney Branch Church, the regaining of which cost much fighting . . . and very many gallant officers and men."[4]

The next day the opposing infantry lines in the Wilderness stood idle, waiting for one side or the other to move. For the foot soldiers this battle was over. While neither side could claim victory, it appeared that Lee had thwarted another Federal drive on Richmond. Grant's first battle as commanding general proved anything but auspicious, prompting some observers to pronounce him a failure—like all the others. The casualty figures alone seemed to confirm such a conclusion. Although the Confederate forces suffered about 11,000 killed, wounded, and missing, the Federal toll approached 18,000. The same people who contemplated Grant's demise no doubt forecast a speedy withdrawal. But Grant, who followed the ghastly events with remarkable calm, never considered retreat. Early that day, he issued orders for his corps to pull out of their positions during the night. Lee was not among those who anticipated Grant's withdrawal. Even as the two great commanders planned their next move, the cavalry still had work to do.

The Cavalry Corps spent much of the seventh regaining the ground it reluctantly abandoned the previous day. General Torbert, "suffering from an abscess" that required surgery, yielded command of the First Division to Wesley Merritt. Under Merritt the division, with Custer's brigade and the Reserve Brigade, commanded temporarily by Colonel Alfred Gibbs, doing the fighting, drove Stuart's cavalry from Todd's Tavern and along the Brock Road toward Spotsylvania Court House before disengaging. Gregg's Second Division advanced on both sides of Merritt. Irvin Gregg's brigade on the right covered the road toward Shady Grove, while Davies on the right "made a handsome attack on the Piney Branch Church road." Action lasted until dark, when both divisions camped near Todd's Tavern in preparation for the next day's movement. Fighting independently, the Cavalry Corps, with its strength of numbers and Spencer carbines, had again bested Stuart's now-demoralized cavalry.[5]

That night, exhausted Federal infantrymen pulled out of line one corps at a time and marched through the smoldering woods by the left flank toward Todd's Tavern. Sheridan issued orders for his troopers to set out early the following morning, occupy the small community of Spotsylvania Court House, and seize the three bridges over the Po River, denying them to the Confederates. Wilson received his orders during the night and moved out accordingly at 5:00 A.M. on the eighth. Gregg and Merritt had not received their instructions when, at 1:00 A.M., General Meade, riding in advance of Warren's V Corps, found the two cavalry divisions camped at Todd's Tavern. Meade ordered Gregg and Merritt immediately to take the road ahead of the oncoming infantry and sent word to Sheridan, advising him of his actions. Thus two crack mounted divisions became part of a cumbersome advance, frustrated by Confederate cavalry and numerous man-made obstructions. An angry Sheridan blamed Meade, their feud now reaching the boiling point, for the subsequent failure to secure the Po bridges. For his part, Meade blamed the cavalry for slowing the infantry and preventing the army from beating Lee to Spotsylvania. But even had Gregg and Merritt proceeded as Sheridan intended, they would have been too late to take and hold the bridges. Nor was the cavalry materially at fault. Once again, Lee made the right move first.

Lee believed that Grant intended a shift to the east, perhaps to Fredericksburg. Once he detected Grant's withdrawal from the Wilderness, however, Lee ordered Major General Richard H. Anderson, who assumed command of Longstreet's Corps when that officer fell dangerously wounded, to move his men to Spotsylvania, in order to protect the approaches to Richmond. Anderson, on his own initiative, pressed his men through the night and crossed the Po on bridges the Federal cavalry failed to secure.

Wilson reached Spotsylvania at dawn and drove Brigadier General Williams Wickham's Brigade of Fitz Lee's Division from the crossroads, but when he turned the Third Division for the Po River bridges, he found Anderson's infantry already there. Sheridan, who caught up with his units, quickly recalled Wilson before he got cut off. Both armies raced for the next bloody confrontation—another horrible meat grinder of a battle that roughly doubled the casualties of the Wilderness, a fight Sheridan and the Cavalry Corps thankfully missed.

Late on the morning of the eighth, Meade summoned Sheridan to his headquarters, where the two hot-tempered generals gave vent to their anger. According to Horace Porter of Grant's staff, "a very acrimonious dispute took place." Both men, exhausted and overwrought from the previous days' exertions, held nothing back. Meade, wrote Porter, went after his cavalry chief "with hammer and tongs," to which Sheridan responded with a tirade "highly spiced and conspicuously italicized with expletives." Sheridan reiterated his belief that if allowed to concentrate his forces for offensive action he could destroy Stuart's cavalry. He went so far as to tell his superior that if he intended to use the cavalry piecemeal for the protection of supply trains and marching infantry he could command the cavalry himself. A visibly irate Meade reported the exchange to Grant, who supposedly replied that if Sheridan thought he could whip Stuart, "Let him start right out and do it." By the end of the day, Sheridan had his orders. Little Phil finally got his wish—independent action with a large mounted force, a showdown with dashing Jeb Stuart. Now he had to make good his prophecy.[6]

The next morning, May 9, the three divisions of the Cavalry Corps turned away from the main army, swung around the Confederate right, and headed southward for the much-awaited clash with Stuart. Although independent of the main army, Sheridan had specific orders from Meade's headquarters: "proceed against the enemy's cavalry, and when your supplies are exhausted proceed via New Market and Green Bay to Haxall's Landing, on the James River, there communicating with General Butler, procuring supplies, and return to this army." Sheridan marched with him some 10,000 officers and men in the three divisions, six batteries of horse artillery, and an abbreviated supply train. Six hundred dismounted troopers and most of the corps' baggage and its ambulances remained with the army. The First Division, still headed by Merritt, led the column, followed by Wilson's command; Gregg's Second Division brought up the rear. Hardly a stealth raid, the blue column stretched for miles and held a slow but steady pace. Stuart's cavalry, as the Union leaders expected, followed.[7]

Late on the first day's march the First Division crossed the North Anna River and advanced on Beaver Dam Station, while Davies conducted a splendid rear-guard action against the pursuing Rebels. That evening, Custer's brigade struck Beaver Dam Station with surprise, seizing the railroad station, two locomotives, three trains, a hundred cars, and ninety wagons containing an estimated 1,500,000 rations and valuable medical supplies for Lee's army, most of which went up in flames. The Wolverines also liberated 375 Federal prisoners. During the night, as the rest of the First Division arrived, the men commenced the destruction of perhaps ten miles of railroad and telegraph wire. In less than a day Sheridan appeared well on the way to proving himself a military prophet with a most lucrative first strike.

On May 10, Sheridan continued toward Richmond basically unmolested. Stuart, determined to interpose his force between Sheridan and Richmond, divided his small command—he had inexplicably pursued the Federal raid with only three brigades. Leaving Brigadier General James Gordon's Brigade to harass the Federal rear, Stuart pushed his remaining brigades—those of Brigadier Generals Williams Wickham and Lunsford Lomax—on a forced march wide of Sheridan's column to reach the crossroads at Yellow Tavern, only a few miles north of Richmond. Here he hoped to pounce on and cripple the Yankee raiders. With his men and mounts completely worn down from a grueling overnight march, Stuart reached Yellow Tavern by late morning on May 11. He mustered no more than 3,000 men to deal with Sheridan's 10,000. But Jeb Stuart never backed down from a fight.

At noon on the eleventh, Merritt's First Division struck Stuart's cavalry, as the Reserve Brigade, commanded by Colonel Gibbs, and Tom Devin's Second Brigade became heavily engaged. After the initial clash the fighting slackened, but as more blue-clad troopers reached the field, Sheridan moved in for the kill. The push came on the Federal right, where Custer dismounted two of his regiments and sent them at Lomax's position, while the 1st Michigan, Lieutenant Colonel Peter Stagg commanding, launched a mounted charge against a weakly defended Confederate artillery position. Supported by the 1st Vermont of Chapman's brigade from Wilson's Third Division, the Michiganders' "brilliantly executed" attack pierced the Rebel line, taking two particularly troublesome guns and many prisoners. The Confederates managed a brief counterattack, but the day was lost. Stuart, who rode to the threatened section and emptied his revolver into passing Federals, took a bullet in the abdomen from the pistol of Private John Huff of the 5th Michigan. The most fabled cavalry commander of the war died the following day in Richmond.[8]

As the fighting raged at Yellow Tavern, Gregg's division turned back Gordon's Brigade, which had snapped futilely at the rear of Sheridan's raid. Never before had this Confederate cavalry suffered such a total defeat. Fitz Lee managed to gather the remnants of Stuart's command and lead it away. The Confederate horsemen were far from finished, though; too many good men remained. Stuart would be missed, but under leaders such as Fitz Lee and Wade Hampton the Rebel cavalrymen still had some fight left in them. Even so, Yellow Tavern marked Sheridan's arrival, and from then onward the war in Virginia became, in many ways, Sheridan's war.

The Federal raiders had no time to enjoy their victory. After tending to the wounded and burying their dead, they managed a brief rest before pushing on at 11:00 P.M., with Wilson's division in the van. The corps moved eastward, skirting Richmond against spotty opposition. The following morning, artillery fire from the Richmond defenses and mounting pressure from the rear caused Sheridan to alter his course. Although he later downplayed the danger, Sheridan found himself in a hazardous position. He ordered Custer's brigade to cross to the north side of the Chickahominy River at Meadow Bridge. But Custer's men discovered the bridge destroyed and the crossing contested by elements of Fitz Lee's cavalry and a battery of artillery. While two of Custer's regiments occupied the Confederates, who held a strong position north of the river, the rest of Merritt's division repaired the bridge. Their labor completed, the First Brigade charged the Rebel position and drove the defenders from the field and for some two miles beyond, taking many prisoners. Among the Confederate casualties was another general, mortally wounded James Gordon, whose brigade had dogged the blue column for days. As the First Division fought for the Meadow Bridge crossing, Confederate infantry from Richmond assailed the Second and Third Divisions. Gregg and Wilson managed to beat back this threat with relative ease, and Sheridan's troopers spent the next several hours tending to the wounded, burying the dead, and grazing their horses. Many passed the time enjoying Richmond papers; Sheridan noted nonchalantly, "two small newsboys having, with commendable enterprise, entered our lines and sold to the officers and men."[9]

Apparently, Sheridan toyed with the idea of attacking Richmond, but recognizing that even if he successfully entered the Confederate capital he could not hold it and casualties would be prohibitive at best, he wisely abandoned the thought. Another argument against further offensive action became the steadily weakening condition of the command. Food and forage were scarce in this fought-over region and, despite the regrettable practice of taking what they could from hard-pressed citizens, troopers found it impossible to live off the land. That afternoon, May 12, the column proceeded without opposition and camped that night near Gaines' Mill. Two days later, after six days of riding and fighting, the Cavalry Corps entered General Butler's lines at Haxall's Landing on the James River southeast of Richmond, having suffered some 450 casualties. Although successful, the raid left men and mounts utterly exhausted and in dire need of food and rest. Leaving the wounded and prisoners with Butler, after a brief three days of recovery the Cavalry Corps marched away from the James to rejoin the Army of the Potomac, unsure where it might be found.

Sheridan's first raid, if not spectacular, rated a clear success, yet it produced few lasting results. Certainly, the Federal cavalry bested its opponent in each encounter, but then it had faced only a portion of the Confederate mounted force. Still, while Sheridan had not destroyed the Rebel cavalry, his men had killed two generals, including the legendary Stuart, and the command had moved deep into hostile territory with relative ease and managed to dictate the terms of battle. More important for the long term was the performance of Sheridan's subordinates. Merritt and Gregg left nothing to be desired as division commanders. In fact, Merritt emerged as Sheridan's workhorse. And Wilson, although Sheridan was loath to admit it, performed solidly. The brigade and regiment commanders proved their capabilities time and again. Custer and his brigade had been spectacular.

While Sheridan raided southward, Grant and Lee continued their incredibly bloody chess match. Each time Grant pressed the initiative, Lee countered. After twelve days of desperate fighting around Spotsylvania, Grant pulled his men from the trenches and commenced another sweep around Lee's right, again trying to place his army between Lee and Richmond, while Lee, again using his interior lines, rushed to stay ahead of the Federal advance. The Army of the Potomac raced toward the North Anna River and on May 23 crossed the river at two places, only to find Lee's army, which struck with characteristic fury. The next day brought more heavy fighting and another stalemate, as the Confederate lines formed an inverted V that divided the Union army and limited Grant's options. On May 24 the Cavalry Corps reunited with the Army of the Potomac on the North Anna front.

The men of the Cavalry Corps had little time to rest and refit; Grant planned another eastward sweep around Lee's right flank, and Sheridan's horsemen would lead the way. On May 27, while Wilson's division demonstrated on the Federal right, the First Division, with Torbert back at the helm, led the army's advance to the Pamunkey River, crossing at Hanovertown on May 28. Unsure of Confederate dispositions, Grant ordered the cavalry forward to develop the situation. Gregg's division moved westward toward Richmond, passing through the crossroads at Haw's Shop and Salem Church before confronting a strong Confederate position manned by Wade Hampton's dismounted cavalry.

Upon Stuart's death, Lee did not name an immediate successor but retained the three-division structure of his cavalry, with Major Generals Hampton, Fitz Lee, his nephew, and W. H. F. "Rooney" Lee, his son, commanding the divisions, all reporting directly to him. Hampton, as the senior commander on the field west of Haw's Shop, had with him the brigades of Williams Wickham and Brigadier General Thomas Rosser and part of the recently arrived brigade of Brigadier General Matthew C. Butler. Butler's Brigade had come up from South Carolina and was in reality mounted infantry; although these men had seen limited action during the war, they carried short Enfield rifles, which they employed with great effect, prompting the Federals to believe they faced regular infantry. The Confederates massed in dense woods behind improvised breastworks of logs and rails, backed by artillery and further protected by swamps. This time the Rebels owned advantages in position and manpower.

General Gregg's men struck this position with admirable fury, initiating one of the most heated cavalry battles of the war. The dismounted action lasted for several hours, with neither side gaining advantage. Late in the day, Sheridan sent Custer's brigade to buttress Gregg. The Wolverines dismounted and took position between Gregg's two brigades, and the Federal line moved forward, driving the Confederates from their position with heavy losses, particularly in Butler's Brigade, which earned Sheridan's praise: "these Carolinians fought very gallantly in this their first fight, judging from the number of their dead and wounded, and prisoners captured." Gregg's and Custer's men suffered about 350 casualties, the bulk of which fell in Gregg's division. But again the Federal cavalry had triumphed.[10]

In what had become an unhappily regular pattern, the Cavalry Corps buried their dead, and those of the Confederates, on the field at Haw's Shop before making a night march to Old Church, where the horsemen found security with the gathering infantry. Sheridan wasted no time in sending pickets forward toward the important road junction of Cold Harbor, only ten miles east of Richmond, the possession of which, Sheridan recalled, "became a matter of deep interest." It was of deep interest to the Confederates as well, and they assembled a strong force in order to hold it. On May 30 the bulk of the First Division took up the fight to gain Cold Harbor, with Merritt's steady Reserve Brigade carrying the load. But the Confederates, Butler's South Carolinians again putting up a stiff fight, held until Custer's Michigan Brigade attacked dismounted and drove the defenders back on Cold Harbor.[11]

On the following morning, Sheridan conferred with Torbert and Custer, who had developed a plan to take Cold Harbor. As a testament to his leadership style and the confidence he had in his lieutenants, Sheridan readily endorsed the plan. That afternoon, Custer's and Merritt's brigades moved against the Confederate position. Another emerging theme of this campaign became the increased use of field works, and here the Rebels had thrown up dirt and rails on commanding ground backed by dismounted cavalry and an infantry brigade. A planned flanking maneuver by Devin's brigade failed to materialize; as Torbert complained, it did not appear that "a very serious attempt was made to carry

*General Wade Hampton. Courtesy of the National Archives*

out my designs." But Merritt detected an opportunity to flank the Confederate left and moved in for the kill. "General Merritt's plan was eminently success-ful," reported Torbert. Indeed, as Merritt's men struck the left, Custer hit the right; the combined thrust routed the defenders and drove them through Cold Harbor. Again the Confederates left their killed and wounded to the Federals.[12]

Sheridan proudly reported that his men "were now beginning to accept nothing less than victory." But again he had no time to celebrate, as General

Lee and the bulk of the Army of Northern Virginia closed rapidly on Cold Harbor. Sheridan had with him at Cold Harbor only the three brigades of the First Division and soon felt compelled to fall back on the main army. He had, in fact, initiated the withdrawal when orders arrived from army headquarters to hold his position "at all hazards." To do this, the battle-weary men reversed the Confederate works and dug in to face the new threat. On June 1, Lee's infantry attacked, but the Federal cavalrymen answered with steady fire from their Spencers and single-shot, breach-loading Sharps carbines, beating back two assaults until relieved by the VI Corps in the late morning. While the First and Second Divisions fought on the Federal left, Wilson's Third Division had been busy on the right, fighting a series of smaller actions in support of the army's advance.[13]

By the end of this latest drive the men and animals of the Cavalry Corps desperately needed rest. Almost a month of near-constant riding and fighting exacted a huge toll on the corps. Human casualties had been heavy but manageable under the circumstances, and many of the wounded would return to duty. Lost and damaged horses, though, continued to be a problem, as army procurement failed to keep pace with demands. For the time being the infantry took up the fight while most of the cavalry enjoyed a welcomed but short-lived respite.

As two great armies concentrated at Cold Harbor, Lee developed a strong position west of Old Cold Harbor, entrenching in preparation for Grant's next thrust. Grant hoped to launch an assault on June 2, but heavy rains and equally heavy skirmishing that day forced him to postpone the attack until the following morning. At 4:30 A.M. on June 3 the Army of the Potomac charged Lee's prepared works, precipitating one of the most horrible slaughters of the war. In a matter of minutes, thousands of blue-clad soldiers fell killed or wounded. By the time Grant called off the attack, 7,000 of his men had become casualties in this sad reminder of the slaughter at Fredericksburg a year and a half earlier. Lee's losses reached perhaps 1,500. Grant always regretted his costly orders at Cold Harbor, but Lee could scarcely celebrate what was his last real victory of the war, because unlike at Fredericksburg the giant Federal army refused to quit.

Although Wilson's division of the Cavalry Corps saw action on the Federal right during the battle, Cold Harbor was an infantry fight. The First and Second Divisions stood idle. For the next nine days the two armies remained stationary in their positions at Cold Harbor, while Grant and Lee plotted their next moves. But as Grant contemplated another sweep around the Confederate right toward the James River, he looked to the cavalry to create a diversion and at the same time cut into Lee's supply lines. On June 5, Meade's headquarters sent Sheridan his new marching orders: "With two divisions of your corps you will move on the morning of the seventh instant to Charlottesville and destroy the railroad bridge over the Rivanna, near that town. You will then thoroughly destroy the railroad from that point to Gordonsville, and from Gordonsville toward Hanover Junction."[14]

For the raid, Sheridan selected, not surprisingly, the divisions of Torbert and Gregg, as well as most of the horse artillery, which combined, with recent losses, numbered perhaps 8,000 officers and men. The column traveled light, each man carrying three days' rations (to last five days) and two days' feed for their horses. Each trooper packed forty rounds of ammunition (another sixty rounds per man went in wagons). On June 7 the command crossed the Pamunkey at New Castle and marched at a walk northwestward toward Gordonsville and the Virginia Central Railroad. The Virginia Central provided a vital link between the sustenance-rich Shenandoah Valley and Lee's army. Feeder lines from Staunton and Lynchburg met at Charlottesville, from which the rails stretched to Gordonsville and, via Trevilian Station and Hanover Junction, on into Richmond. In addition to wrecking this lifeline and diverting Confederate attention from Grant's intended crossing of the James southeast of Richmond, Sheridan had orders to unite with Major General David Hunter's command near Charlottesville and bring that force back to the Army of the Potomac. It was an ambitious plan for exhausted soldiers and worn-out horses, but Sheridan had momentum and he had good reason to believe that the once-feared Rebel cavalry posed little threat. As it turned out, the so-called Trevilian Raid proved that the Confederate horsemen had plenty of fight left in them.[15]

When Lee learned of Sheridan's departure, he reasonably assumed the target of the Federal raid to be the Virginia Central and quickly ordered Wade Hampton, with his own and Fitz Lee's Divisions, probably less than 6,000 men in all, to move by a shorter direct route and intercept the raiders. Hampton might not have been Jeb Stuart, but the present emergency demanded his more restrained talent. Although a bold and determined fighter, the burly South Carolinian was no gambler; he believed, as Sheridan did, in concentrating his force, in conserving his mounts, and in fighting under the most favorable conditions possible—unlike Stuart, who frequently wore down his men and mounts and would give battle against almost any odds. Hampton, one of the South's richest men and a self-taught natural warrior, was one of few men without a West Point pedigree to rise to high command in Lee's army. It fell to Hampton to stop Sheridan and restore the luster to the Confederate cavalry.

Sheridan's march proceeded in easy stages along the North Anna River, being careful not to overburden the horses. He intended to strike the railroad at Trevilian Station and commence destruction from that point to Gordonsville, several miles to the west. By June 9, Sheridan knew that the Confederate

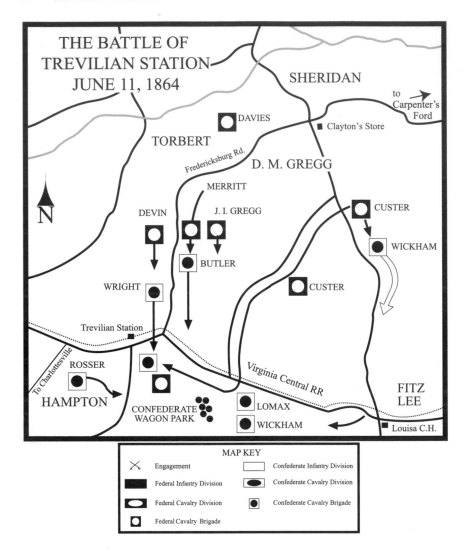

THE BATTLE OF
TREVILIAN STATION
JUNE 11, 1864

SHERIDAN

to
Carpenter's
Ford

DAVIES

Clayton's Store

TORBERT

Fredericksburg Rd.

D. M. GREGG

MERRITT

DEVIN          J. I. GREGG

CUSTER

WICKHAM

BUTLER

CUSTER

WRIGHT

Trevilian Station

ROSSER

To Charlottesville

HAMPTON

Virginia Central RR

FITZ
LEE

CONFEDERATE
WAGON PARK

LOMAX

WICKHAM

Louisa C.H.

MAP KEY

| ✕ | Engagement | | Confederate Infantry Division |
|---|---|---|---|
| ▬ | Federal Infantry Division | ⬭ | Confederate Cavalry Division |
| ◧ | Federal Cavalry Division | ⊙ | Confederate Cavalry Brigade |
| ◘ | Federal Cavalry Brigade | | |

cavalry had taken the bait and moved to block his advance. The following day, Sheridan's column crossed to the south of the North Anna and made camp within striking distance of Trevilian Station. But the "boldness of the enemy's scouting parties" that evening, Sheridan reported, "indicated the presence of a large force." Indeed, Hampton won the race to Trevilian Station.[16]

Before sunrise on June 11, Sheridan had his two divisions in motion, intending to strike Hampton's forces at Trevilian Station. Torbert's division, with

Merritt's Reserve Brigade leading the advance, marched down Fredericksburg Road from Carpenter's Ford on the North Anna, followed by Devin's Second Brigade and Gregg's division. Custer's brigade took an alternate parallel route toward the same objective. Hampton planned to block Torbert's advance with Brigadier General P. M. B. Young's Brigade (Colonel Gilbert J. Wright commanding) and Bulter's undaunted South Carolinians while Rosser's Brigade and Fitz Lee's Division struck the Federal flanks. Another furious cavalry battle ensued—one considered by many the hottest of the war. The Battle of Trevilian Station became a cauldron of confusion and carnage that seriously threatened to terminate Sheridan's run of success.

Fighting dismounted, Merritt's veterans struck the Palmetto State warriors and drove them back to dense woods, where Butler's men mounted another tenacious stand, perhaps half a mile from Trevilian Station. While Merritt's and Devin's brigades engaged in a brutal struggle with Butler's and Young's Confederates, Custer marched undetected around the action and fell upon Hampton's lightly defended wagon park and the led horses of Butler's and Young's commands at Trevilian Station. The impetuous Custer sent Colonel Russell Alger's 5th Michigan to take the unexpected prizes at hand. In short order, Alger's men swooped in upon the surprised defenders, capturing 800 men, 1,500 horses, and fifty wagons, plus caissons and ambulances. Alger imprudently left some men to guard his prize and took off in pursuit of fleeing Rebels. Fitz Lee's Division arrived from Louisa Court House, cutting off Alger from the rest of Custer's command and recovering all that Alger had captured as well as the men he left behind as guards, and soon took Custer's train and headquarters wagon. The arrival of Lee's column also scattered part of the 6th Michigan, sent to aid Alger. In a scene that anticipated the events on the Little Bighorn in 1876, Custer found himself trapped behind enemy lines and badly outnumbered.

Hampton, alerted to Custer's move, ordered Rosser from his flanking position to meet the threat and also pulled troopers from the fight on Fredericksburg Road. With Lee's two brigades moving from the southeast, Rosser from the west, and elements of Butler's and Young's Brigades from the north, the Confederates converged on Custer's position. Surrounded, Custer formed something of a hollow square out of what remained of his brigade—the 1st and 7th and part of the 6th Michigan Cavalries—and managed to hold his ground with desperate fighting.

Sheridan then added weight to the attack on the Carpenter's Ford road, throwing in Irvin Gregg's brigade of the Second Division. He also sent Davies's brigade to snap at Fitz Lee's flank in order to relieve some of the pressure on Custer. Late on this miserably hot day, Merritt, Devin, and Irvin Gregg broke Butler's line north of Custer's position to relieve the First Brigade. Perhaps it

*General George Armstrong Custer. Courtesy of the Library of Congress*

was a sign of Custer's famous luck that he and his brigade survived the battle, but as Torbert reported, "Much credit is due to General Custer for saving his command under such trying circumstances." Yet all of the "Boy General's" efforts would have come to naught without the tenacious fighting of Merritt's and Devin's men. The reunited corps pushed Hampton's Division to the west and Lee's to the southeast, gaining Trevilian Station and taking 500 Confederate prisoners. When the fighting ended, Sheridan could claim a tactical victory but nothing more. His command had been badly mauled, and during the night, Lee's Division marched to join Hampton west of Trevilian for a renewed effort to block Sheridan's further advance.[17]

On June 12, another very warm day, Gregg's troopers commenced destruction of the railroad, while Torbert's division marched westward to secure the crossroads where the Charlottesville Road split from the Gordonsville Road. Sheridan abandoned the idea of uniting with Hunter, who had failed to reach Charlottesville, and citing concerns over the presence of Rebel infantry, inadequate ammunition supplies, and the burden of transporting the wounded and prisoners, he decided to terminate the raid and return to Grant's army. Torbert's advance along the Gordonsville Road, preparatory to that return, turned into another bitter fight made all the worse by the deadly heat. Torbert's three brigades hit the combined weight of Hampton's and Lee's Divisions, but after several attempts to dislodge the Confederates from their improved position, withdrew with heavy losses. Sheridan and his men would have to return on the route by which they came. The Rebel cavalry under its new commander earned a bit of redemption.

The retreat began that night. Sheridan's assertions to the contrary, the marginal victory of the previous day, followed by an unqualified reverse, amounted to failure, which a few miles of temporarily wrecked railroad could never offset. He had lost almost a thousand men killed, wounded, missing, and captured, and this time he left his most dangerously wounded behind in temporary hospitals along with hundreds of suffering Confederates, carrying the ambulatory in an odd assortment of wagons and carriages. Halting frequently to attend to these damaged soldiers, the battered command crossed the North Anna early on the thirteenth and stopped to allow the horses to graze and drink before the march entered the barren countryside of Northern Virginia. Hampton paralleled Sheridan's retreat, but his command and his horses suffered as well, and he refused to engage his enemy as he moved eastward in easy stages toward the James.

For the next eight days, Sheridan's column cut a circuitous route through war-scarred Northern Virginia, shadowed all the while by Confederate horsemen. Again the men had to forage for sustenance, and again the citizenry suffered. But the suffering became general on this hot, dusty march. In addition to looking after their own needs, the men of the Cavalry Corps had to feed and treat a thousand wounded men and prisoners, and soon an army of African American refugees joined the column as well. To make matters worse, the jaded mounts could not bear the burden imposed upon them. Hundreds of horses broke down and were shot—an ugly military expedient done to keep horses that would recover with a few days' rest from being rehabilitated for use by the Confederates.

The depleted command arrived at the former Army of the Potomac base near White House on the Pamunkey on June 21. Sheridan discovered that Grant had moved the army across the James River to attack Petersburg from the east and had established a new base at City Point. Back in May, while Grant and Lee fought the Battles of the Wilderness and Spotsylvania, Ben Butler's Army of the James moved up that river in an effort to attack lightly defended Richmond from the south in conjunction with Grant's drive from the north. As Lee slowed Grant's advance, General P. G. T. Beauregard assembled a ragtag force that turned Butler away from the capital and back into his prepared works at Bermuda Hundred on the James. Butler's bridgehead became the staging point for Grant's army when it sidestepped Richmond to strike the important railroad center at Petersburg. On June 16, 17, and 18, Grant flung his forces at the Petersburg defenses, but Beauregard managed to beat back these assaults until Lee arrived with most of his main force. Reluctantly, Grant began siege operations.

At White House, Sheridan found much of the army's supply train and some infantry Grant had left behind. After establishing contact with Grant's headquarters, Sheridan received orders to "break up the White House depot" and escort more than 900 wagons to the new base at City Point—not a duty that he relished or that his command was particularly prepared to undertake in its distressed state. The troopers got little rest over the next two days as the men tore down the depot and prepared for what promised to be a most difficult mission. Sheridan understood his encumbered command's vulnerability to attack from the nearby Confederates; in fact, an attack appeared certain. On June 23 the First Division led the trains to the Chickahominy River crossing while David Gregg's division covered the right flank. Tom Devin's brigade, supported by several infantry companies of U.S. Colored Troops, beat back a vigorous probe by Brigadier General John R. Chambliss's Brigade of Rooney Lee's Division, and the wagon train crossed in good order.[18]

The procession continued the next day toward Charles City Court House. Sheridan posted Gregg's division at St. Mary's (Samaria) Church, between the Chickahominy and the James, with orders to hold off the Confederates until the train reached the James River. Torbert's men faced only minor opposition as they led the wagons safely to the James, while at St. Mary's Church, Gregg received the bulk of Hampton's cavalry. Badly outnumbered and fighting in oppressive heat, the Second Division put forth a stubborn effort, suffering heavy losses before it gave way. The division withdrew in "some confusion," leaving its dead and seriously wounded on the field, but it did its job. "This very creditable engagement," Sheridan reported, "saved the train, which should never have been left for the cavalry to escort." It was the kind of performance now expected of Gregg and his men.[19]

Gregg's action allowed the train to reach the James essentially unmolested. Over the next several days the trains, men, and mounts ferried across the river, the last of the troopers crossing on June 28. The First and Second Divisions of the Cavalry Corps rejoined the Army of the Potomac after twenty-one days of marching and fighting. The raid, for all intents and purposes, had failed; it bought no strategic advantage that could not have been achieved by keeping the cavalry with the main army. Besides the harrowing victory at Trevilian Station on June 11 and the destruction of a few miles of rail and telegraph wire that the Rebels quickly repaired, the Federal raiders had little else to show for three weeks of arduous campaigning. Exceptionally high attrition among men and horses limited the command's usefulness for weeks to come. The campaign, though, continued the maturation of the Cavalry Corps. Losses among field- and company-grade officers could not easily be filled, but the division and brigade commanders again performed well, often superbly, and Sheridan kept the command together and maintained amazingly high morale under most demanding circumstances. Fortunately for the Cavalry Corps, the Union could supply replacements for the lost troopers and horses; therefore, the campaign, while unsuccessful, turned out far from devastating. When it returned to the field, Sheridan's cavalry would be more formidable than ever.

# ≥ 3 ≤

# "War Is a Punishment"

$\mathcal{S}$heridan's arrival on the south side of the James did not bring immediate relief for the two returning divisions of the Cavalry Corps. Before getting any rest, the seriously depleted divisions of Torbert and Gregg received orders to rescue the Third Division, whose own raid had come to peril south of Petersburg. In the absence of the First and Second Divisions, Wilson's Third Division ran itself ragged trying to fulfill all of the army's demands. To make matters worse, Grant ordered Wilson to stage a raid on the three rail lines leading into Petersburg and Richmond—the Weldon, which entered Petersburg from the south; the Southside, connecting Petersburg with the Shenandoah Valley; and the Richmond & Danville, which split from the Southside line to feed the Confederate capital.

Supported by the Cavalry Division of the Army of the James, Brigadier General August V. Kautz commanding, Wilson launched his raid on June 22. With 5,000 troopers, Wilson struck the Southside and Danville lines, doing significant damage, but on the return march the raiders found their path blocked by Confederate cavalry, freed for action after Sheridan crossed the James. Promised Federal infantry support failed to materialize. Forced to divide his command and cut his way through the opposition, Wilson lost hundreds of men captured, his supply train, and his artillery before reaching the safety of Union lines on July 1 and before Sheridan's relief column could render any aid. Wilson's casualties came to 1,500; losses in horseflesh were equally high. Grant, Meade, and Sheridan considered the raid a success, the destruction of Rebel rail lines more than compensating for the exceptionally high losses suffered by the Third Division.

On July 2 the Cavalry Corps began a three-week period of much deserved rest, interrupted only by light picket duty. During that time, the corps received replacement men and mounts and badly needed supplies. In recognition of their service during the Wilson raid, George Chapman and John McIntosh garnered promotions to brigadier general, but their commands remained undermanned. The corps had yet to regain its full strength when called upon for another raid.

With the advance on Petersburg stymied, Grant and Meade reluctantly authorized a novel plan brought forth by a regiment in General Burnside's IX Corps to dig a mine beneath the Confederate line, pack it with dynamite, and explode it, creating a huge gap through which the Federal infantry would storm. To pull Confederate troops from the planned point of attack, Grant ordered a diversion north of the James River by Winfield Scott Hancock's II Corps. Sheridan, with Torbert's and Gregg's divisions, was to exploit the bridgehead and with Kautz's small division raid the Virginia Central Railroad. The crossing went as planned, but Lee's ability to shift troops rapidly from one point to another ended all hope for the raid. The cavalry fought sharp actions on July 27 and 28 and withdrew on the 29th.

On July 30, Torbert's and Gregg's divisions recrossed the James and rode to the opposite end of the Federal line to join Wilson's division for an attack on the Confederate right in conjunction with the mine explosion scheduled for that day. The mine charge detonated early that morning, blowing a huge crater in the Confederate trench line. But the infantry exploitation went horribly wrong. Stunned Rebels quickly responded to the emergency, pouring intense fire into the attackers as they flooded the crater. The Battle of the Crater became a mammoth disaster, resulting in almost 4,000 Federal casualties. Fortunately for the cavalrymen, Meade canceled their portion of the assault. The Siege of Petersburg continued for another eight months, but it would do so without Sheridan and most of the Cavalry Corps.

When Grant laid out his plans for the grand offensives of 1864, the primary efforts—those against Lee's main force in Northern Virginia and Joe Johnston's army in Georgia—received the lion's share of attention and resources. But numerous ancillary campaigns figured prominently in Grant's design to win the war by the year's end. The most significant of these campaigns involved control of the rich and scenic Shenandoah Valley. Although removed from the worst of the fighting for most of the war, the Valley held special importance, materially, militarily, and psychologically. Nestled between the Appalachian range and the Blue Ridge, it stretched along the western border of old Virginia, north from Lexington to the confluence of the Shenandoah River and the Potomac River at Harpers Ferry, where it opened into Maryland and the back door to the Federal capital. By 1864 it represented one of the last major sources of food for Lee's beleaguered army. But from the beginning of the conflict the Valley had been fought over, parts of it changing hands numerous times. Stonewall Jackson made his reputation here with the brilliant campaign of 1862; Lee used the Valley as an invasion route for his two failed attempts to take the war to the North. Now, as fighting stagnated around Petersburg and Atlanta, the Shenandoah and its inhabitants stood to suffer the grim reality of total war.

The Shenandoah Valley had been, for the most part, an unhappy place for the Federals, and the opening clashes of the 1864 campaign offered nothing in the way of change. In concert with Grant's move into the Wilderness, German-born Major General Franz Sigel moved southward up the Valley in order to deprive Lee of its bounty and pin down Confederate troops in the region. But Sigel's advance came to an abrupt halt when, on May 15, Major General John C. Breckinridge's ragtag Rebel force defeated the Federals at New Market. Major General David Hunter replaced Sigel and commenced a march of destruction up the Valley, routing the badly outnumbered Confederates at Piedmont on June 5. Hunter then occupied Lexington, where on June 11, the same day that Sheridan and Hampton fought at Trevilian Station, he ordered the burning of the Virginia Military Institute before moving on to Lynchburg. Breckinridge, who had joined Lee's army, quickly led his command back to the Valley. Lee, concerned about his tenuous rail link at Lynchburg, on June 12 ordered Lieutenant General Jubal A. Early, recently promoted to command the Second Corps of the Army of Northern Virginia, to march with his entire corps to Lynchburg. On June 17 and 18, Hunter made halfhearted probes of the reinforced Confederate position at Lynchburg before retreating into West Virginia, leaving the Valley to Early and the gate to Washington wide open.

After terminating the immediate threat to Lee's rail communications, Early prepared to take his command, reorganized into two small infantry corps under Breckinridge and Major General Robert Rodes, assorted cavalry units, and artillery, for a diversionary raid down the Valley and threaten the vulnerable Federal capital, stripped as it was of men to feed Grant's blue monster in Virginia. Lee hoped that this thrust might compel Grant to loosen his grip on Petersburg and Richmond by sending off a sizable portion of his force to deal with Early or perhaps to launch a costly attack on the Confederate trenches.

On June 28, as Sheridan's battered force reached the James after the un-successful Trevilian raid, Early assembled at Staunton his 14,000-man force, shockingly small for the proposed work at hand, and began a spirited march northward down the Valley. By July 4 the exuberant column had reached Harpers Ferry. Bypassing the Federal garrison there, Early's raiders crossed the Potomac and moved into Maryland on July 6. That same day, Brigadier General John D. Imboden's cavalry destroyed sections of the Baltimore & Ohio (B&O) Railroad while Brigadier General John McCausland's cavalry occupied Hagerstown, exacting a $20,000 reparation from the town for Hunter's depreda-tions in Virginia. On July 9 the gray ranks passed through Frederick, where Early demanded and received a $200,000 cash ransom, but the next day the crusty, profane Confederate commander found his path blocked by a hastily assembled Federal force under Major General Lew Wallace. Wallace, who commanded the Middle Department from his headquarters in Baltimore, gathered what men he could find and rushed to Monocacy Junction, south of Frederick on the

*General Jubal A. Early. Courtesy of the National Archives*

road to Washington; he hoped to delay Early's advance long enough for reinforcements to come up from Grant's army. By the time Early arrived, Wallace's
force had been augmented by a division from the Army of the Potomac's
VI Corps, rushed from Virginia to meet the emergency.

After a hot contest in which Wallace lost more than a quarter of his 7,000
men, the Federals broke and retreated in disorder, yielding to Early the road
to Washington. But Wallace's valiant stand bought valuable time, a full day
as it turned out, to prepare the capital for Early's arrival. Still, panic gripped
Washington, fueled by wildly exaggerated estimates of the raiders' strength—
some as high as 30,000—and the certain knowledge that the city's defenses
were manned by unsteady militia and walking wounded. Much of the fear

dissipated when the balance of Major General Horatio Wright's VI Corps filed into Washington, followed closely by elements of the XIX Corps, recently shipped to Virginia after operations in Louisiana.

The Confederates approached Washington's outer defenses on July 11. Early planned an assault for the following day, but during the night he learned from informants that indeed two veteran corps had filled or soon would fill the forts that ringed the Federal capital. After some lively skirmishing on July 12, Early pulled away and headed for the Potomac and a return to the Valley. The Federals mounted an ineffectual pursuit while Hunter's troops, after a frustrating absence, reentered the fray under Sheridan's old friend George Crook. Despite a minor Union victory at Cool Springs, the raiders managed to reach the Valley. At this point, the VI Corps began its return to Washington, only to be sent back after Early bested Crook at Kernstown on July 23. Before the Federals could get a grip on things, the Confederates again moved down the Valley in what appeared to be another strike against Washington. At Martinsburg, West Virginia, on July 28, the Confederates destroyed an important railroad facility, and two days later two Rebel cavalry brigades under McCausland occupied Chambersburg, Pennsylvania. When local leaders refused the general's demand for an exorbitant ransom, the raiders put the town to the torch, another act of reprisal for Hunter's wanton activities in the Valley, surrendering, if it mattered at this stage, whatever moral high ground the Confederacy might have occupied.

After a month of marching, some hard fighting, and much mischief, Early showed no sign of slowing down. It appeared to Grant, who initially paid little attention to the Valley, that Early's activities warranted a more robust response. But Early's wide-ranging activities brought into play four separate and often overlapping Federal departments, conflicting lines of command, and no shortage of confusion. Grant had had about enough of this rather formidable diversion. All along, he wanted to deal with Early without a substantial disruption of his main effort, but the time had come to devote whatever resources might be required to end this menace once and for all and then lay waste to the Valley. The most effective way to accomplish this goal was to bring the various departments involved under one unified command—something he had considered for weeks. But to whom could he assign this essential role? He proposed his old friend William Franklin, but political opposition—mostly Lincoln's—quashed that idea; he considered the quarrelsome Meade and even the zealous Hunter, but in the end he settled on Sheridan—a decision Lincoln only reluctantly endorsed.

Although Grant wanted Sheridan involved, Chief of Staff Halleck and Secretary of War Stanton thought him too young for such a command. Also, Hunter ranked Sheridan by virtue of seniority. So when Grant ordered Sheridan to the Valley, the cavalry commander's role had yet to be defined. Hunter's reaction would provide that definition. Grant wrote to Halleck on August 1: "Unless General Hunter is in the field in person, I want Sheridan put in command of all the troops in the field, with instructions to put himself south of the enemy and follow him to the death. Wherever the enemy goes let our troops go also. Once started up the Valley they ought to be followed until we get possession of the Virginia Central Railroad." On August 2, Sheridan was relieved, temporarily, of his duties with the Army of the Potomac, and ordered to report to Washington, even as Grant and Halleck discussed the various contingencies. Hunter selflessly made it easy on everyone by stepping aside.[1]

On August 7 the War Department announced: "1. The Middle Department and the Departments of Washington, of the Susquehanna, and of West Virginia will constitute the Middle Military Division. 2. Maj. Gen. P. H. Sheridan is assigned by the President to the temporary command of the Middle Military Division." That same day, Grant welcomed Sheridan to his new command: "What we want is prompt and active movements after the enemy in accordance with instructions you already have. I feel every confidence that you will do the very best, and will leave you as far as possible to act on your own judgment, and not embarrass you with orders and instructions." Sheridan could ask nothing more. Since taking charge of the Cavalry Corps he had argued for an independent command—his Virginia raids only confirmed (in his mind at least) the correctness of his belief that he could achieve great things—and now, still only thirty-three years of age, he commanded an army. For the job at hand, no one was better suited.[2]

What Grant had in mind, what he understood to be necessary, involved not simply victory but victory accompanied by the kind of devastation that would render the Valley useless to the Confederacy—militarily and materially—and discourage civilian support for the war. In two often-recalled dispatches to Halleck in July, Grant articulated these views. Federal troops in the Valley, he wrote, should be prepared "to eat out Virginia clear and clean as far as they go, so that crows flying over it for the balance of this season will have to carry their provender with them." He wanted to "make all the Valley south of the Baltimore and Ohio Road a desert as high up as possible," elaborating, "I do not mean that houses should be burned, but all provisions and stock should be removed, and the people notified to move out."[3]

Sheridan, perhaps concerned about how posterity might judge him, added his thoughts on the subject to a campaign report filed after the war: "I do not believe war to be simply that lines should engage each other in battle, as that is but the duello part—a part which would be kept up so long as those who live at home in peace and plenty could find the best youth of the country to enlist in their cause . . . and therefore do not regret the system of living on the enemy's country. These men and women did not care how many were

killed or maimed, so long as war did not come to their doors, but as soon as it did come in the shape of loss of property, they earnestly prayed for its termination. As war is a punishment, and death the maximum punishment, if we can, by reducing its advocates to poverty, end it quicker, we are on the side of humanity."[4]

Sheridan's new command, pulled together in the heat of emergency, was a conglomerate force with few common threads. Horatio Wright's veteran VI Corps from the Army of the Potomac formed its backbone. The Connecticut-born Wright, who graduated second in his 1841 West Point class and built a distinguished career as an engineer officer prior to the war, was a respected and well-liked soldier who inherited the VI Corps following the death of popular John Sedgwick in the Wilderness. Although Sheridan's senior—in age and in military service—by eleven years, Wright never made it an issue. His

*General Horatio Wright. Courtesy of the National Archives*

three divisions contained some of the Union's toughest campaigners, including their commanders. Brigadier General David A. Russell, a New York–born West Pointer (class of 1845), had been Sheridan's friend and commander during the prewar days in the Pacific Northwest. His daring leadership style had earned him the respect and admiration of his men and fellow officers. Russell's First Division included brilliant Brigadier General Emory Upton, who led the Second Brigade. At twenty-four, Upton, a burgeoning military theorist, had risen to brigade command on his audacious battlefield performance at Spotsylvania, where he spearheaded an attack that almost broke Lee's army. Brigadier General George Washington Getty, a career artillery officer from the District of Columbia who graduated from West Point in 1840 (with Sherman and George Thomas) and fought in Mexico, assumed command of the Second Division prior to the Battle of the Wilderness, where he received a dangerous wound. Although fairly new to the corps, Getty already owned a fine reputation. The Third Division, which fought tenaciously at Monocacy Junction, took its orders from another solid veteran, Brigadier General James B. Ricketts of New York. An 1839 graduate of West Point, Ricketts had been wounded several times and spent many months as a prisoner of war. Like his fellow division commanders in the VI Corps, he enjoyed the respect of his comrades, respect earned in battle.

The two-division XIX Corps, just off an unhappy experience in the Red River Campaign and commanded by Maryland-born Brigadier General William Emory, presented something of an unknown quantity. At fifty-three, Emory ranked among the oldest Federal officers still leading troops in the field—having graduated from the academy in the year of Sheridan's birth (1831). After a distinguished career as an engineer, Emory languished under the ineffectual leadership of George McClellan and Nathaniel Banks. His assignment to the Middle Military Division offered a new lease on life for Emory and the XIX Corps. When Sheridan met his new army, he found only Brigadier General William Dwight's First Division of the XIX Corps present for duty. Almost singular among Sheridan's division commanders, Dwight was of questionable character and dubious quality. Dismissed from West Point in 1853, he became a brigadier general of Volunteers in 1862 and had seen some hard fighting, but as Banks's chief of staff during the Red River Campaign, his primary function, apparently, had been to ship contraband cotton to mills in his native Massachusetts. The Second Division, still en route to the field, was led capably by Brigadier General Cuvier Grover of Maine. Graduated near the top of his West Point class of 1850, Grover had commanded a brigade during the early fighting in Virginia before leading a division under Banks in Louisiana.

Sheridan's friend and former West Point classmate Brevet Major General Crook commanded Hunter's former command, now designated the Army of West Virginia but also known as the VIII Corps. The Ohioan graduated from

*General William Emory. Courtesy of the National Archives*

the academy near the bottom of his 1852 class and served on the frontier prior to the war. His war service had been diverse and generally successful. After leading troops in Western Virginia and at Antietam, earning a commission as brigadier general of Volunteers in September 1862, he led a cavalry division in the Army of the Cumberland before returning to head a division in West Virginia. In July he assumed command of Hunter's field forces, and despite his loss to Early at Kernstown, he held Sheridan's trust and admiration. In addition to his demonstrated skill as a leader of men, Crook possessed strong battlefield awareness and knowledge of the area. He thus became an invaluable confidant for the new army commander. Crook's two division commanders, both only colonels—Joseph Thoburn and Isaac Duval—came from civilian backgrounds but had led troops, mostly in Western (West) Virginia since early in the conflict. Promising Ohio politician-turned-warrior Colonel Rutherford B. Hayes commanded a brigade in Duval's Second Division. Although barely the size of a full division, the so-called Army of West Virginia could provide a formidable kick if properly employed.

The cavalry complement provided Sheridan with certain familiarity and some new challenges. Torbert's division of the Cavalry Corps, ordered to Washington on July 30, remained detached for service in the Valley. A few days later, at Sheridan's request, Wilson received orders to join Torbert with his division. Hunter's West Virginia cavalry, two brigades under New York–born Brigadier General William Averell, gave Sheridan an additional mounted division. Averell, an 1855 graduate of West Point, had held various cavalry commands in the Army of the Potomac, becoming a brigadier general of Volunteers in September 1862. The following March his cavalry division scored the first victory of the war against Stuart's command at Kelly's Ford, but he was banished from the Army of the Potomac for an allegedly lethargic performance during the Chancellorsville Campaign. A string of recent successes in West Virginia and in the Valley notwithstanding, Averell faced a rocky tenure under Sheridan.

Surely, Sheridan welcomed his workhorse First Division and was no doubt pleased to have Wilson's men join the command, but for some unexplained reason, and somewhat surprisingly, Gregg's stalwart Second Division, rather than perhaps Wilson's, stayed with the main army. Equally surprising was Sheridan's selection of Torbert as chief of cavalry for the Middle Military Division. Torbert had thus far performed well in the role of cavalry commander, and his division clearly had become Sheridan's favorite. But Gregg offered more experience and likely inspired more respect among the horsemen. Torbert's appointment posed something of a problem, since Averell ranked him by seniority and refused to accept orders from his junior until Sheridan gave him no choice. The time had passed for this kind of military formality.[5]

On the upside, Torbert's promotion facilitated the concurrent, and well-deserved, elevation of Wesley Merritt to command the First Division. As they remained technically attached to the Army of the Potomac, the First and Third Divisions retained their numerical designations while Averell's command, still part of the Department of West Virginia, became the Second Cavalry Division in the new organization. All of this created a documentary nightmare. Sheridan's force remained essentially provisional—the various units that constituted the so-called Army of the Shenandoah belonging, at least administratively, to other organizations—but the basic idea of a unified command in the Valley had been achieved.

Sheridan established his headquarters at Harpers Ferry and waited for the component parts of his army to concentrate around nearby Halltown, West Virginia, before assuming the offensive. Contrary to the popular impression of Sheridan as an impetuous warrior unleashed upon the Valley with over-whelming force, he displayed great patience and even caution in preparing for his duties. In fact, prior to assuming command, Sheridan endured an excru-ciating interview with Edwin Stanton, who openly opposed his appointment. The dour head of the War Department impressed upon him the importance of success but, more pointedly, stressed the political necessity of avoiding failure. With Grant bogged down at Petersburg and Sherman stalled around Atlanta, a Federal defeat in the Valley would probably doom Lincoln's already shaky chances for reelection.[6]

Sheridan, therefore, spent hours going over maps with the gifted young lieutenant John R. Meigs, whose impressive knowledge of the Valley Sheridan much admired. The Valley, with its mountains and gaps, offered myriad oppor-tunities for the kind of disaster Stanton feared. It had after all contributed to the ruination of many a Federal general. Sheridan resolved not to let the Valley defeat him. "It always came rather easy to me to learn the geography of a new section, and its important topographical features as well," he wrote; "the region in which I was to operate would soon be well fixed in my mind."[7]

The nature of his force—hardly a ready-made juggernaut—also con-tributed to Sheridan's initial prudence. The VI Corps, although well led and re-liable, had been worn down by constant fighting and marching and showed some displeasure with its current assignment. Grover's division of the XIX Corps had yet even to reach the Valley, leaving only Dwight's division of that corps on hand when Sheridan arrived. Crook's two small infantry divisions had been run ragged and were demoralized. Among the cavalry, only Merritt's division was present and ready for duty; the disgruntled Averell's command was scattered and poorly mounted, and Wilson's division, late to receive its marching orders, endured further delay in its laborious transport to Washington, where Wilson managed to have his First Brigade armed with Spencer repeaters.[8]

Still, the substantial Federal presence at Halltown did convince Early to pull back his raiding parties from north of the Potomac and concentrate along the Valley Turnpike near Martinsburg, West Virginia, where he could con-tinue to menace the Baltimore & Ohio Railroad. Although the Army of the Shenandoah left much to be desired, Sheridan ordered a general advance on August 10 that succeeded in driving the Confederates from the Lower Valley to a strong position at Fisher's Hill. After pushing as far as Strasburg on the fourteenth, Sheridan learned that reinforcements from Lee's army (reportedly two infantry divisions and Fitz Lee's cavalry) were en route and threatened his flank. Faced with a foe of undetermined strength and having at his disposal only some 21,000 men of all arms, Sheridan ordered a withdrawal to Hall-town. The movement featured many skirmishes, including Merritt's successful clash at Front Royal with Major General Joseph B. Kershaw's Division as it approached from Petersburg. By August 21 the Federals, now including Grover's XIX Corps division and Wilson's cavalry, had reestablished themselves at Hall-town as an emboldened Early closed in.

Over the next few weeks, Sheridan and Early maneuvered and skirmished and waited for an opportunity. Most of the activity involved cavalry: "the cavalry was employed every day in harassing the enemy, its opponents being principally infantry," Sheridan reported. "In these skirmishes the cavalry was becoming educated to attack infantry lines." This, of course, happened by design, the cavalry being the outstanding element of Sheridan's army. Merritt's First Division had reached elite status, while Wilson's had matured nicely. Significantly, Sheridan's army boasted an incredibly high ratio (more than 1 to 5) of cavalry to infantry, and his cavalry, when combined, far outnumbered the Rebel horses. The high esprit de corps that existed in the mounted arm, at least among Merritt's and Wilson's men, seemed to spread through the entire army. By mid-September, largely due to Sheridan's inspired leadership, the army exuded great confidence and stood poised to strike—if only the Confederates would oblige. Sheridan could ill afford to delay his major action much longer. Although Sherman's capture of Atlanta on September 1 brought some confirmation of Grant's sanguinary approach and brightened Lincoln's reelection hopes, it did nothing to relieve the anxiety on the Potomac. The Northern press and the Lincoln administration openly questioned the wisdom of Grant's decision to give Sheridan an army. Grant also needed to see results, and quickly, so he journeyed to the Valley to lend encouragement and offer a course of action. By the time Grant arrived at Charles Town, however, the opportunity Sheridan awaited had presented itself. He prepared to march, and Grant, withholding his own plan, readily endorsed that of his prized subordinate.[9]

On September 15, Sheridan learned of Kershaw's Division's return to Lee's army. Three days later, Averell reported that Early had divided his force, sending two of his four remaining infantry divisions to Martinsburg, leaving two near Winchester. Sheridan hoped to destroy the divided Confederate force in detail. The Army of the Shenandoah would strike first at Winchester and then turn on Early's forces at Martinsburg. At 2:00 A.M. on September 19, Merritt's and Wilson's cavalry divisions began the army's advance, initiating a bloody new phase of the war. Any doubts about Sheridan's fitness for command would soon be erased.

# ⇘ 4 ⇙

# "To the Bitter End"

$\mathcal{G}$eneral Early, having had things pretty much his way since coming to the Shenandoah Valley, allowed himself to be deceived by Sheridan's deliberate approach. "The events of the last month had satisfied me," he later wrote, "that the commander opposed to me was without enterprise, and possessed an excessive caution which amounted to timidity." These sentiments echoed the indictments leveled by critics in Washington at the time. But as General Merritt accurately pointed out, Sheridan's "caution was fortunate at this time," adding, "his fearlessness and hardihood were sufficiently displayed thereafter." Early's overconfidence gave Sheridan the opening he needed. "He had come out to fight," Merritt wrote, and "fight he would to the bitter end."[1]

Early's contempt for his younger adversary's generalship had seduced him into a foolish venture. With his two best and largest divisions—Rodes's and Major General John B. Gordon's—he set off to harass Union work crews on the B&O near Martinsburg, something he had done with relative impunity for the past several weeks (much to the displeasure of railroad officials and the Lincoln administration). He left only the small divisions of Major General S. Dodson Ramseur and Brigadier General Gabriel Wharton (under the direction of Breckinridge) to cover Winchester. But at a telegraph station near Martinsburg, Early learned of Grant's visit to Sheridan and reasoned logically that such a meeting presaged the long-anticipated Federal advance. Seemingly unshaken, he quickly ordered Rodes and Gordon back to within reach of Winchester. Although outnumbered roughly three to one, the Confederate commander remained confident. After all, he had learned his trade under Lee and Stonewall Jackson; he knew that long odds did not necessarily foretell defeat. Nor did a divided command necessarily pose a problem—Second Manassas (Bull Run) and Chancellorsville offered vivid reminders of what an outnumbered, divided Confederate army could accomplish. Like Lee, Early relied on audacity more than numbers. And his Army of the Valley, while small, contained

51

some of the best officers and men the Confederacy could muster, including many veterans of Jackson's 1862 campaign; others had held the Sunken Road at Sharpsburg (Antietam). These tough, battle-tested soldiers had faced long odds from the start and could be counted upon to rise to this occasion. Early, though, made their jobs considerably tougher. Even if he managed to reunite his army, it would number at best 14,000 of all types of arms, and Sheridan was on the way with more than 40,000 men.[2]

Early did manage to get Rodes's and Gordon's Divisions to within supporting distance of Winchester before the Federals struck, but his two divisions at Winchester remained dangerously exposed. Wilson's cavalry led the main Union advance—the VI and XIX Corps—westward from Berryville toward Opequon Creek, which ran south to north some three miles west of Winchester. Crook's two divisions, with a longer march, followed on this line and represented the army's mobile reserve. Meanwhile, Merritt's and Averell's mounted divisions crossed the lower Opequon and united at Stephenson's Depot on the Martinsburg Pike in order to hit Winchester from the north.

The Battle of Opequon, or Third Winchester, began in the predawn hours of September 19, when Wilson's division crossed Opequon Creek and pressed through an inclining ravine known as Berryville Canyon, which opened to a plateau east of Winchester. McIntosh's First Brigade led the way, bursting through the canyon and driving the unprepared Rebels—elements of Ramseur's Division—from the canyon's exit. But the outgunned Southerners fought tenaciously before falling back on prepared positions east of Winchester. Wilson's men accomplished their job, opening the way for the infantry, but it had been an unexpectedly tough and costly fight. General McIntosh, who received a serious leg wound that necessitated amputation of the limb and ended his active war service, became the first serious casualty among Sheridan's top lieutenants—but the day was young. Unfortunately for Sheridan and his army, gross blunders in the deployment of Wright's VI Corps negated any early advantage and cost Sheridan the opportunity to destroy Ramseur's Division before help arrived.

Contrary to orders, Wright placed his lengthy supply train on the narrow road between his corps and the trailing XIX Corps, causing a massive bottleneck that delayed the planned full-scale attack by six hours, hours Early used to complete the concentration of his forces at Winchester. As the opposing infantry filed into position, both sides exchanged lively artillery fire. By late morning the VI and XIX Corps finally cleared the canyon and prepared for the much-delayed attack, with Getty's division on the left, south of the Berryville Road, Ricketts's men in center astride the road, and Grover's division of the XIX Corps deployed in the woods on the right. Russell's and Dwight's divisions stood in reserve. Crook, still further back, was, according to Sheridan, to join Wilson's cavalry, which had formed on the far left, for a flanking attack on the

*General John McIntosh. Courtesy of the Library of Congress*

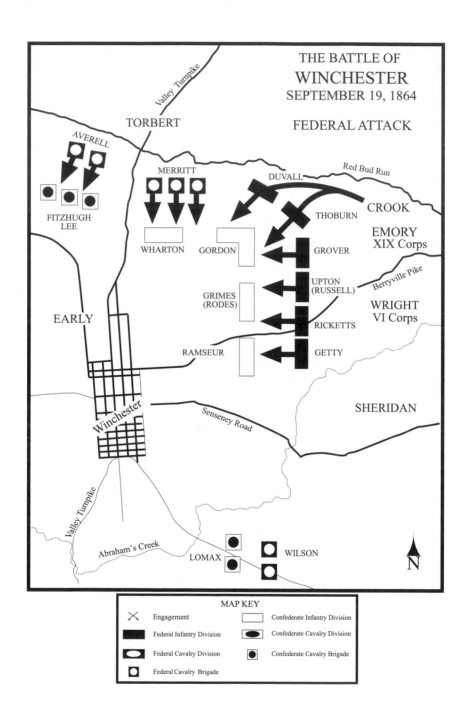

THE BATTLE OF
**WINCHESTER**
SEPTEMBER 19, 1864

FEDERAL ATTACK

Valley Turnpike

TORBERT

AVERELL

MERRITT

DUVALL

Red Bud Run

CROOK

THOBURN

FITZHUGH
LEE

WHARTON

GORDON

GROVER

EMORY
XIX Corps

UPTON
(RUSSELL)

Berryville Pike

GRIMES
(RODES)

WRIGHT
VI Corps

EARLY

RICKETTS

RAMSEUR

GETTY

Winchester

Senseney Road

SHERIDAN

Valley Turnpike

Abraham's Creek

LOMAX

WILSON

N

MAP KEY

✕   Engagement     ▭ Confederate Infantry Division

◼ Federal Infantry Division     ⬛⬤ Confederate Cavalry Division

◖◗ Federal Cavalry Division     ◙ Confederate Cavalry Brigade

◘ Federal Cavalry Brigade

Confederate right. Facing the Federals, south to north in front of Winchester, were the small but ever-dangerous divisions of Ramseur, Rodes, and Gordon. Major General Lunsford Lomax's Division of cavalry held the Confederate right flank opposite Wilson.

Just before noon the blue line moved forward. Getty and Ricketts made steady progress against the Confederate right and center, and Grover did even better on the left, scattering a brigade of Gordon's Division but in the process opening a gap between his division and Ricketts's to his left. Colonel Warren Keifer's Second Brigade of Ricketts's division attempted to close the interval just as Rodes and Gordon unleashed a furious counterattack in which Rodes, one of the most highly regarded division commanders in the Confederacy, fell mortally wounded. The onslaught, though, checked the Federal advance and threatened to wreck Sheridan's entire plan by driving back the Federal right. But Little Phil had plenty of cards to play. At this crucial moment, he ordered in his immediate reserve—David Russell's First Division of the VI Corps, the Second Brigade of which belonged to dynamic Brigadier General Emory Upton, who less than a month past his twenty-fifth birthday had already established himself as a rising talent in the Union army. Upton, an 1861 graduate of West Point, earned his star for a fierce attack at Spotsylvania Court House back in May. Sheridan now called for a repeat performance.[3]

Russell deployed two of his brigades to block the Confederate advance but held Upton's brigade to strike the Rebels in flank as they drove forward. The intense fighting grew desperate as the Southerners pressed on. When the opportunity presented itself, Upton's brigade fixed bayonets and, spearheaded by Colonel Ranald Slidell Mackenzie's 2nd Connecticut Heavy Artillery (serving as infantry), smashed into the rapidly advancing gray ranks. Twenty-four-year-old Mackenzie, who graduated at the top of his West Point class of 1862 and had in his brief career already collected three wounds—one of which took two fingers from his right hand—galloped ahead of his troops "with his hat aloft on the point of his saber . . . through a perfect hailstorm of Rebel lead and iron, with as much impunity as though he had been a ghost." General Russell experienced no such luck. Already struck by a bullet in the chest—a wound Sheridan thought "must have proved mortal"—Russell continued to lead his men until "killed by a piece of shell that passed through his heart." The death of this much-admired officer, Sheridan recalled, "oppressed us all with sadness, and me particularly." But Upton's flank assault achieved the desired result; it broke the Confederate attack and allowed Sheridan to reform his line. For the time being, fighting abated as both sides anticipated future developments.[4]

Sheridan later wrote that he hoped to employ Crook's men as a flanking column on the far left. "As my lines were being rearranged, it was suggested to me to put Crook into the battle, but so strongly had I set my heart on using him to take possession of the Valley pike and cut off the enemy," he reported, "that I resisted this advice." Two additional factors probably contributed to Sheridan's reluctance to commit Crook to the main battle line: first, Crook's men remained far to the rear and would require valuable time to get into position; second, Sheridan expected at any moment to hear evidence of Torbert's advance from the north. But with no word from Torbert and fears of another Rebel attack on his right mounting, Sheridan ordered up Crook. As for Torbert's cavalry—Merritt's and Averell's divisions—the going had been frustratingly slow thanks to unexpected Rebel resistance.[5]

Before sunrise, Colonel Charles Lowell's Reserve Brigade of Merritt's division forced a crossing of Opequon Creek at Seiver's Ford northeast of Winchester and established a presence on the opposite bank, while Devin's brigade remained east of the stream. Less than a mile downstream (north), Custer's brigade faced stiffer opposition, but the young cavalier employed his men, both mounted and dismounted, with admirable skill in gaining the west bank of the creek, where they linked with Merritt's other brigades. Memories of this day prompted some inspired prose from Merritt: "The glorious old First Division was never in better condition. Officers and men, as they saw the sun appear bright and glorious above the horizon, felt a consciousness of renewed strength, a presentiment of fresh glory to be added that day to their already unfading laurels. They felt like men who were willing to do and die, that they were not deceived the history of the day proves." By sunrise the cavalry had completed a good day's work, but plenty remained to do. As Merritt recalled, "The rich crimson of that fine morning was fading away into the broad light of day when the booming of guns on the left gave sign that the attack was being made by our infantry." The main event had begun, and soon enough the cavalry would be expected to play its part.[6]

The cavalry, however, displayed no sense of urgency. The First Division stood east of Stephenson's Depot, awaiting the arrival of Averell's men. Soon, though, events at Winchester compelled Early to withdraw Wharton's Division, elements of which had harassed the Union cavalry all morning, leaving only two overworked cavalry brigades to confront the Yankee horsemen. At 1:30, Merritt brought forward Devin's brigade and ordered an attack that pushed the Rebels through Stephenson's Depot, where Averell joined the advance. With the Confederates falling back on Winchester, the Federal cavalry prepared to follow in grand style—five brigades abreast, all mounted, all well in hand. As with Merritt, the events of the day moved Custer to grandiloquence: "the line of brigades as they advanced across the open country, the bands playing the national airs, presented in the sunlight one moving mass of glittering sabers. This, combined with the various and bright-colored banners and battle flags, intermingled here and there with the plain blue uniforms of the troops, furnished one of the most inspiring as well as imposing scenes of martial grandeur ever witnessed upon a battle-field. No encouragement was required to inspirit either man or horse. On the contrary, it was necessary to check the ardor of both until the time for action should arise." The time for action had arrived.[7]

As this spectacular blue line trotted forward, three small Southern cavalry brigades commanded personally by Fitzhugh Lee stood no chance of halting it. But, typically, Lee charged the oncoming Federals, creating some momentary havoc before giving way. The Confederate commander suffered a leg wound that took him out of action, and what remained of his dogged troopers broke for the main Rebel position. "At this time (3:00 P.M.)," Merritt reported, "the field was open for cavalry operations such as the war has not seen." Indeed, the Federal cavalry, 7,000 strong, now prepared to deliver the coup de grace to Early's army at Winchester, but not before the infantry launched a last furious assault.[8]

At 3 o'clock, as the cavalrymen cleared the final obstacle north of Winchester, Crook's two divisions, having reached their staging points on the Federal right next to the XIX Corps, advanced smartly against ever-formidable Confederate resistance. General Crook, with Duval's Second Division, managed to slip beyond Gordon's exposed flank, compelling the fiery Georgian to fall back and refuse his left as Thoburn's First Division drove against Rodes's Division, now commanded by Brigadier General Bryan Grimes. Duval's advance bogged down in the swampy morass of Red Bud Run, allowing the Confederates to pull back in orderly fashion. Wharton's Division, which had been moved repeatedly, arrived to bolster Gordon and Grimes just as Duval's division, led by Rutherford B. Hayes's First Brigade, emerged from Red Bud Run and linked with Thoburn's men. New lines formed as artillery from both sides spewed forth withering fire. An hour into the attack, Crook tried forcefully to induce regiments of the XIX Corps to support his attack, but General Emory refused to issue the order. Young Upton, who joined Crook in this futile effort, soon came to the rescue.

Finally, at 4 o'clock, informed of Torbert's approach, Sheridan issued orders for a general advance. The VI Corps, with Upton commanding Russell's division on the right, Ricketts in the center, and Getty on the left, moved forward in conjunction with Crook. The renewed Federal effort combined with the imminent arrival of the mighty Yankee cavalry prompted a further restriction of the Confederate line, well conducted under heavy fire. The Southerners formed an inverted L close to the town, with Gordon's and Wharton's Divisions refused northward and Rodes's (under Grimes) and Ramseur's Divisions facing the oncoming VI Corps to the east. While Crook pressed Gordon, Upton unleashed his second major assault of the day. Again, Mackenzie and the 2nd Connecticut Heavy Artillery led the way. As the boyish, dark-tempered colonel dashed ahead of his men, "his horse was cut in two by a solid shot" from a

Rebel cannon that "grazed the rider's leg." Undeterred by his fourth wound, Mackenzie tied a handkerchief around his bleeding leg and continued on foot. Upton, also in the thick of things, received a life-threatening wound when a shell fragment cut a huge gash in his thigh that almost severed the femoral artery. Sheridan, who briefly attended his new division commander, ordered Upton to a hospital, but the general applied a tourniquet to his damaged limb and continued to direct his units from a stretcher until victory was assured. Such was the nature of this new generation of officers.[9]

Across the front, Federal soldiers fought. Sheridan rode among the regiments, inspiring officers and men to further heroics, waiting for the cavalry to strike. Early's outnumbered and outgunned army had on this long day met every threat with remarkable resilience and tenacity, surpassing any reasonable expectation, and had inflicted heavy casualties on the attackers, all for naught. Early had nothing to contest the mounted storm sweeping down from the north.

The Federal troopers had been in the saddle for most of fifteen hours when they arrived on the northern outskirts of Winchester and broke like a mighty wave upon the harried defenders. Averell's division, advancing west of the Martinsburg (Valley) Pike, veered right toward the Confederate rear, where it engaged two Rebel cavalry brigades in a desperate fight while Merritt's saber-wielding First Division charged into the northward-facing line held by Gordon's and Wharton's Divisions. Custer's brigade struck with fury, followed by Lowell's Reserve Brigade and Devin's Second Brigade. "The enemy's line," according to Merritt, "broke into a thousand fragments under the shock." This represented the first fully realized employment of mounted cavalry as a major strike force against infantry in a large battle during the war, and it confirmed long-held beliefs among horsemen that they were good for much more than scouting and raiding and flank protection, that they could in fact decide battles. The charge of the First Division, Custer gloated, "stands unequaled, valued according to its daring and success, in the history of this war." This bit of tactical innovation, in this war at least, belonged to Sheridan and sprang from an abiding confidence in his cavalry. Of course, he possessed an awesome weapon in this large and well-equipped mounted command, but no other army commander on either side had thus far so effectively employed all branches of his force in a single major battle. Sheridan's new model gained immediate currency and would prove unstoppable as the war drew to a close.[10]

As the cavalry plunged into the top of the inverted L, Mackenzie led Upton's brigade against the apex as the balance of the VI Corps pounded away against Grimes's and Ramseur's positions. Southerners resisted in small pockets before yielding to the overwhelming force. Under these hellish circumstances, Early managed to withdraw what remained of his army while Ramseur's Division, which retained its organization, mounted a rear-guard action that allowed the Confederates to save their trains and most of their artillery. As the sun set over the mountains to the west, the battered Rebel columns marched dejectedly southward up the Valley road toward Strasburg, an exit left open thanks to Lomax's two small cavalry brigades, who thwarted Wilson's inexplicably feeble efforts to cut the turnpike and deny Early his only realistic escape route.

The Battle of Opequon, as the Federals called it, ended as Sheridan hoped it would, but the desired result came with much more difficulty and at a considerably higher price than he could have expected. True, the Union forces finally had gained a victory big enough to erase the legacy of failure in the Shenandoah Valley, inflicting in the process some 4,000 casualties (almost half of which came in the form of captured and missing) and taking several artillery pieces, stands of colors, and hundreds of small arms. But it took a Herculean effort and 5,000 casualties to defeat a badly outnumbered and divided foe. David Russell was dead; Upton and McIntosh, who played vital roles in the day's success, survived their wounds but would not return to Sheridan's army. Duval, who led Crook's flank attack, and George Chapman, commanding Wilson's Second Brigade, also suffered wounds but would return to duty. At 7:30 that night, as an ineffectual Federal pursuit died in the darkness, Sheridan wired Grant with news of his great triumph in this "most stubborn and sanguinary engagement."[11]

The following day, as his army followed the Confederates to Fisher's Hill, Sheridan received congratulatory telegrams from his superiors. From Washington a grateful Lincoln sent a short note: "Have just heard of your great victory. God bless you all, officers and men." Secretary of War Stanton followed with words of appreciation and some tangible rewards: "Please accept for yourself and your gallant army the thanks of the President and this Department for your great battle and brilliant victory of yesterday. The President has appointed you a brigadier-general in the Regular Army, and you have been assigned to the permanent command of the Middle Military Division. One hundred guns were fired here at noon to-day in honor of your victory." General Grant also ordered a 100-gun salute (with live ammunition) on the Petersburg front, but in typical fashion remained focused on unfinished business. "If practicable," he admonished his triumphant lieutenant, "push your success and make all you can of it."[12]

Although Early readily acknowledged his defeat, he refused to credit the martial prowess of his adversary. "A skilled and energetic commander," he believed, would have destroyed the Army of the Valley. "As it was," Early wrote years later, "considering the immense disparity in numbers and equipment, the enemy had very little to boast of." Citing particularly Sheridan's failure to crush Ramseur's Division before help arrived and the vast superiority of the Federal cavalry, he concluded: "When I look back to this battle, I can but attribute my escape from utter annihilation to the incapacity of my opponent." The indictment held some undeniable truths; Sheridan had missed a rare opportunity to destroy an enemy army and, as Early pointed out, suffered 1,000 more casualties than did he. But Early could not deny that Sheridan's force had dealt him a crippling blow. As for casualties, the 5,000 Federal losses (700 killed, 4,000 wounded, and 300 missing) amounted to roughly one-eighth of the total engaged, while Early's 4,000 represented at least one-quarter of his force—a devastating toll by any reckoning. Losses were equally heavy among Confederate leaders: gallant and gifted division commander Rodes was dead, as were brigade commanders Brigadier General Archibald Godwin and Colonel George S. Patton (grandfather and namesake of the World War II hero), and Brigadier General Zebulon York had lost an arm. As the smoke cleared over Winchester, all that really mattered was that Sheridan had scored a much-needed Federal victory in his first full-scale battle as an army commander and that Early still had an army in the Valley.[13]

After an agonizing twenty-mile march with only brief periods of rest, the bloodied remnant of the Confederate Army of the Valley moved into positions along a ridge called Fisher's Hill that stretched across the Valley south of Strasburg. It offered the strongest position available and the only opportunity to fight at advantage. Early's men had occupied this same ground, and improved it with field works, back in August, when Sheridan, unsure of Rebel dispositions, declined to attack. Now with only 10,000 troops, not even enough adequately to man these formidable heights, Early hoped to turn back Sheridan a second time.

The victorious Yankees moved out of their camps around Winchester before dawn on September 20, heading southward to complete the destruction of Early's Confederates. Wilson's cavalry division led the way before it veered off the Valley Turnpike to the southeast toward Front Royal, while Averell's men marched southward along the Back Road, which ran parallel to and west of the pike. Merritt led the main advance, the VI and XIX Corps marching abreast on both sides of the pike, followed by Crook's two divisions, the artillery, and the massive wagon train. Merritt's troopers brushed back the few feeble attempts by Rebel cavalry to slow the march, and by early evening the army moved into position north of Strasburg, with Crook's men well back. Sheridan, as usual, personally reconnoitered his adversary's disposition and found it every bit as daunting as it had been in August. That night he met with Wright, Emory, and Crook to formulate a plan of action. He dismissed a frontal assault as out of the question, so discussion focused on alternatives, and the favored alternative became a flanking movement by Crook. Since the Rebels manned an excellent observation post atop Massanutten Mountain, Crook moved his divisions that night to a concealed position amid dense woods north of Cedar Creek to avoid detection.[14]

*General George Crook. Courtesy of the Library of Congress*

The Army of West Virginia remained hidden throughout the next day, while Sheridan developed the battle plan. Before sunrise on the twenty-first, Torbert took two brigades of Merritt's division to join Wilson at Front Royal in order to slip behind Early and cut his line of retreat up the Valley, leaving Devin's brigade to guard the army's trains. After some heavy fighting, Wilson took Front Royal, and Merritt's arrival late in the day induced the Confederate cavalry to withdraw. By late morning the VI and XIX Corps had pressed forward around Strasburg to assume positions behind Tumbling Run and before the Confederate lines on Fisher's Hill. By the morning of the twenty-second, after some brisk fighting, heated exchanges of artillery fire, and much shifting, the Federal infantry stood ready to exploit whatever hell Crook unleashed. Crook's men, meanwhile, rested.

But early on the twenty-second, Crook led his two divisions toward Little North Mountain and the Confederate left flank, the men taking the extra precaution of wrapping their canteens and other metal accoutrements in cloth to minimize noise. Further to disguise Crook's movement, Sheridan ordered lively demonstrations along the main line by the VI and XIX Corps. Still unaware of Crook's approach, Early watched the Federal activity on the twenty-second with mounting concern. Although he held a strong defensive position, his small army was stretched thin, and he began to doubt his ability to hold if Sheridan attacked, as it appeared he intended to do. The Confederate commander, therefore, issued orders that afternoon to withdraw during the night. Unfortunately for Early, his orders did nothing to stop Crook's advance, which continued unnoticed and unopposed. For their part, Crook's men negotiated the dense thickets and ravines, which fostered their concealment, with quiet determination, working their way along the eastern slope of Little North Mountain, well beyond the exposed western flank of the Confederate line.

When late in the afternoon the divisions of Hayes and Thoburn burst with a mighty yell down the mountain, Lunsford Lomax's 1,000 dismounted and demoralized Rebel cavalrymen had nothing for them and broke, exposing the entire Confederate line to destruction. Ramseur attempted to rally his division for a stand, but now the VI and XIX Corps, with Sheridan trailing Wright's men, joined the attack, driving frontally up the ridge and into Early's crumbling line. What resistance Confederate commanders could muster proved futile under such overwhelming force, and soon the disorganized Southerners streamed southward.

Measured against the recent carnage at Winchester, the clash at Fisher's Hill hardly counted as a major battle. That the attacking Federals suffered fewer than 600 casualties testified to the swiftness and completeness of their victory, which also explained the astonishingly low Rebel losses in killed and wounded— less than 250—and the more understandable 1,000 men missing and captured.

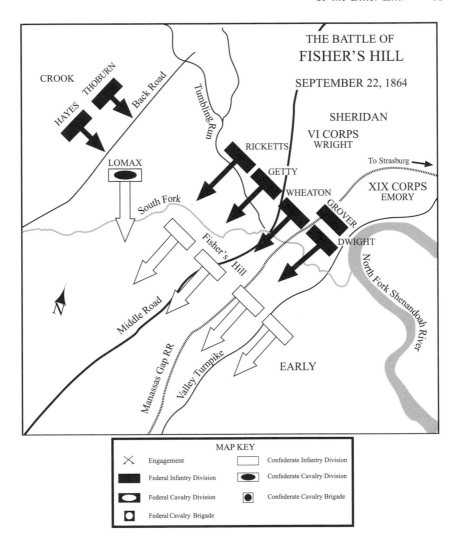

The Federals also took fourteen field pieces. All told, Early lost a tenth of his army and much of his artillery. But it could have and should have been worse. Darkness, rain, and Yankee disorganization prevented a thorough pursuit that the routed Southerners were ill disposed to contest. And fortunately for Early and his men, the anticipated blocking movement by Sheridan's cavalry, designed to deny a Confederate escape, failed to materialize.

At 11:30 that night, Sheridan wired Grant with the news of "a most signal victory over the army of General Early." He offered sketchy details of the battle at Fisher's Hill and explained that his First and Third Cavalry Divisions had been sent down the Luray Valley in order to cut the Valley Turnpike and block the Confederate retreat. He added that "if they push on vigorously to the main valley, the result of this day's engagement will be still more signal." In a telegram to Grant sent from Woodstock the following morning, Sheridan again predicted "great results" from his cavalry. This time, though, the horsemen let him down.[15]

After gaining Front Royal on the twenty-first, Torbert had his troopers in motion early on the next day, marching southward toward Luray, where they expected to turn west and strike the Valley Turnpike at New Market. But the advance came to an abrupt halt at Milford, where Wickham's Rebel cavalry, commanded by Colonel Thomas Munford, manned a strong position. The Federal cavalry briefly tested the Confederate line before Torbert, unwilling to risk a costly battle, ordered a withdrawal to Front Royal. Sheridan grew enraged when he learned of this setback, which rendered hollow the success at Fisher's Hill. Writing years later, Sheridan admitted, "to this day I have been unable to account satisfactorily for Torbert's failure." It was rather inexplicable in light of the recent boldness displayed at Winchester.[16]

Although Sheridan never regained complete confidence in Torbert, he reserved his immediate wrath for Averell, who failed to pursue aggressively the defeated Confederates from Fisher's Hill, leaving the task to the infantry. When Averell arrived at temporary army headquarters near Woodstock on the twenty-third, he exchanged some "hot words" with the commander. Yet, hoping to exploit the presence of a mounted division, Sheridan ordered Averell to join Devin's brigade, which now pressed the Federal pursuit to Mount Jackson. Again, Averell failed to perform up to his commander's expectations when his tardy support of Devin, in Sheridan's mind, dashed any chance of victory at Mount Jackson. Averell's uninspired performance, while only one source of Sheridan's mounting displeasure, proved sufficient to cause his removal. Late that night, Sheridan relieved this troublesome outsider, temporarily turning over the Second Cavalry Division to Colonel William Powell. On this day, Averell may well have paid for Torbert's sins, but his demise had been in the making since Sheridan came to the Valley. Averell left the army immediately, but the shakeups continued. On September 25, Grant telegraphed Sheridan to send "either Torbert or Wilson to report to Sherman to command his cavalry." Although this represented a prime opportunity to rid himself of Torbert, who continued to perform timidly as chief of cavalry, Sheridan selected Wilson, for whom he harbored even less regard, for transfer to Sherman's Western force. The ouster of Averell and the transfer of Wilson opened a division command for the deserving Custer. Sheridan originally slated the golden-haired "Boy General" for the Second Division but ended up giving him Wilson's division, retaining the competent Powell as Averell's replacement. Custer's ascent proved pleasing to both the army commander and the men of the Third Division.[17]

Sheridan's disappointment in his mounted force notwithstanding, in short order he had pushed deep into the Upper Valley, dealt the Confederates two crushing defeats, and stood prepared to finish the job. Not only had Sheridan become a national hero but also his victories at Winchester and Fisher's Hill, coming on the heels of Sherman's capture of Atlanta, all but guaranteed Lincoln's reelection, which meant that the war would be decided on the battlefield.

By September 25, Early's army had melted into the Blue Ridge beyond Front Royal to await the return of Kershaw's Division and Tom Rosser's cavalry brigade, while the pursuing bluecoats pulled up at Harrisonburg. Over the next several days, Sheridan's troopers laid waste to the Valley between Harrisonburg and Staunton. What the army could not use, it burned, destroying a reported 2,000 grain-filled barns and seventy mills, and making off with thousands of cattle and sheep. Meanwhile, Grant planned ahead. He proposed that Sheridan, with Early's force clearly whipped, take his army over the Blue Ridge, strike Charlottesville, and move along the Virginia Central Railroad to Richmond— a move that might well have ended the war months sooner. But Sheridan, who proved more conservative as an army commander than he did as a chief of cavalry, argued against such a move, citing a lack of transportation and, absurdly, an inability to sustain his army in the field. Grant relented, and Sheridan contented himself with devastating the Valley as he backtracked toward Winchester.

This utter, often wanton, destruction of the rich Valley occasioned terrible human suffering and became one of the most unsavory aspects of the war, and in this effort Sheridan's men rivaled or surpassed Sherman's more notorious merchants of misery in thoroughness. Sheridan and his superiors considered such business regrettable but fully justified as a military expedient. Southerners, though, would never forgive or forget this burning season.

# ⋉ 5 ⋊

# "All Sorts of Barbarity"

$\mathcal{A}$fter whipping the Rebels twice in quick succession and especially after such a one-sided affair as the clash at Fisher's Hill, even the most pessimistic Federal officer had to believe that Jubal Early and his dauntless little army were finished. Certainly Sheridan and Grant wanted to believe it, and most likely they did, which permitted them to think ahead. Grant continued gently to press his preference for a strike over the Blue Ridge against Charlottesville and the Virginia Central Railroad, while Sheridan remained adamant that his army lacked the transportation and the resources required to realize Grant's expectations. Also, some consideration had to be given to what the Confederates might do. President Lincoln, for one, needed reassurance: "I am a little afraid lest Lee sends re-enforcements to Early, and thus enables him to turn upon Sheridan." Grant calmly replied that he intended to discourage such detachments by increasing the pressure on Lee. Reports that Lee had ordered Joseph Kershaw's much-traveled division back to the Valley along with one of the South's most storied cavalry units—the Laurel Brigade—caused only mild concern.[1]

On October 1, 1864, Sheridan wired Grant to update the commanding general on the progress of his troopers' incendiary activities and once again beg off a move against Charlottesville. "The rebels have given up the Valley," he wrote. "I think the best policy will be to let the burning of the crops of the Valley be the end of this campaign, and let some of this army go somewhere else." So as the Federal high command pondered the next move, the Valley burned.[2]

As ancillary objectives of the Valley Campaign, the loathsome work of stripping the Valley of its material usefulness to the Confederacy and of sapping its inhabitants' desire to support that cause had been underway to some degree since Sheridan took charge of the Middle Military Division. But in the aftermath of Winchester and Fisher's Hill, as the Valley lay virtually unprotected, the scope of destruction and the precision with which the Yankees carried it out rose to levels unprecedented in American warfare. With the Federal army concentrated at Harrisonburg, Sheridan called forth the final destruction of the upper Valley. In a September 28 dispatch to General Merritt, Sheridan's chief of staff, Lieutenant Colonel James Forsyth, directed the cavalry commander to leave enough troopers to protect the various gaps in the Blue Ridge and with his own First Division and Custer's Third Division press forward to the vicinity of Staunton. The order was clear and simple: "Destroy all mills, all grain and forage, you can, drive off or kill all stock, and otherwise carry out the instructions of Lieutenant-General Grant." For emphasis, Forsyth included a copy of Grant's August 26 instructions to Sheridan: "Do all the damage to railroads and crops you can. Carry off stock of all descriptions, and negroes, so as to prevent further planting. If the war is to last another year, we want the Shenandoah Valley to remain a barren waste." With only the admonition that "no villages or private houses will be burned," the cavalry fanned out across the Valley, from the Blue Ridge to the Alleghenies, and went to work.[3]

During the next week, until October 6 when Sheridan ordered the general withdrawal, and for three days thereafter as the army fell back on Strasburg, the Federal troopers carried out their charge with alarming efficiency. After burning crops, destroying mills, and killing what stock they could not herd away from the Staunton–Port Republic area, the cavalry formed a cordon across the Valley behind the retiring infantry. Custer's Third Division on the west covered the Back Road, Merritt's men took the middle, marching on both sides of the main turnpike, while Colonel Powell with Averell's old command moved up the Luray Valley. They brought total devastation, their progress marked by the towers of smoke rising from torched barns and mills.

Colonel James H. Kidd, commanding Merritt's First Brigade, noted, "one could have made a chart of Custer's trail by the columns of black smoke which marked it." While some of the soldiers may well have fancied the work, most decidedly did not. Kidd recalled one instance when he led his troopers in an effort to save a home threatened by flames. But such attempts to minimize human suffering paled in comparison to the obvious toll this bitter application of total war exacted on the people of the Valley. "The anguish pictured in their faces," Kidd wrote, "would have melted any heart not seared by the horrors and 'necessities' of war." Indeed, few of those who experienced "the burning," soldier and citizen alike, emerged unscathed: "it was a disagreeable business and," Kidd admitted, "I did not relish it."[4]

By the time the army reached the familiar environs of Strasburg, the cavalry had amassed a staggering record of devastation. Sheridan reported on October 7 the destruction of "over 2,000 barns, filled with wheat, hay, and farming implements; over 70 mills, filled with flour and wheat." His troopers had driven off 4,000 head of livestock, captured a "large number" of horses, and "killed and issued to the troops not less than 3,000 sheep." The soldiers had burned acres of corn, vital leather tanneries and their valuable contents, iron furnaces, and locomotives and rolling stock. The value of property lost reached several million dollars; but no monetary figure could be attached to the suffering that followed in the wake of such a man-made catastrophe. The citizens of the Upper Valley faced a bleak existence at best. Sheridan closed his report to Grant with a chilling promise: "When this is completed the Valley, from Winchester up to Staunton, ninety-two miles, will have but little in it for man or beast."[5]

Another unsavory aspect of the Valley Campaign came to a head during this time. Since Sheridan's arrival in the Valley and the commencement of the campaign against Early, Southern guerrilla bands, including spectral Lieutenant Colonel John S. Mosby's 43rd Virginia Battalion—his Partisan Rangers—had harassed Federal supply trains and outposts. The name Mosby alone struck fear into teamsters and isolated pickets, not to mention a good many officers. Sheridan and other Union leaders considered such Southern partisans irregulars— criminals to be dealt with outside the rules of war; Mosby regarded himself and the members of his band as legally constituted protectors of their homeland, a view shared by the Confederate government. In reality, while Rebel guerrillas had caused a good deal of mischief and created more than a bit of consternation among the Yankee brass, they had not significantly impacted operations. But as the hostilities intensified and nerves grew raw, a grizzly sideshow opened. The killing of a Federal soldier by "bushwhackers" and many similar incidences occurred demanding brutal retaliation, and such retaliation yielded equally ugly countermeasures. Two such events brought the guerrilla war to the forefront.

On September 23 near Front Royal a large band of Mosby's Rangers (Mosby not among them) attacked an apparently undefended wagon train only to be surprised by Colonel Lowell's Reserve Brigade and routed. In the fight, Lieutenant Charles McMaster fell mortally wounded. The story spread that Mosby's men shot the officer as he tried to surrender, and when Lowell's men brought in six prisoners—one a local youth—their execution was a given. Mosby later blamed Custer, whose men participated in the execution, but Merritt or Torbert gave the order. Federal troopers unceremoniously shot four captives, including the boy, and hanged two more. To one of the hanged men the soldiers affixed a warning that such a fate awaited all of Mosby's men. When Mosby learned of these executions, he vowed to hang an equal number of Custer's men. This war within a war lasted for the duration of the conflict, and more atrocities loomed.[6]

The controversial death of Sheridan's chief engineer on October 3 sparked another reprisal. Lieutenant John R. Meigs, son of Quartermaster General Montgomery Meigs, was a gifted engineer—top of his West Point class of

1863—for whom Sheridan held great fondness. Young Meigs had been scouting near Dayton with two assistants when he was killed in a melee with three Confederate troopers. One of the aides escaped to inform Sheridan that guerrillas gunned down Meigs in cold blood. Sheridan deemed the killing the act of bushwhackers who had been "secretly harbored by some of the neighboring residents." He therefore determined to teach "these abettors of the foul deed—a lesson they would never forget," ordering that all houses in Dayton and within five miles of the area be burned. The task fell to Custer and his new command, the Third Cavalry Division, but before the burning got too far, and much to the relief of many a soldier, Sheridan canceled the order. Writing after the war, General Early categorically refuted Sheridan's version of events, berating Little Phil for "inflicting on non-combatants and women and children a most wanton and cruel punishment for a justifiable act of war."[7]

In a poignant letter to his wife, Colonel Lowell commented on the week's sad events: "I was very glad that my Brigade had no hand in [the Dayton burning]. . . . I was sorry enough the other day that my Brigade should have had a part in the hanging and shooting of some of Mosby's men." A Harvard graduate who had joined the regulars at the outbreak of the Civil War and later raised and commanded the 2nd Massachusetts Cavalry before succeeding Merritt in command of the Reserve Brigade, Lowell expressed what numerous officers and men must have been thinking: "I believe that some punishment was deserved,—but I hardly think we were within the laws of war, and any violation of them opens the door for all sorts of barbarity. . . . The war in this part of the country is becoming very unpleasant to an officer's feelings."[8]

Distracting though they were, such episodes failed to dull the fighting edge of Sheridan's army, even as it retraced its steps down the Valley, trailing hundreds of refugees, including Dunkers, Mennonites, and liberated slaves. Early's men, forced reluctantly to stand aside as the Yankee horsemen did their worst, offered little opposition, but despair and pride and the arrival of additional troops inspired more aggressiveness as Sheridan's withdrawal began. The arrival of Rosser and his Laurel Brigade brought new optimism. This unit, after all, had gained renown under Jeb Stuart, and Rosser, a Virginia-born Texan, joined Early's command with the unfortunate (and possibly self-imposed) appellation of "Savior of the Valley." But the Laurel Brigade, like most Southern units, fielded but a shadow of its former self, numbering only 600 men when it reached Early's army during the first week of October. Still, Rosser's horsemen and Joseph Kershaw's 3,000 proven foot soldiers, Early believed, covered his losses at Winchester and Fisher's Hill and allowed him once again to duel with Sheridan. So as the Yankee columns moved northward down the Valley, burning as they went, Early resolved to follow, sending Rosser with two divisions of cavalry ahead to snap at the rear of the retiring Federals. But on October 8, as

*General Thomas Rosser. Courtesy of the Library of Congress*

Rosser and his emboldened troopers became more than an annoyance, Sheridan resolved to "finish this 'Savior of the Valley.'"[9]

That night, Sheridan summoned General Torbert to his headquarters and informed his chief of cavalry that he "expected him either to give Rosser a drubbing next morning or get whipped himself," and that he planned to watch the action from nearby Round Top Mountain. Apparently, Torbert's inability to seal the deal at Fisher's Hill remained a sore subject. After another day of destruction, Merritt's division went into camp along the pike south of Strasburg and just north of a stream known as Tom's Brook; Custer's men stopped some six miles to the northwest on the Back Road. After leaving Sheridan's tent, Torbert issued orders for an all-out attack by the two divisions the following morning. Custer's men, with farther to ride, moved out in the early hours of October 9 to strike Rosser, who led his own brigade and the remnant of Fitz Lee's Division— Wickham's Brigade, commanded by capable Thomas Munford, and Colonel William Payne's Virginians. Later that morning, Merritt's men splashed across Tom's Brook to assail Lomax's Division, which held positions south of the stream.

This would be something of a coming-out party for Custer as a division commander. Not only was Custer new to his position but also both brigades of the Third Division featured new leaders. Alexander C. M. Pennington, an 1860 West Point graduate and a gifted artillerist before entering the Volunteers as colonel of the 3rd New Jersey Cavalry, replaced the fallen McIntosh at the head of the First Brigade. Colonel William Wells had commanded the Second Brigade since George Chapman went down at Fisher's Hill. A merchant by trade, Wells enlisted in 1861 as a private in the 1st Vermont Cavalry and rose to colonel of the regiment during the course of the Valley Campaign. At twenty-seven, he was the eldest of the three new commanders.

Merritt's First Division remained the veteran organization of the Cavalry Corps, with twenty-nine-year-old Lowell firmly entrenched at the head of the Reserve Brigade and steady Tom Devin still commanding the Second Brigade. Colonel James H. Kidd, 6th Michigan, who replaced Custer as head of the First Brigade, offered continuity and a proven record of success with the Wolverines. New leadership notwithstanding, the Cavalry Corps anxiously wanted to get back to the business of fighting.

At 7:00 A.M., Federal troopers spurred across Tom's Brook to initiate the action. Custer's men found Rosser's command well deployed behind improvised works and well supported by artillery. The Yankees fought methodically, applying pressure to the Rebel center while jabbing at Rosser's flank. But the Virginians (these were all Virginia regiments) held against heavy pressure, until a three-regiment mounted charge, personally led by Custer, buckled their left flank, followed quickly by a frontal assault led by Pennington and Wells on the center. Rosser's command dissolved under the pressure, fleeing in every direction as blue-jacketed troopers swarmed over the camp, capturing men, animals, and just about everything on wheels. As Sheridan observed, "the retreat quickly degenerated into a rout the like of which was never before seen."[10]

Merritt's division struck Lomax in much the same fashion and with much the same result. These Confederates, armed only with rifles, could not stand up to the concentrated saber charges of a better mounted and much better equipped foe. Like Rosser's men, Lomax's troopers stood firm until a flank attack obliterated their line, and like Rosser's men they broke for the rear, through Woodstock and up the Valley. To make matters worse, the nearest infantry support rested more than twenty miles distant. They were on their own with nowhere to hide. The magnitude of the Federal triumph became, as Wesley Merritt put it, "merely a question of the endurance of horseflesh." The pursuit, unchecked and unrelenting, continued, in the case of Merritt's division, for twenty-six miles. "Never has there been, in the history of this war," Merritt bragged, "a more complete victory than this of Tom's Creek." Yankee troopers, many of whom who had been on the receiving end of similar thrashings, dubbed this day's action the "Woodstock Races."[11]

All hyperbole aside, this result was just what Sheridan had in mind when he "decided to have Rosser chastised." And there could be no doubt that Rosser, a West Point classmate of Custer's and Merritt's, had been thoroughly chastened, along with the rest of Early's cavalry. Confederate casualties in the battle of Tom's Brook were never reported but likely numbered into the hundreds. Sheridan and his subordinates reported more than 300 prisoners captured, along with eleven pieces of artillery, more than forty wagons, ambulances, and caissons (including the headquarters wagons of the Confederate commanders), forges, harnesses, dozens of horses and mules, and a wagonload of rifles. All of this bounty came at a cost of nine troopers killed and forty-eight wounded.[12]

With the Confederate cavalry clearly wrecked and with no sign of Early's infantry, on October 10, Sheridan resumed his retrograde movement. The XIX Corps and Crook's Army of West Virginia (VIII Corps) moved into camp north of Cedar Creek, between Strasburg and Middletown, where Custer's and Merritt's divisions of cavalry soon joined them. Here along Cedar Creek the army enjoyed a few precious days of relative inactivity. The VI Corps, though, moved on to Front Royal, preparatory to its planned return to the Army of the Potomac. Powell's cavalry meanwhile mounted an ineffectual raid toward Gordonsville, returning to the main army on the fourteenth. Again, Sheridan let himself believe that Early was finished, and again Early would prove him wrong. Although neither commander knew the other's intentions, both Sheridan and Early planned ahead. But this time, Old Jubal held the initiative; what he could accomplish with it remained to be seen.

At Tom's Brook, Rosser invited disaster by placing his command within easy reach of the Federals but miles from any infantry support. Now only days after his cavalry's ignominious showing, Early risked a similar fate by pressing forward his entire army.

On October 12, Sheridan wired Grant: "I believe that a rebel advance down this valley will not take place," and he issued orders for the VI Corps to continue overland to Alexandria. While the Federal commanders debated future operations, Early, believing that Sheridan had indeed sent off much of his command, pushed his five small infantry divisions to within striking distance of the Union camps at Cedar Creek and began to lob shells into the startled Yankees. Generals Emory and Crook took action, sending Thoburn's division of Crook's command to investigate this new menace. Thoburn's men soon confronted Kershaw's Division in a spirited fight south of Cedar Creek that drove the Federals back, but well-directed Yankee artillery and the speedy arrival of reinforcements compelled Kershaw to break off his pursuit. The Confederates withdrew to the familiar environs of Fisher's Hill, knowing that Sheridan still had plenty of firepower. The Federals, on the other hand, learned that Early's army apparently refused to die.[13]

This became a frustrating time for Sheridan. Not only had Early reappeared in undetermined strength but also Little Phil had to contend with a barrage of messages from General Halleck, prodding him to adopt Grant's proposal for a strike against Gordonsville and the Virginia Central and to plan accordingly. Although Grant had bowed to Sheridan's views throughout the campaign and always stopped short of issuing direct orders, perhaps Little Phil could sense his autonomy slipping. On October 13, he notified Halleck that if such an advance were to be made he would need all of his men and intended, therefore, to recall the VI Corps, pending further developments. At this untimely juncture Secretary Stanton intervened to resolve the impasse between his two commanders, requesting that Sheridan come to Washington for a "consultation."[14]

Sheridan had toyed with the idea of launching an offensive once Wright's men reached the Cedar Creek encampment but abandoned the notion to accept Stanton's invitation. Anxious to resolve the stalemate over future operations, he spent the fourteenth seeing to the disposition of his army, and on the following day departed for Washington, leaving competent Horatio Wright in command. He rode to Front Royal with four members of his staff and most of the army's cavalry, which he planned to throw against the Virginia Central at Charlottesville while he and his staff moved on to Washington. But distractions continued to dog the fiery general. At Front Royal on the sixteenth he received a dispatch from Wright: a coded message intercepted from a Rebel signal station indicated that General James Longstreet was marching with a large force to join Early. Sheridan correctly assumed it to be a bluff, but he acted prudently, wiring Halleck to confirm his suspicion. Promptly, Grant reported no major Confederate departures from the Richmond-Petersburg front. If Longstreet was coming to the Valley, he was traveling alone. Confident in Wright's ability to handle any situation, Sheridan prepared to resume his journey but not before ordering most of the cavalry to return to Cedar Creek should Early, Longstreet, or both attack. Finally, he sent a short message to Wright: "make your position strong. . . . Look well to your ground and be well prepared. Get up everything that can be spared."[15]

The journey continued to Rectortown, where Sheridan and his staff boarded a train for Washington. Arriving at the capital on the morning of the seventeenth, Sheridan met only briefly with Stanton and Halleck and came away satisfied: "the upshot was," he wrote, "that my views against [operations east of the Blue Ridge] were practically agreed to." Two engineer officers were assigned to return with Sheridan in order to fix the location for a "defensive line in the valley" that could be maintained while the bulk of his army relocated to Petersburg. The details agreed upon, Sheridan and his augmented entourage boarded a special train for Martinsburg. On the eighteenth the group, escorted by 300 troopers, continued on horseback to Winchester, where Sheridan, hearing nothing alarming from Cedar Creek, decided to spend the night.[16]

Back along Cedar Creek, the Army of the Shenandoah settled in for what could become a lengthy stay, establishing a strong position according to Sheridan's instructions. But after weeks of marching and fighting, and all the horror of war, the men fairly basked in the lovely fall setting. "We are in glorious country," Colonel Lowell wrote to his mother, "with fine air to breathe and fine views to enjoy." Surely, one would be hard pressed to find a more inviting location at this stage in the war. But the area presented problems as well, cut as it was by the meandering Cedar Creek and Meadow Brook, which created deep ravines and ridges that separated commands and, in the event of an attack, could hamper rapid troop movements. And while the army achieved a certain degree of concentration, some units remained isolated and vulnerable to attack.[17]

Posted east of the Valley Turnpike and north of Cedar Creek, Crook's corps and Colonel Howard Kitching's recently organized Provisional Division presented the most obvious weakness, with Thoburn's division dangerously exposed well south of the next closest division—that of Rutherford B. Hayes. Most of Powell's cavalry, supposed to protect the eastward approaches to Crook's flank, remained near Front Royal (Sheridan had told Wright to bring in Powell, but this adjustment had not been completed). Only Colonel Alpheus Moore's small brigade covered the flank that stretched from Cedar Creek to Middletown. The XIX Corps occupied the ground between the pike and Meadow Brook, covering Cedar Creek, which protected the corps' right flank. A deep ravine cut by Meadow Brook separated the XIX and VI Corps, which pitched its tents between the two streams just southwest of Middletown. The cavalry divisions of Merritt and Custer ranged to the west of the VI Corps, patrolling the Back Road and protecting the army's right and rear. An attack, if it came, would almost certainly be from this direction. Artillery batteries made good use of the many ridges, covering any gaps and potential avenues of attack. But a full-scale attack, any attack for that matter, the Federal commanders deemed unlikely. In fact, a reconnaissance on the eighteenth revealed no Rebels in the vicinity. Another such effort was scheduled for the following morning.

While the Yankees soaked up the autumn splendor, Early faced a moment of truth. He could not sustain his army for long in the burned-out and
picked-over land south of Cedar Creek; he had to fight or quit the Valley. The
latter option, of course, would free Sheridan to send the bulk of his force to
Petersburg, which was precisely what General Lee hoped to prevent by sending valuable troops—Kershaw's and Rosser's commands—to augment Early's
forces. If Early did not intend to strike with his full force, he might just as well
bring it all to the trenches of Petersburg. The crusty Virginian knew what he
had to do. On October 17, he sent General John B. Gordon, his most capable
division commander, along with the gifted engineer and cartographer Captain Jedediah Hotchkiss, to the top of Massanutten Mountain, which offered a
lovely panorama of the Valley below, to plot the disposition of Sheridan's army
and divine a route of approach for a surprise flank attack. With field glasses,
Gordon and Hotchkiss had a clear view of the Yankee position and carefully
identified the various infantry camps and artillery placements. More important,
they found their path to glory.

During the morning of the eighteenth, Gordon presented his plan for
a surprise attack to Early and the division commanders. The plan, bold and
brilliant, called for a stealthy march along the base of Massanutten, between
the mountain and the North Fork of the Shenandoah River. The path was so
narrow and the stream so high that the Yankees gave no regard to an attack from
this direction—with good reason. This daring proposal required the old Second Corps, under Gordon's direction and including the divisions of Brigadier
General Clement Evans (Gordon's), Dodson Ramseur, and Brigadier General
John Pegram, to ford the cold Shenandoah twice and march undetected at night
in order to be in position to attack the Federal eastern flank before dawn on
the nineteenth. Kershaw's Division would cross Cedar Creek concurrent with
Gordon's attack and hit Thoburn's exposed command, while Gabriel Wharton's
Division pressed down the Valley Turnpike with the army's artillery. Rosser,
meanwhile, would engage the Yankee cavalry west of Middletown, creating
the impression that the attack was indeed coming from that direction. In an
interesting side plot, Colonel William Payne's cavalry would precede Gordon's
column but strike ahead to Belle Grove Plantation, Sheridan's headquarters, in
an effort to capture the "Scourge of the Valley." Over some objection, but with
Gordon's forceful advocacy, Early adopted the plan.[18]

That crisp, clear evening, with rations prepared and noisy accoutrements
discarded, Payne's cavalry followed by Gordon's foot soldiers moved out of
their camps, crossing the North Fork of the Shenandoah south of Strasburg
and marching single-file in bright moonlight around the base of Massanutten.
Gordon recalled how "the long gray line like a great serpent glided noiselessly
along the dim pathway." Later that night and into the next morning, Kershaw,

*General John Brown Gordon. Courtesy of the National Archives*

Wharton, and Rosser moved their divisions to assigned staging points and waited for 5:00 A.M., the appointed hour for the attack to begin. Considering the limited time available to plan and prepare such a bold strike and the difficulty, particularly of Gordon's flanking march, in moving an entire army at night, it was rather astonishing that all units reached their launching points unnoticed ahead of schedule. A heavy fog now kept the attackers concealed.[19]

Shortly after 4:00 A.M., Payne's troopers charged across the river, drawing gunfire from Yankee pickets, before dashing off in search of General Sheridan. Gordon's men followed, shrouded in fog, moving quickly and unnoticed to within a few hundred feet of the vulnerable eastern flank of the Federal army. Kershaw's Division slipped across Cedar Creek and formed in front of Thoburn's isolated command, while Wharton and the artillery prepared to dash down the pike once the fighting began. Although by now Payne's troopers had caused some alarm, reports from Union outposts of threatening movements received remarkably little attention as they climbed the ladder of command. Contrary to popular legend, though, this was not a sleeping army caught completely unawares. The XIX and VI Corps had taken routine precautions and had posted heavy guards, and the cavalry, alerted to the presence of Rosser's troopers, who attacked Union pickets at about 4:00 on the Back Road, had struck tents and was ready for action by daybreak. But nothing likely could have prepared this resting army for the hell Early had in store for it. A combination of factors contributed to the Confederates' ability on this morning to achieve surprise. Faulty deployment, especially of Thoburn's division, provided the attackers with an opportunity to, by crushing this exposed division, trigger a chain reaction that could engulf the entire army. The Rebels on Crook's front and flank managed through stealth and fire discipline not to disclose their presence. Thus, many Federal officers assumed that any commotion that morning had to be the scheduled XIX Corps reconnaissance. Finally, none of Sheridan's lieutenants considered an attack of this magnitude on this front a realistic possibility. But realistic it was, as the men in blue soon discovered to their horror. Clearly, flawed Federal dispositions and simple neglect had opened the door for a stunning Confederate attack, but the Rebels had to be credited with imaginative planning and flawless execution during the advance, aided though they were by forces of nature.[20]

Considerable disagreement later ensued over who struck first and when, but within minutes of each other, just before daybreak, Gordon and Kershaw unleashed their divisions on Crook's unsuspecting corps. Stepping ghostlike out of the dense fog with orders not to fire until they gained the Yankee works, Kershaw's battle-hardened veterans quickly overran Thoburn's outposts and, with a thunderous volley of musket fire, stormed the main works, gathering up prisoners and seizing field pieces, which they soon turned on the bluecoats. Confounded, Thoburn's regiments, most of which were only stirring when

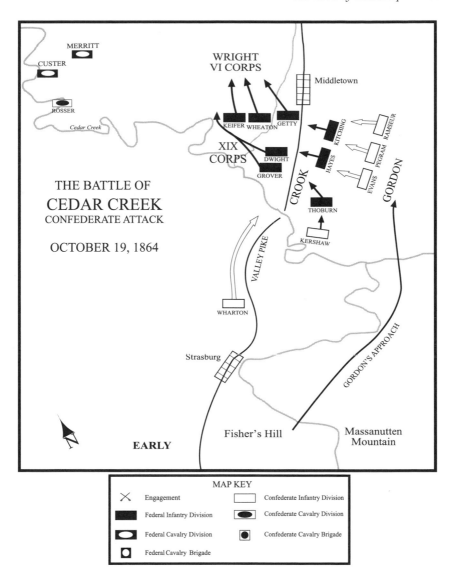

THE BATTLE OF
**CEDAR CREEK**
CONFEDERATE ATTACK

OCTOBER 19, 1864

MAP KEY

| | | | |
|---|---|---|---|
| ✕ | Engagement | ▢ | Confederate Infantry Division |
| ▬ | Federal Infantry Division | ⬭ | Confederate Cavalry Division |
| ⬮ | Federal Cavalry Division | ◉ | Confederate Cavalry Brigade |
| ▢ | Federal Cavalry Brigade | | |

the attack began, broke, some grudgingly, others on contact, and fled toward the XIX Corps position one mile away. Fog and smoke obscured the field, and confusion abounded. Even at this early point in the attack, hungry Rebels treated themselves to the breakfast their enemy had been preparing. It hardly mattered, as Kershaw's attack completely routed Thoburn's division and opened the way to the now exposed XIX Corps and the rest of Crook's command.

Concurrent with Kershaw's advance, Gordon sent his three divisions forward against the underprepared positions of Hayes's Second Division and Kitching's Provisional Division. Hayes, an Ohio lawyer and burgeoning politician who had turned himself into a pretty solid soldier, had some warning of the impending onslaught, but his men had yet to form fully when Gordon's screaming warriors struck. Spearheaded by Gordon's own division under Clement Evans, the gray line burst from the fog into the Federal camp. As Crook, Wright, and Emory looked on, Hayes's division, already destabilized by refugees from Thoburn's command, essentially shattered on impact, and its commander, a future president of the United States, knocked unconscious when his horse went down under him, barely escaped capture. Meanwhile, Dodson Ramseur's men made quick work of Kitching's division. In well less than an hour the Confederates had crushed Crook's entire corps, capturing hundreds of men, many half-dressed or still in their tents, seven pieces of artillery, and assorted wagons and ambulances. Among the casualties was Colonel Thoburn, who went down with a mortal wound. The remnant of the Army of West Virginia streamed rearward, some units managing to maintain order, some pausing to make a futile stand, but most melting into a growing flood of panic-stricken humanity that threatened to pull the remaining Federal corps in with it. Crook, a hapless witness to the disintegration of his proud army, rallied a small portion of the command near Belle Grove Plantation long enough to save most of his supply train, before being driven beyond Meadow Brook. Writing years later, a bitter Crook blamed the disaster that befell his command on the cavalry: "had the cavalry pickets [Powell's division, a brigade of which was in the area] been where we had every reason to expect them, the surprise never could have happened." But there was plenty of blame to go around, and Crook knew it.[21]

Kershaw and Gordon now converged on the XIX Corps. Unlike Crook's corps, the XIX Corps had plenty of warning, its men standing to arms behind substantial fieldworks west of the pike. Aware of the crisis developing on his left—and that the collapse of Crook's line exposed his own flank and rear—General Emory prepared to meet the oncoming Confederates. To buy the time he needed to adjust his lines, Emory sacrificed Colonel Stephen Thomas's brigade of Dwight's Second Division, sending it into the woods across the pike and into the path of the gathering storm. This brigade suffered massive casualties in frenzied close-quarters fighting before falling back on Emory's refashioned line behind the confluence of Cedar Creek and the Valley Turnpike. Confederate artillery (including captured Federal pieces) pounded away as the divisions of Evans and Kershaw closed on the XIX Corps. Despite intense musket fire and withering blasts of canister from rapidly firing Yankee guns, the attackers soon swarmed around Emory's uncovered flanks. Brutal hand-to-hand combat followed, but regiments broke one by one until the XIX Corps lost all order and followed Crook's men in flight, falling back across Meadow Brook, where Emory and Grover attempted to rally the corps. Again, outright panic mixed with orderly withdrawal, but the result was the same—another Federal corps had been shattered. Now only the stalwart VI Corps and the cavalry stood between the Confederates and one of the most shocking victories of the war.

In less than two hours the Confederate attackers had, it seemed, more than made up for a month's worth of ill treatment at Sheridan's hands. They had driven two experienced Federal corps—five infantry divisions in all—from the field in great disorder; they had captured some 1,500 thunderstruck Yankees and killed or wounded hundreds more; Early's men had grabbed eighteen field pieces thus far, and the day was young. Considering the sorry performances put forth by the Rebels at Fisher's Hill and since, this fog-bound reversal of fortune must have felt all the more miraculous to the reeling Federals. To Early's ragged foot soldiers, the attack at Cedar Creek represented something of an encore; they had delivered miracles before.

For Horatio Wright a very bad day got steadily worse. Alerted by the opening salvos of the battle, the temporary army commander had been in the saddle all morning, dashing from one point to the next and receiving a slight wound to the face in the process. Now, with the VIII and XIX Corps routed and running for the rear, Wright looked to his own corps to stem the Rebel advance. These veterans responded to the predawn violence in orderly fashion, striking tents and forming for battle long before it came their way. Initially, Wright ordered James Ricketts, commanding the corps, to advance in support of Crook and Emory, but with nothing left for it to support, the VI Corps braced itself behind Meadow Brook west of Middletown and waited its turn. Even before the Rebel infantry struck, terrified refugees from the shattered commands of Crook and Emory passed through the line, breaking cohesion and spreading despair, and General Ricketts was already down with a dangerous wound. Although many of these men in blue could recall calamitous performances at Bull Run and Chancellorsville, the Army of the Shenandoah had not experienced defeat, much less the kind of catastrophe that appeared to be in the offing. A heavy, almost unfathomable burden—the fate of the army and the campaign—fell squarely upon the VI Corps as it grimly awaited its time of reckoning.

At about 7:30 Kershaw's Division, following the routed XIX Corps, charged up the slope occupied by the VI Corps only to be turned back by volley fire from Colonel Warren Keifer's (Ricketts's) Third Division, which held the corps' right flank. Getty's Second Division on the left and the First Division, commanded by Brigadier General Frank Wheaton, in the center, adjusted to meet the next charge, while Emory continued to reform his corps behind Keifer's right flank. Kershaw's men attacked again, and again Keifer's line held, but an abortive Yankee counterattack backfired, giving Kershaw's relentless Southerners the upper hand. In ferocious hand-to-hand fighting and desperate struggles for prized field pieces, Kershaw's Deep South regiments overwhelmed Keifer's division, sucking in part of Wheaton's First Brigade in the process. Meanwhile, Gordon's attack merged with Kershaw's, striking Wheaton's Second Brigade, commanded by Colonel Joseph Hamblin, with tremendous fury. Hamblin fell wounded during the ensuing melee, and Ranald Mackenzie, already shot through the heel, assumed command of the Second Brigade. The high-strung New Yorker, who won praise for his performance at Winchester, directed an orderly withdrawal under heavy pressure, pausing briefly to make a stand before giving way under continued pressure. Mackenzie's horse then went down, throwing its rider, who secured another mount only to be knocked to the ground by a shell blast. Now Mackenzie and his 2nd Connecticut Heavy Artillery (fighting as infantry) fled with the rest of Wheaton's division in retreat. The First and Third Divisions reformed beyond Middletown as attention turned to the last Federal unit south of the village—Getty's Second Division.[22]

Getty, his line compromised by the collapse of the First and Third Divisions, directed an orderly withdrawal to a strong new position near the Middletown cemetery, and here this excellent division repulsed repeated Confederate attacks. When the divisions of Ramseur and Pegram failed to dislodge Getty's men in heavy fighting, Early, who had moved forward and assumed direct command of his army, ordered in Gabriel Wharton's small division, yet it too failed to drive the stubborn Yankees. Finally, Early ordered a concentrated artillery barrage that did the job. Getty's stand lasted more than an hour and, although forced to retire to yet another position about a mile beyond Middletown, the division had bought the Federals the time they needed to regroup. At this point the Confederates had achieved a victory of enormous proportion—they held 1,300 prisoners and twenty-four captured cannons and had driven seven quality infantry divisions from the field—the most significant Rebel triumph since Chancellorsville, one that could in a single day make good all the losses of this otherwise dismal campaign. It was not yet 10:00. All that remained to be determined, it appeared, was the magnitude of the Federal defeat. Could this Yankee army be destroyed?

Unfortunately for Early, his triumphant little army found its pursuit of that lofty goal challenged by the very bane of its existence—the Federal cavalry. The intimidating presence and considerable firepower of this mighty blue monster brought the Rebel advance to a halt at Middletown. Had Early possessed a mounted arm of any consequence (he had only 300 troopers of Payne's brigade on his right flank), he likely could have sealed the victory before the Yankee horsemen came into play, but he had nothing of the sort. Torbert's men held the pike north of the village and appeared poised to contest a continued advance by

*General Ranald Slidell Mackenzie. Courtesy of the National Archives*

Early's forces. Merritt's and Custer's divisions had been in the saddle since well before light. Much of their effort thus far had been dedicated to stemming the flow of panicked infantrymen—a distasteful duty for sure. Rugged Tom Devin's brigade did most of this dirty work, "it being necessary in several instances to fire on the crowds retiring," the veteran wrote, "and to use the saber frequently." With his infantry falling back on Middletown, General Wright had ordered both cavalry divisions from the extreme right to the left in order to shore up the disintegrating army and to hold the Valley Turnpike. Torbert left three of Custer's regiments to deal with Rosser out to the west and sent Merritt and Custer to support the main army north of Middletown, and here they rendered valuable service. When the gray lines pushed through the village, they ran into Merritt's men, whose Spencer repeaters stopped the Rebels cold. Lowell's Reserve Brigade dismounted and formed behind a stone wall, pouring a heavy fire into the advancing Confederates, while Devin and Kidd launched periodic saber charges.

For many of the Confederates on this part of the field, this clash was their first hard fighting of the day, and they came back for more. A firestorm raged north of Middletown as the Yankee horsemen and the Rebel foot soldiers went at each other. Union officers found the Confederate artillery particularly impressive and all too deadly, but of his own men, Merritt reported, "Never did troops fight more elegantly than at this time; not a man shirked his duty." The men of the Cavalry Corps, under withering fire and almost completely exposed, "held their ground," in Torbert's words, "like men of steel." Custer noted with perhaps more accuracy than many wished to admit: "But for the cavalry the enemy would have penetrated to the rear of our army, which at that time was in no condition to receive an attack from any direction." Early, fearing that the Federal cavalry would overlap his right flank and apparently content with his already impressive achievement, halted any further advance. With hours of daylight remaining and his vengeful army champing at the bit, according to Gordon and many observers since, Early presently surrendered his chance for glory and redemption.[23]

A great controversy arose over what happened next. Gordon, the architect of the day's success, claimed that he encountered Early at Middletown during this lull and advocated vigorously for an all-out assault that would finish the Federals. But, maintained the handsome Georgian, Early declined to act, satisfied with his considerable gains, and therefore failed to capitalize on this rare chance to crush an entire Yankee army. For Gordon, this behavior revived painful memories of fatal delays and lost opportunities: "my heart," he wrote, "went into my boots." Early, however, held to the belief, and had ample evidence to support it, that his army was in no condition to press on, citing the fact that his men had been up all night and were "much jaded." He also pointed to the sad truth that his ranks "were much thinned by the absence of the men engaged in plundering the enemy's camps." The plundering began at Thoburn's camp before sunrise. To these scarecrow-like campaigners, who knew hunger all too well and had fought long and hard in rags and often barefooted, the richly provisioned Yankees left a bounty that could hardly be ignored. Many a Southerner found this treasure—food and clothes, boots and blankets—irresistible. Clearly, such activities took a toll on the army, but so too did five hours of hard fighting across a fog- and smoke-obscured field, which left Early's various divisions badly in need of reorganization before a move such as Gordon contemplated could be launched. Finally, there remained the "immense force of cavalry . . . which of itself rendered an advance extremely hazardous." Jubal Early seemed possessed of a peculiar and completely understandable reverence for this cavalry. Given the situation as he saw it, Early opted for caution and consolidation; he wanted to hold what had been won. It was, perhaps, the prudent decision, but it became one Old Jubal would never live down.[24]

The morning fog had burned off and an uneasy lull, punctuated by sporadic musket and artillery fire, settled over the field north of Middletown. The stage set, actors in place, the curtain now opened on one of the most famous episodes of the Civil War.

## ⊻ 6 ⊼

# "The Ablest of Generals"

$\mathcal{O}$n the night of the eighteenth, Sheridan bedded down at a private residence in Winchester, about a dozen miles from the encampment on Cedar Creek. Early the next morning an officer from the local garrison woke him with news that the rumble of artillery fire could be heard from the direction of Middletown. Sheridan inferred that the noise emanated from the scheduled reconnaissance by Cuvier Grover's division. He tried to go back to sleep, but the officer returned to report that the ominous sounds continued. Sheridan still believed the distant cannonading to be Grover's gunners "banging away at the enemy," but he dressed, ate a quick breakfast while the horses were saddled, and at about 9:00 mounted his prized black charger Rienzi. With his staff and a small escort, he rode toward Cedar Creek. All too soon, he confronted the first evidence that something had gone terribly wrong at Cedar Creek—"the appalling spectacle of a panic stricken army." Hundreds of dazed soldiers and harried teamsters struggling to control their loads told of the disaster befalling his command.[1]

"On accosting some of the fugitives," Sheridan wrote, "they assured me that the army was broken up, in full retreat, and that all was lost." The general summoned a brigade from Winchester to corral the refugees and, detailing part of his staff and escort for the same purpose, he rode on with two aides and some twenty troopers. His concern turned to the rest of the army, which was for all he knew in full flight. "I felt that I ought to try now to restore their broken ranks," he recalled, "or, failing in that, to share their fate because of what they had done hitherto." Onward he rode into a thickening wave of damaged men, largely unable to stem the flow. The road grew so congested that Sheridan and his entourage had to take to the fields. At Newtown, he encountered Major William McKinley of Crook's staff. The future president of the United States, wrote Sheridan, "spread the news of my return through the motley throng there." He spurred Rienzi onward, often outdistancing his escort by several yards, exhorting groups of retreating soldiers to return with him, cussing as he promised the army would sleep this night in its camps on Cedar Creek. As the strange-looking little man on the huge black horse passed, dazed men regained their composure and began to follow the commander back to the field. "I am happy to say," reported Sheridan, "that hundreds of men, when on reflection found they had not done themselves justice, came back with cheers." At about 10:30, Sheridan reached Getty's position north of Middletown, joining his corps commanders as they surveyed the scene. His soon-to-be-famous ride from Winchester brought him to the battlefield at roughly the same time that Early suspended his attack.[2]

General Wright, blood-soaked from the wound to his chin, provided a brief account of the morning's disaster and apprised his chief of the current situation. Sheridan quickly dismissed the idea of a retreat to Winchester and soon issued instructions for a realignment of the army. Fearing a Rebel attack at any minute, he wanted the troop movements completed quickly, and they were, but it still took time. He had the new line formed on Getty's position north of Middletown and west of the pike, with Keifer, then Wheaton, moving in on Getty's right; Grover and Dwight of Emory's corps extended the line westward. Merritt continued to hold the army's left flank east of the pike, but Custer returned to the right flank alongside Dwight's division. Wright resumed direct command of the VI Corps, and Getty, who performed so well in Wright's stead, returned to his division, relieving Brigadier General Lewis Grant, who had also done a fine job. By noon the new line had taken shape, and each minute it grew stronger as refugees returned to the ranks. At about half past noon, still expecting a Rebel attack, Major George "Sandy" Forsyth of Sheridan's staff suggested that the commander show himself to the men by riding along the new line. As Sheridan recalled, "I crossed to the front and, hat in hand, passed along the entire length of the infantry line." As he passed each unit, he shouted, in his often-profane style, words of encouragement, words designed to fire the soul of these hard men. The soldiers responded with almost rapturous cheers.[3]

In one of the truly remarkable occurrences of the war, Sheridan's mere presence on the field, which he made obvious by dashing from one sector to another, instantly revived the spirit of a demoralized army. Men who had stood and fought now cheered; many, if not most, of those who ran now returned to fight. Officers, some older than Sheridan, greeted him emotionally; Custer raced up on horseback to hug him. Some Civil War commanders possessed great skill, others sheer determination, a few, it was said, had luck; Sheridan wielded magic. The confidence his soldiers placed in him at this stage no doubt owed much to his recent string of battlefield successes, but that fact only partially explained his uncanny influence over officers and men in battle. He inspired his troops as few army commanders could. As if shocked back to life by some inexplicable force, the Army of the Shenandoah reassumed its swagger.

Sheridan's return did not save his army from destruction. Wright and Getty and the Cavalry Corps had pretty much achieved this feat before he arrived. Not only was Getty's division holding its new line but also Wheaton and Keifer had reformed behind Getty, and to their right, Emory continued to rally his corps. Custer and Merritt showed no signs of backing down; if anything, the cavalry had to stifle the impulse to attack. "Custer, himself, was riding along the front of his command," Colonel James Kidd wrote, "chafing like a caged lion, eager for the fray." As things stood at 10:30, Early displayed little inclination to press the initiative, and Wright appeared prepared to hold his position. No, Little Phil could not take credit for rescuing his army from the brink of annihilation, but almost as certainly the subsequent events of this most extraordinary day would not have transpired without him. Sheridan, then, came not as a savior but as a redeemer.[4]

The Confederates too had formed a new line north of Middletown. Wharton's Division (plus Brigadier General William Wofford's Brigade from Kershaw's Division) remained east of the pike, where it had been checked by Merritt's cavalry, while John Pegram's men covered the pike and the village; both commands placed sharpshooters in the town's buildings. West of the pike, opposite the main Federal line, Ramseur's, Kershaw's, and Evans's Divisions fell in, backed closely by Colonel Thomas Carter's artillery. Rosser's small command ranged far to the west, but it offered no protection for Evans's flank, just as Payne's even smaller unit provided little comfort for Wharton on the right. With the army reasonably closed up after noon, at 1:00 P.M., Gordon directed a feeble three-division (Ramseur, Kershaw, and Evans) advance against the section of the Union line held by the XIX Corps and Wheaton's division of the VI Corps. What Early had ordered as an assault to drive the Federals from their new line amounted to nothing more than a probe to see what the Yankees had left, which proved to be more than enough. Emory's men easily turned back the effort with volley fire from their swelling ranks. Gordon recalled his forces to a line a few hundred feet in advance of the previous one. Early now seemed committed to rest on the day's accomplishments; apparently, he feared losing more than he wanted to complete the victory; perhaps he simply doubted his army's ability to break the ever-strengthening Federal line. "I determined, therefore," Early wrote, "to try and hold what had been gained, and orders were given for carrying off the captured and abandoned artillery, small-arms, and wagons." Although low stone walls and rail fences offered some cover for his army, Early made no attempt to improve the position or to pull back Gordon's wing, which stood too close to their enemy to have much reaction time in the event of a Union attack. If Early intended to protect his victory, this approach appeared to be a hazardous way of doing it. The tide of this battle had definitely turned.[5]

Again a lull fell over the field. Men in both armies used the respite to refresh themselves as best they could. Sheridan wanted to unleash his aggrieved army, but still haunted by the apocryphal signal that hailed Longstreet's approach, he hesitated, especially when reports reached him that indeed a large force of infantry had passed through Front Royal, pushing aside Powell's cavalry, seemed to confirm his fears. He ordered Merritt to grab some informants, which the cavalryman did by raiding a nearby artillery position. The prisoners admitted that Kershaw's Division represented the extent of Longstreet's involvement, as Powell soon substantiated. The only Rebels on his front were Lomax's horsemen, and they posed no threat. Satisfied with this intelligence, Sheridan waited only for returning soldiers to fill his ranks.[6]

Shortly before 4:00 the commander issued orders for a general assault, a left wheel by Emory's XIX Corps to fall on Gordon's right and drive eastward toward the pike as the rest of the Federal line charged the Confederate center, sweeping the rebels from the field. At the hour, Dwight's division stepped off and soon from right to left the other divisions followed. The Confederates, outnumbered and poorly situated, nonetheless met the advance with characteristic vigor. Grover's division followed Dwight's men into the fray, losing its capable commander to wounds. Next, at the center of the Union line, came Wheaton's division, spearheaded by Ranald Mackenzie's brigade. Prior to the attack, Sheridan came upon the wounded Mackenzie and ordered him to the rear, but the young warrior pleaded to remain with his command. The army commander relented, and moments later, shell fragments tore into Mackenzie's upper chest, knocking him from his horse. Although forced to relinquish command, he still refused to leave the field. Finally, Keifer and Getty sent their men forward. Along the line, heavy fighting raged, but the Rebels held.[7]

Over on the left, where Merritt's cavalry division halted the Confederate advance, the bluecoats had beaten back several sorties and endured nasty cannonading during the afternoon. Now Sheridan's Old Guard charged boldly forward. The Confederates answered with equal tenacity and double loads of canister. Colonel Lowell, already "suffering acutely" from a painful wound, led his Reserve Brigade into a blizzard of lead and, recalled Wesley Merritt, "fell in the thickest of the fray, meeting his death as he always faced it—calmly, resolutely, heroically." His loss, Merritt wrote, "cast a gloom on the entire command." General Torbert added, "He was the beau ideal of a cavalry officer." The men of the First Division had no time to mourn the fallen Lowell, because their comrades in Custer's Third Division, on the far right of the Union line, were about to steal the show.[8]

After dispatching Rosser's division with ease (Rosser was never a factor in this fight) and somewhat belatedly, Custer's division charged thunderously into the confusion created by the XIX Corps's advance. Gordon had warned Early that his thin line, especially his flank, could not withstand a full-blooded advance, but Early, transfixed by the threat posed by Merritt to his right, had

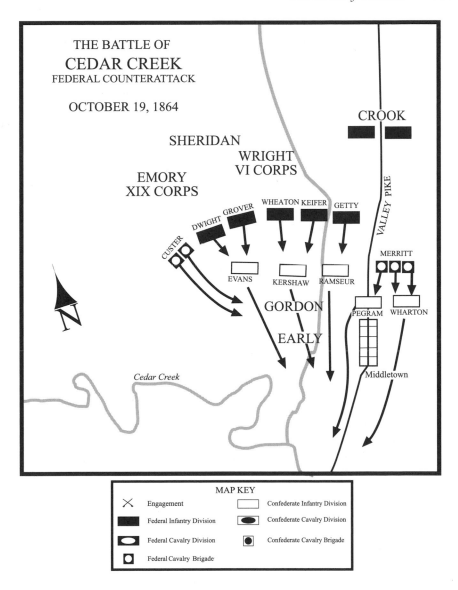

THE BATTLE OF
# CEDAR CREEK
FEDERAL COUNTERATTACK

OCTOBER 19, 1864

MAP KEY

| | | | |
|---|---|---|---|
| ✕ | Engagement | ▭ | Confederate Infantry Division |
| ▬ | Federal Infantry Division | ⬬ | Confederate Cavalry Division |
| ⬭ | Federal Cavalry Division | ⊡ | Confederate Cavalry Brigade |
| ▫ | Federal Cavalry Brigade | | |

not adjusted, opening the door once again for catastrophe. At about 4:30, Custer's troopers stormed into Gordon's flank, stampeding the Southerners. This onslaught triggered a chain reaction that rolled along the Rebel line. Gordon's Division broke, exposing Kershaw's, which followed suit, and finally Ramseur's. The attack proved too much for these hearty campaigners. Once again their commander had placed them in peril, and once again they suffered the consequences.

As always, pockets of resistance formed only to be overwhelmed, as the Yankee infantry joined the chase. In one of these pockets fell Dodson Ramseur, whose only wish this day was to gain victory enough so that he could visit his wife and newborn child. One of the finest division commanders in the Southern army, young Ramseur was loaded into an ambulance headed for the rear. On the Confederate left, Merritt's men finally broke the stubborn ranks of Pegram and Wharton. Soon all resistance ceased, and in a bitter replay of Winchester and Fisher's Hill, the long-suffering Army of the Valley streamed southward in what Custer ungenerously dubbed "a headlong and disgraceful manner." As darkness fell over this twice-lost field, the terrible blue cavalry pursued the shattered Confederates with a feverish relentlessness. "It was no longer a question to be decided by force of arms, by skill, or by courage," Custer reported. "It was simply a question of speed between pursuers and pursued; prisoners were taken by the hundreds, entire companies threw down their arms, and appeared glad when summoned to surrender." It had taken Sheridan's army little more than an hour to turn defeat into victory.[9]

Efforts by numerous Rebel commanders, including the much-respected Gordon and an ever-cursing Early, failed to rally the panic-stricken soldiers, who splashed across Cedar Creek and headed for their old camps at Fisher's Hill. The flood of humanity swept around and then blocked hundreds of wagons, ambulances, caissons, and guns, including the captured Federal field pieces, leaving all ripe for the picking. Troopers from Colonel William Wells's brigade of Custer's command, pursuing from the west, charged into this mass of men, animals, and equipment, converging near Strasburg with Tom Devin's men, spearheading Merritt's advance. Out of the darkness, these blue demons, according to Confederate engineer Jed Hotchkiss, "dashed along, killing horses and turning over ambulances, caissons, &c., stampeding the drivers, thus getting 43 pieces of artillery, many wagons, &c., as there was nothing to defend them as we had no organized force to go after them. Only a few Yankee cavalry did it all."

Indeed, the two commands snatched up an astonishingly lucrative bounty. Not only did they recover almost everything the army lost that morning (except 1,300 prisoners whom the Confederates managed to retain) but also they took possession of most of Early's artillery and almost everything else on wheels. More than 300 horses and mules fell into Union hands, as did hundreds of small arms and assorted equipment. In one of the captured ambulances, the cavalrymen found mortally wounded Dodson Ramseur, whom they took to Belle Grove Plantation, where Union surgeons tried in vain to save his life. Ramseur spent his final hours surrounded by friends, old West Point classmates like Custer and Merritt, and died the following morning. This counterattack completed the most stunning reversal of fortune to transpire on one field on one day during the war. Some 6,000 Federal officers and men and 3,000 Confederates were killed, wounded, or missing. Captain Hotchkiss remarked bitterly: "Thus was one of the most brilliant victories of the war turned into one of the most disgraceful defeats, and all owing to the delay in pressing the enemy after we got to Middletown; as General Early said, 'The Yankees got whipped and we got scared.'"[10]

Regrettably, Early blamed his men for the horrible turn of events. "But for their bad conduct," he messaged Lee's headquarters, "I should have defeated Sheridan's whole force." In his report, Early revealed just how little he understood his foe: "Sheridan's forces are now so shattered that he will not be able to send Grant any efficient aid for some time. I think he will be afraid to trust the Eighth and Nineteenth Corps." Sheridan, of course, could and would send Grant plenty of very good help. As for his trust in the battered VIII and XIX Corps, thanks to Early it really did not matter if Sheridan trusted these commands or not. Early might strike again before this war finally ended, but as of sundown on October 19, he no longer posed a serious threat to Federal operations.[11]

As Sheridan had promised, much of the army slept that night in the old camps along Cedar Creek. Over the next few days, as news of the incredible battle spread, the little, emaciated general became the toast of the Union, surpassing for the moment all other Northern heroes. The drama of Cedar Creek irresistibly aroused the public imagination, spawning poems and patriotic readings and something akin to worship for the unlikely champion. On October 20, General Grant ordered his customary 100-gun salute (with live ammunition aimed at Confederate positions at Petersburg) in honor of Sheridan's triumph. In a note to Secretary Stanton, the commanding general praised his hot commodity: "Turning what bid fair to be a disaster into a glorious victory stamps Sheridan, what I have always thought him, one of the ablest of generals." Two days later a handwritten message from President Lincoln arrived at Sheridan's headquarters: "With great pleasure I tender to you and your brave army the thanks of the nation and my own personal admiration and gratitude for the month's operations in the Shenandoah Valley, and especially for the splendid work of October 19, 1864." Lincoln had good reason, beyond the battlefield victories, to be grateful—Sheridan's Valley Campaign had, along with Sherman's triumph at Atlanta, guaranteed the president's reelection. Writing from Georgia, General Sherman extended his regards: "You have youth and vigor, and this single event has given you a hold upon an army that gives you a future better than older men can hope for." The high-strung conqueror of Atlanta closed with a sanguine charge to his younger colleague: "I shall expect you on any and all occasions to make bloody results." The most tangible reward for thirty-three-year-old Sheridan came from the War Department: promotion to major general in the regular army.[12]

Sheridan might have won the praise for Cedar Creek, and deservedly so, but even he admitted that the surprise attack that threatened to destroy his army "might have befallen" him had he been commanding the army instead of Wright. Most of his officers seemed content to bask in his considerable glory and let him take the credit. But true to form, Little Phil presently took care of the people who took care of him. He requested brevet promotions to major general of U.S. Volunteers for Getty, Grover, Wheaton, and "the brave boys, Merritt, and Custer." Mackenzie, Devin, Powell, and Lowell (posthumously) soon received well-deserved promotions to brigadier general of Volunteers. Crook's long-anticipated promotion to major general of Volunteers arrived shortly after the battle. Even Rutherford Hayes, whose division was wrecked, garnered a star. All of this recognition took time, but Sheridan badgered General Halleck and the War Department until all of the promotions came through. In the weeks following the victory at Cedar Creek, dozens of officers sewed on new stars or counted their brevets, but not Wright (already a major general) or Emory, the old regular, who remained a brigadier. Strangely, twenty-eight-year-old Warren Keifer, who commanded a division most of the day, picked up only a brevet to brigadier rather than the full rank, which he earned and never received. A grateful nation thus showered this conquering army with lavish recognition. Even Sheridan's war horse Rienzi, whom the general renamed Winchester, became a national hero as the voice of Thomas Buchanan Read's famous poem "Sheridan's Ride."[13]

Sheridan, though, attracted some critics, such as Early, who maintained that the new hero had not accomplished all that he should have or could have with such a superior force, a valid indictment for sure. Another reasonable point of contention involved Sheridan's continued avoidance of Grant's desired strike against the Virginia Central, which many believed could have shortened the war. To some, Sheridan was not worthy of praise; he lacked strategic vision and tactical skill, and if not for his outstanding cavalry and heavy infantry columns he, not Early, would have suffered disgrace in the Valley. This Irish upstart was lucky, not good. Good arguments could be made on all of these points, but the critics rather missed the essential point—he won. There was no denying his impact on the battlefield—his influence on men in battle, his ability to adapt to battlefield conditions, or his spectacularly successful use of cavalry. No other army commander employed the mounted arm in such a prominent role. Sheridan deserved credit for that and for cultivating young talent like Merritt, Custer, and Mackenzie. He had done many things well in his brief career as an army commander. He delivered three dramatic victories when his nation needed them, and he won in Virginia, where Yankees usually lost. While perhaps he could have accomplished more than he did, he had accomplished a great deal.

Although not among the critics of the new celebrity, Ulysses S. Grant, for one, believed that Sheridan could indeed accomplish more. Only a day after learning of his esteemed subordinate's Cedar Creek heroics, the commanding general returned to a familiar tune. In a brief message to Sheridan, Grant again called for a strike at the Virginia Central: "If it is possible to follow up your great victory until you can reach the Central road, do it." Again Sheridan rated such a move "impracticable." Apparently content to hold his position in the Lower Valley as a very nasty winter approached, Sheridan in early November moved his army into camps near Kernstown, south of Winchester. Early, meanwhile, gathered his remaining forces at New Market, sending forth an occasional reminder of his resilience in the form of small cavalry thrusts, which the Yankee horsemen easily repulsed. In mid-November, Kershaw's Division returned to General Lee. Sheridan, though, retained most of his army into December. He had some unfinished business.[14]

Early no longer posed a serious threat, but partisan bands throughout the region, particularly Mosby's Rangers, continued to prey upon Federal outposts and railroads. So, instead of moving against the Virginia Central, Sheridan turned his attention to John S. Mosby and his guerrillas. These "irregulars" had not prevented Sheridan's men from doing their worst, but they managed to tie up thousands of troops pulled from the firing line to guard supply trains and railroads. With efficient hit-and-run tactics, they grabbed payrolls, derailed trains, and generally made life miserable for hapless rear-echelon commanders, who appeared incapable of dealing with the Gray Ghost and his stealthy Rangers. And the odious business of retaliation and retribution continued. The October killings of quartermaster Colonel Cornelius Tolles and medial inspector Dr. Emil Ohlenschlager within Union lines, attributed to Mosby's men, rekindled the anger aroused by the earlier "murder" of Lieutenant Meigs. Mosby, for his part, had not forgotten the brutal executions back in September of six of his men, an act he blamed on Custer, or the recent hanging of one of his Rangers by order of Colonel Powell. The Virginian vowed to hang an equal number of Custer's men, a course of action readily condoned by General Lee. During October and into November, Mosby's men took a number of Custer's troopers and on November 6, twenty-seven unlucky Yankees drew slips of paper; seven pulled marked slips, condemning them to hang. The executions the next morning, staged purposefully close to Custer's camp, went badly, as two prisoners escaped and two others were wounded and left for dead trying to flee; three troopers were hanged. Mosby later sent a note to Sheridan in which he explained his motive and offered to let these hangings be the end of it, lest some future outrage compel him to reciprocate. Sheridan apparently accepted the proposal. This agreement did not end the conflict between Sheridan and the Southern irregulars—guerrillas still had to be dealt with—but hereafter both commanders took steps to avoid atrocities.[15]

In the wake of Cedar Creek, life got no easier for Sheridan. Not only were guerrillas running unchecked over much of his department but also Early's diminished command remained a nuisance if not a true concern. The weather became a problem as well, with bitter cold and frozen precipitation hindering operations and making camp life miserable for men and beasts. And then there was Grant. Throughout November the general pressed Sheridan to mount an offensive against the Virginia Central, which, Grant maintained, continued to carry vital sustenance to Lee's army. To each prod, Sheridan demurred, citing weather and the uncertainty of his situation in the valley. If Sheridan did not intend to use his troops for offensive purposes, Grant reasoned, he could send them to Petersburg. But Sheridan resisted this suggestion, too. Grant still avoided issuing Sheridan direct orders, but hero or not, Sheridan was verging on insubordination. Grant would not wait on Sheridan forever. Finally, in late November, Halleck, perhaps trying to break the impasse, suggested to Sheridan that if he did not intend to raid the Virginia Central it might be a good time to go after Mosby.[16]

Sheridan always claimed that Mosby and his Rangers actually benefited his efforts in the field by keeping his army closed up and alert. Besides, to deal with these guerrillas would require a disproportionately large force, which Sheridan had refused to devote to such an expedition. Now he could, replying to Halleck, "I will soon commence on Loudoun County, and let them know there is a God in Israel." On November 28, Merritt's division descended upon Mosby's stronghold east of the Blue Ridge, with orders to strip it of its material usefulness by consuming or driving off all stock and burning all crops, barns, and mills, "bearing in mind, however, that no dwellings are to be burned and that no personal violence be offered to the citizens." Merritt returned to the Kernstown camp on December 3, as Sheridan recalled, "having carried out his instructions with his usual sagacity and thoroughness." But while Merritt laid waste to the Loudoun Valley, Rosser's Rebels, uncontested, captured a Federal post on the B&O Railroad in West Virginia, taking some 700 prisoners and destroying warehouses and tracks. It was going to be that kind of winter for Little Phil.[17]

Also during this time, Grant apparently ran out of patience. "My impression now," the lieutenant general wrote Sheridan on November 28, "is that you can spare the Sixth Corps with impunity." Sheridan complied, sending off his best infantry over the next few days. He also broke up Crook's command, releasing the First Division and the Provisional Division for service with Grant, while Crook with the Second Division moved to Cumberland, Maryland, to strengthen defenses in that vital area. But Grant remained fixated on the Virginia Central. On December 4, even as the VI Corps departed, Grant queried, "Do you think it possible now to send cavalry through to the Virginia Central road?" Sheridan remained impertinent if not insubordinate. "I have contemplated a cavalry raid," he replied, but added, "I have not estimated the breaking of the road as very important." Grant, showing great restraint, ignored this breach, but he did not drop the subject. On December 9, to news that Gordon's and Pegram's Divisions had left Early, Grant tried again: "If the weather holds favorable you can make a successful offensive campaign. Try it if you can." He followed this request with a more direct appeal three days later, informing Sheridan in no uncertain terms that the Virginia Central remained vital to Lee's beleaguered army and essentially giving Little Phil the option of making the raid or detaching more troops. Amazingly resistant, Sheridan shot back, "It is impossible to do anything toward the Central road until the present inclement weather is over. The snow is now seven inches deep and the cold intense." He also continued to contradict Grant on the value of the railroad.[18]

Whether worn down by Grant's intransigence or sensing the erosion of his stature as a result of his stubbornness, Sheridan on December 19 sent forth his cavalry in unbearable conditions. Torbert, with Merritt's and Powell's divisions, struck out for the Virginia Central at Gordonsville, while Custer mounted a diversionary advance on Early's position near Staunton. Torbert's column, after an agonizing march in sleet and freezing rain, made it to Gordonsville before Lomax's cavalry and infantry, rushed to the area from Richmond, discouraged further progress. General Merritt commented that it was "difficult to imagine a more disagreeable duty for a mounted soldier." The effort proved "demoralizing to men and ruinous to horses." After five days of exposure and frustration, Torbert's command limped, frostbitten, back to Kernstown. Custer never made it to Staunton; his division, surprised in camp near Harrisonburg by Rosser's troopers, beat a hasty retreat. This failed effort ended offensive operations for the winter.[19]

What had been a very good year for Sheridan now ended sourly. His behavior after Cedar Creek grew decidedly curious; he seemed to have lost his fighting edge while growing increasingly insolent. Perhaps the constant frustration of guerrilla activity and the burden of often-mindless administrative duties contributed to his behavior. He was clearly run down by months of campaigning. Whatever the case, a nasty exchange with Secretary of War Stanton brought the problem to a head. When Sheridan responded angrily to a telegram forwarded by the War Department from the governor of West Virginia concerning numerous reports of Rebel activity in the region, Stanton fired back in his usual caustic manner. "It has been supposed that such information might be useful and desired by you," Stanton wrote, "as it is by other commanders who are your seniors in the service, without provoking improper insinuations against State authorities or disrespectful reply." The secretary, who unlike Grant refused to excuse such behavior (even from a national hero), put Sheridan in his place, informing the Valley commander that future reports from his office "will be expected to be received with the respect due the Department of which you are a subordinate." Sheridan's rant proved all the more embarrassing when in early January, Rebel cavalry raided the post at Beverly, West Virginia, capturing, killing, or wounding more than 600 Federal soldiers. The final blow came on February 21, 1865, when partisans under Jesse McNeill dragged Sheridan's old friend Crook and Brigadier General Benjamin Kelley from their beds in Cumberland, Maryland (both generals eventually were exchanged). But by that time, Sheridan's winter of discontent was coming to an end.[20]

On February 20, Grant sent Sheridan his most forceful directive yet. "As soon as it is possible to travel I think you will have no difficulty about reaching Lynchburg with a cavalry force alone," Grant wrote. "From there you could destroy the railroad and [James River] canal in every direction, so as to be of no further use to the rebellion." Sheridan could then "push on and join Sherman" in North Carolina or return to Winchester. If this provided insufficient motivation, the lieutenant general closed with a stern admonishment: "I would advise you to overcome great obstacles to accomplish this." By now, though, Sheridan seemed to have recovered his old aggressiveness. In less than a week, he assembled his fighting force, tied up what loose ends he could, and made ready to march.[21]

For Sheridan, the coming campaign represented something of a throwback to his earlier campaigns in Virginia. Having sent away most of the infantry, he prepared to march with essentially the same commands he brought with him when he first came to the Valley—the First and Third Cavalry Divisions and some horse artillery—leaving behind a small contingent to protect the B&O Railroad and the approaches to Washington. But many of Sheridan's longtime lieutenants would not be going along. Wright's VI Corps was already at Petersburg, as was one of Crook's old divisions; Crook himself awaited exchange in a Confederate prison. Emory remained at Winchester with Dwight's division, while Grover's division sailed from Virginia for duty at Savannah, Georgia. Colonel Powell resigned his commission under mysterious circumstances in January, and his Second Cavalry Division was broken up. George Chapman, who returned from his wound, replaced Powell but remained in the Valley with only a small brigade, while Colonel Henry Capehart's four regiments joined Custer's Third Division, giving that command a third brigade. The most glaring subtraction from Sheridan's lean new field force was Alfred Torbert. "General Torbert, being absent on leave at this time," Sheridan wrote, "I did not recall him." Torbert had always been an ill fit among Sheridan's lieutenants and, as the commander mentioned matter-of-factly, he "had disappointed me." Newly breveted Major General Wesley Merritt became chief of cavalry, a well-earned promotion for Sheridan's most dependable officer. Tom Devin, who received his long-overdue promotion to brigadier, assumed command of the First Division.[22]

On February 25, Merritt got his marching orders, and two days later almost 10,000 troopers in the First and Third Divisions, two sections of horse artillery, and a scaled-back supply train, all under Sheridan's personal direction, proceeded southward as heavy rain melted the snow that still covered the Valley. Brushing aside feeble blocking attempts by Rosser's cavalry, the blue juggernaut arrived at Staunton and the Virginia Central on March 2. Jubal Early, condemned to rot in the Valley for his failures, no longer possessed an army to contest Sheridan's advance. He had in fact scarcely a division—2,000 troops under Gabriel Wharton and Rosser—which he assembled at Waynesboro, a few miles east of Staunton, where the railroad passed through the Blue Ridge. Here he made a final stand, hoping to discourage the Federal approach to Charlottesville. On learning of Early's disposition, Sheridan dismissed the idea of moving on to Lynchburg, as Grant had directed, against which he could march with scant opposition, and immediately sent Merritt with Custer's division to deal with Early. That afternoon, Custer found Early's force hopelessly arrayed before Waynesboro. He dismounted a brigade to work against Wharton's exposed left flank while he charged the main line with his two remaining brigades. Alexander Pennington's men quickly collapsed the flank, and the rout was on. Custer's troopers swarmed through and around the shattered Rebel regiments and bagged almost all of them. Much of Rosser's command managed to escape, as did Early, Wharton, and a few other officers and men, but the Yankees took everything else—all of Early's wagons and artillery, seventeen battle flags, and 1,600 officers and men. This engagement finally brought the termination of Early's command. Sheridan sent these trophies of war back to Winchester under a heavy escort and commenced the destruction of the Virginia Central. "This decisive victory," Sheridan wrote, "closed hostilities in the Shenandoah Valley."[23]

The next day, Custer reached Charlottesville, where the mayor surrendered the keys to the city. The column stayed there for two days while destruction of the railroad continued. Devin's division then probed toward Lynchburg, but stopped at the James River and began destruction of the canal northeast of the town. While Devin worked eastward along the James, Custer's men moved along the Virginia Central, ripping up track as they went. Sheridan claimed that he planned to reunite his command and cross the James in order to strike the Southside line east of Lynchburg but that the Rebels had burned all of

*General Wesley Merritt. Courtesy of the Library of Congress*

*General Thomas Devin. Courtesy of the National Archives*

the bridges, preventing his crossing. So, "knowing that it was impracticable to join General Sherman," wrote Sheridan, "I now decided to destroy still more thoroughly the James River canal and the Virginia Central railroad and then join General Grant in front of Petersburg." Again, Sheridan took full advantage of Grant's discretionary orders and did what he wanted to do. He had no intention of backtracking to the Valley nor did he ever truly contemplate a rendezvous with Sherman, and he as much as admitted it in his memoirs: "feeling that the war was nearing its end, I desired to have my cavalry to be in at the death."[24]

The united command moved along the James, smashing up the canal, destroying millions of dollars worth of tobacco, grain, and other valuable produce, and liberating hundreds of slaves, who now followed the column as it turned northward. The troopers again struck the Virginia Central in the vicinity of Louisa Court House, tearing up track in both directions. During this long and productive but incredibly miserable march, Sheridan sent word to Grant that he was coming in and asked to have provisions waiting for his men when they reached White House on the Pamunkey River. Swinging to the north of Richmond, the column arrived on March 18 at White House, where the men found provisions waiting in lavish quantities courtesy of General Grant. Sixteen days in the saddle in horrible rainy weather had left the command very much worn down. As usual, the journey had been particularly rough on the horses, many of which were now unfit for duty. The men and mounts needed rest, but no such luxury awaited them. Sheridan recalled that "as each day brought us nearer to the Army of the Potomac, all were filled with the comforting reflection that our work in the Shenandoah Valley had been thoroughly done, and," he continued, "every one was buoyed up by the cheering thought that we should soon take part in the final struggle of the war."[25]

# "In at the Death"

Phil Sheridan's meteoric rise to prominence all but assured for him an important future in the U.S. Army; now he determined to play a conspicuous role in the climactic event of the war—the final defeat of General Robert E. Lee. He wanted, as he wrote, to have his men "in at the death," and he had made extraordinary efforts, to the point of ignoring General Grant's wishes, to see that it happened. But in getting his cavalry to Grant's lines around Richmond and Petersburg in time to realize this desire, Sheridan's men and horses suffered bitterly. They needed rest. Many men needed to be rearmed and remounted, and hundreds of the still serviceable horses needed shoes. On March 20, Wesley Merritt reported 1,323 dismounted troopers and 2,161 unserviceable mounts, and an astonishing 427 men without weapons—more than one-third of the command required remounting. If Sheridan's cavalry hoped to be in on the kill, it would take heroic labor, of the most inglorious kind. But the Union could provide, and soon an army of farriers accompanied by field forges arrived at White House to see to Sheridan's animals, while procurement officers scrambled to acquire new mounts. Still, Sheridan recalled, "nothing like enough horses were at hand to replace those that had died or been disabled on the mud march from Staunton to the Pamunkey River."[1]

At almost any other stage of the war the cavalry might have taken weeks to recover its fighting trim, yet time was not among the gifts Grant could bestow. In his first dispatch to Sheridan at White House, Grant outlined, without a sense of urgency, his plan to have Sheridan reinforced for a raid on the Southside and Danville Railroads—the last lifelines to Lee's army—and again threw out the option to join Sherman's forces in North Carolina. But on March 21, Grant's tone changed: "I do not wish to hurry you," he began, which in this case meant that Sheridan had better prepare to move. The general in chief believed accurately that Lee would attempt to cut his way out of his trenches and to join Joseph Johnston's forces in North Carolina, and he wanted "a large and properly commanded cavalry force ready to act." Sheridan replied the next day that he would march on the twenty-fifth with all available troops.[2]

As promised, the column marched across the peninsula to Harrison's Landing, across the James from Grant's headquarters at City Point. The following day, Merritt led the command to its staging area on the Military Railroad outside of Petersburg, while Sheridan visited Grant to settle a couple of nagging issues and to ascertain more clearly his role in the coming campaign. Grant welcomed his returned cavalry chief and listened as Sheridan reviewed his march from the Valley to Petersburg. Grant then addressed one of Sheridan's concerns—his status. Having essentially surrendered command of the Middle Military Division by joining Grant, Sheridan wanted to know where he stood in the command structure. The commanding general put any fears Little Phil might have harbored about his autonomy to rest by allowing him to retain the position of army commander, answerable only to Grant. Sheridan, therefore, avoided an uncomfortable reunion with George Meade. As to the recurring and loathsome prospect of joining Sherman, Grant told Sheridan not to worry; the reference to such a move in the recent orders was nothing more than a "blind," a fallback clause for the records should something go wrong.

Later that day, Sheridan joined Grant and President Lincoln, who came down from Washington to be closer to the action, for a cruise on the James. He found the president in a gloomy mood, troubled that a bold Federal sweep around the south side of Petersburg would expose the base at City Point to attack and give Lee new life. Just two days before, Confederate General John B. Gordon had launched a surprise predawn attack against the Federal position known as Fort Stedman, not far from City Point. Although the attack ended in disaster when Brigadier General John Hartranft's division of the IX Corps counterattacked, Lincoln apparently feared another such attempt. Sheridan claimed to have assured the president that Lee had shot his bolt. Besides, Lee was about to have his hands full.[3]

Sheridan stayed the night at City Point and returned to his command the following day only to be summoned back by Grant for an impromptu meeting with Sherman. This order raised the unpleasant possibility that Grant had changed his mind about keeping Sheridan's cavalry with him. Little Phil arrived late in the night to find his brother generals in deep discussion. When Sherman intimated that Sheridan's cavalry might join him in North Carolina, Sheridan vehemently protested. "My uneasiness made me somewhat too earnest, I fear," he recalled. Grant again assuaged his fiery subordinate, and Sheridan let it go at that. Not so Sherman; he stirred his junior army commander from bed early the next morning in a futile final effort to win Sheridan's support but, wrote

Sheridan, "when he saw that I was unalterably opposed to it turned the conversation into other channels."[4]

After spending a second night at City Point, Sheridan joined his command at Hancock Station, where his two divisions from the Valley reunited with the old Second Division, minus reliable David Gregg, who resigned in February for personal reasons. As the only substantial cavalry force with the Army of the Potomac for more than seven months, the Second Division had seen rough duty. Gregg, though, had not protested when Sheridan took Torbert to the Valley as chief of cavalry, nor did he seem to mind that Custer and Merritt became heroes while he performed thankless tasks around Petersburg. Apparently, he simply lost his desire to fight. Henry Davies headed the division in Gregg's absence but for unmentioned reasons never attracted consideration for the permanent command. If Sheridan had a say in the search for a new Second Division chief, he did not mention it. Grant wanted Ranald Mackenzie for the job, but Davies ranked Mackenzie. He offered the position to Brigadier Generals Romeyn Ayres and Samuel Crawford, both V Corps division commanders, and both turned him down (perhaps unwilling to serve under Sheridan should he return). Grant then rejected Meade's suggestion to move August Kautz from the Army of the James. Next, Frank Wheaton of the VI Corps, whose division fought so well at Cedar Creek, declined the position for reasons of health. Finally, on March 18, Grant turned to recently exchanged George Crook, Sheridan's closest friend in the service. Perhaps it just worked out this way, but Little Phil must have been pleased to have Crook back in the fold.[5]

Sheridan likely derived great pleasure from seeing the old Cavalry Corps reunited, but the current arrangement, like his Valley command, involved overlapping administrations and creative management as it contained elements from three different armies. In order to accommodate Sheridan as an independent army commander, the troops he brought with him from the Valley constituted the Army of the Shenandoah, and Merritt continued to direct the First and Third Divisions as chief of cavalry. The Second Division belonged administratively to the Army of the Potomac, and since Crook ranked Merritt he reported to directly to Sheridan. Adding to the confusion, on March 31, Grant attached the Cavalry Division, Army of the James, to Sheridan's force. This small, two-brigade division belonged to boyish-looking but battle-tested Ranald Mackenzie, who displaced General Kautz at Grant's insistence. Grant wanted the outstanding, oft-wounded combat officer for the Second Division but, frustrated in that effort, he went to rather extravagant lengths to give Mackenzie the position with the Army of the James. The additions of Crook and Mackenzie to what became known as the Cavalry Corps or Sheridan's Cavalry Command gave it a decidedly personalized aspect. Merritt and all four

*General Henry Davies Jr. Courtesy of the Library of Congress*

division commanders—Crook, Custer, Devin, and Mackenzie—played prominent roles in the Valley Campaign and attracted Sheridan's appreciation. These
were his men—his old West Point classmate and his brave boys—and they led
the most formidable cavalry force America had ever seen.[6]

*Sheridan and His Lieutenants Late in the War: Merritt, Sheridan, Crook, James Forsyth, and Custer. Courtesy of the National Archives*

At the onset of the final campaign of the war, Sheridan commanded an "army" of some 15,000 men, comprised exclusively of cavalry and horse artillery—a command that presaged the mechanized divisions of future wars. Nothing like it had been employed in this war, and its impact would prove the wisdom of Sheridan's vision when he first implored Meade to cut him loose back in May 1964. Devin's First Division remained essentially unchanged except for the brigade commanders. Colonel Peter Stagg, the capable leader of the 1st Michigan, now headed Custer's and James Kidd's old First "Michigan" Brigade. Young Colonel Charles Fitzhugh, plucked from the regular artillery to command the 6th New York, led the Second Brigade, replacing Devin, while experienced Brigadier General Alfred Gibbs, a regular before the war, took the fallen Charles Lowell's place at the head of the Reserve Brigade. The First and Second Brigades of Crook's Second Division remained in the familiar hands of Henry Davies and Irvin Gregg respectively. Colonel Charles H. Smith of the 1st Maine, a veteran of the division, commanded the recently created Third Brigade. Custer's Third Division retained the organization with which it left the Valley: former regular artillerist Colonel Alexander Pennington led the First Brigade; Colonel William Wells, who rose from private to lead the 1st Vermont, commanded the Second Brigade; and Colonel Henry Capehart led the Third Brigade. Three batteries of regular horse artillery accompanied these divisions. Mackenzie's Cavalry Division from the Army of the James had seen much action under Kautz and included the brigades of Colonel Robert West, 5th Pennsylvania, and Colonel Samuel Spear, 11th Pennsylvania—both had served as enlisted men in the regular army prior to the war. Sheridan's all-cavalry force boasted an impressive level of experience; it was well led, well armed, and reasonably well mounted. And, thanks to the efforts of its commander, it stood uniquely positioned to play the featured role Sheridan envisioned.[7]

During the long siege of Petersburg, General Lee continued to extend his trenches westward in an ongoing effort to protect his vital rail links to the Virginia heartland and the Deep South. And through a series of actions, Grant had cut the Weldon road and extended his own position westward past Hatcher's Run. On March 28, Grant ordered the V and II Corps to press farther westward to Dinwiddie Court House, beyond Lee's southwestern flank. Sheridan was to get there first and try to draw out a large portion of Lee's command, which could then be crushed between Sheridan and the converging infantry. Should Lee's men not oblige, Sheridan could then move against the Southside and Danville lines and wreck them. Again, Grant inserted the option of joining Sherman, but this time Sheridan let it pass.[8]

Early the next morning, Crook led the command toward Dinwiddie. Marching in the same muddy conditions of the past weeks, Crook's and Devin's divisions arrived at 5 P.M. Custer's division, detailed to escort the trains, remained well back, nursing wagons through the quagmire. Major General G. K. Warren's V Corps moved into position on Sheridan's right, followed into line by Major General Andrew A. Humphreys's II Corps. Three army corps now faced Lee's flank, poised to strike. Buoyed by the prospects before him, Grant gave up all ideas of cutting railroads or supporting Sherman. In a message to Sheridan that night, Grant wrote, "I now feel like ending the matter." His blood was up, he could sense the kill. He told his cavalry commander to forget the railroads and "In the morning push round the enemy if you can and get onto his right rear." Heavy rainfall began that night and continued throughout the following day, as Devin's and Crook's men pushed on to the important crossroads of Five Forks and Lee's flank.[9]

The troopers had only started out when Sheridan received Grant's order to cancel the planned advance due to the bad weather. Incredulous, Sheridan mounted his powerful gray pacer Breckinridge and with a small escort rode through the muck to Grant's forward headquarters on Gravelly Run to correct what "would be a serious mistake." Braving deep mud and volley fire from startled Yankee pickets, Sheridan arrived at Grant's soggy camp. His very presence produced an uplifting effect on the staff, and soon his self-assurance (he claimed) won over Grant, who closed their brief discussion: "We will go on." Sheridan believed that with the help of his former collaborator Horatio Wright and his VI Corps the cavalry could turn Lee's flank and usher in the rout of the Confederate army. The VI Corps, however, occupied the middle of the Federal line before Petersburg and could not yet be moved. Grant offered the V Corps, which Sheridan declined. Even so, on his return to Dinwiddie, Sheridan visited General Warren's headquarters for a brief conference but found the V Corps commander asleep in the late afternoon. Sheridan cared little for Warren, who returned the sentiment in spades, and when they finally chatted about the coming action, Sheridan recalled, Warren spoke "rather despondently of the outlook." When he returned to his headquarters, Sheridan learned that the Rebels were concentrating at Five Forks and digging in. He reported this situation to Grant on the morning of the thirty-first. Like a child who believed if he asked enough times he would get what he wanted, Sheridan again requested the VI Corps, and Grant again turned him down. He could have the V Corps, he could even have the II Corps, but the VI Corps was out of the question. Sheridan stubbornly decided to take Five Forks on his own, without infantry support.[10]

General Lee, not about to let the Yankees turn his flank without a fight, had dispatched five brigades of infantry under Major General George Pickett, of Gettysburg fame, to join the cavalry already forming at Five Forks under Fitzhugh Lee. During the night of the thirtieth, Pickett moved most of his force farther west, beyond Five Forks, in position to assail Sheridan's left flank as his cavalry advanced on the crossroads, which was precisely what happened.

On March 31, Merritt sent Stagg's and Fitzhugh's brigades of Devin's division and Davies's brigade of Crook's division to develop the situation at Five Forks. Charles Smith's brigade moved to the northwest of Dinwiddie to cover the left flank and western approaches. Gibbs's and Gregg's brigades formed the mobile reserve just north of Dinwiddie. This area turned out to be poor cavalry country, swampy, with thick patches of woods. The Confederate plan unfolded early in the afternoon, when Rooney Lee's and Tom Rosser's Divisions surprised Smith's command along Chamberlain's Creek, but Smith's men, fighting dismounted, threw back the initial Rebel assault. Davies's brigade, marching to Smith's relief, ran squarely into Pickett's infantry and was driven northeastward, back on Stagg and Fitzhugh. Pickett's infantry and the cavalry pushed across the creek, splitting the Federal cavalry and placing themselves between Five Forks and Dinwiddie. Davies, Stagg, and Fitzhugh got caught north of the breach while Smith, Gibbs, and Gregg stood between the Confederate salient and Dinwiddie. On both sides of the Rebel advance, Sheridan's men discovered themselves in serious danger of being overwhelmed.[11]

Pickett pressed eastward, driving Devin and Davies toward the exposed V Corps flank. But as the Confederates crossed above Dinwiddie, Merritt unleashed Gibbs and Gregg against the Rebel flank. This abrupt action halted Pickett's force, which now turned on its assailants, allowing Devin and Davies to circle back to Dinwiddie. Sheridan, meanwhile, sent for Custer, ordering him to leave one brigade with the trains and rush with the rest of his division to Dinwiddie. The horse artillery also broke loose from the mud and rushed to the field of battle. Sheridan determined to hold the Dinwiddie crossroads "at all hazards." While waiting for Custer, he selected a final defensive line and ordered Gibbs, Gregg, and Smith to retire to the new refused position, "but to contest every inch of ground." Custer's command arrived as the others pulled back, and Capehart's men loosed a ferocious volley at the Confederate horsemen as they charged Smith's retiring ranks. As the rest of Custer's command filled the gaps in Sheridan's new line, Pickett paused. Sheridan, Merritt, Custer, and numerous staff officers rode along the line, encouraging the troopers. "The cavalcade drew the enemy's fire, which emptied several of the saddles," Sheridan recalled, including that of a correspondent from the *New York Herald*, who fell wounded. Near sundown Pickett sent his infantry forward in handsome lines of battle. The Federal horse artillery opened, but the dismounted troopers held their fire until the Confederates had moved well into range of their carbines and then poured forth a "shower of lead" from thousands of repeaters, driving the attackers back—but not far.[12]

The day had not gone as Sheridan expected; in fact, he came close to calamity. The Confederates not only dashed Sheridan's optimistic designs but also punished Warren's V Corps a few miles down the line. Pickett's partial success, though, left his command—a sizable portion of Lee's available force—in serious jeopardy of being cut off and annihilated. Such became the topic of a flurry of messages sent between Sheridan, Grant, Meade, and Warren during the night of the thirty-first. Sheridan's first messages regarding the setback at Dinwiddie Court House sent alarm through the Federal high command, but as the situation stabilized, thoughts turned more sanguine. By late evening a contemplated rescue mission had turned into an offensive. Ironically, in light of his sour relations with Sheridan (and especially with regard to future events), it was Warren, apparently, who first proposed that his entire corps march to support the cavalry and crush Pickett's exposed force. At 10:45, Grant informed

Sheridan that Warren's corps and Mackenzie's Cavalry Division from the Army of the James would join him at Dinwiddie and that Sheridan was to take command of all troops sent to him. But Grant placed Warren's time of arrival, impossibly, at midnight—less than two hours after the orders were cut. This ridiculously overoptimistic clause would destroy Warren's life.[13]

Beginning at midnight, Sheridan waited in mounting exasperation for Warren to appear on Pickett's flank. Around 3:00 A.M. on April 1, he sent Warren instructions for his corps to attack at daylight, emphasizing the great opportunity they had to destroy a significant portion of Lee's army. But before the Federals could spring their trap, Pickett realized his vulnerability and during the predawn hours began to withdraw his forces to the prepared works at Five Forks. At daybreak, Merritt pressed his two divisions forward, snapping at Pickett's columns as they fell back to Five Forks; with no sign of Warren's infantry, a full-scale attack was out of the question. Later that morning, Ayres's V Corps division and Mackenzie's cavalry arrived at Dinwiddie, too little too late to catch the Rebels in the open—most of Pickett's men had reached the protection of their breastworks. Sheridan paced and cursed as he watched his chance slip away.[14]

The Confederate line at Five Forks stretched for almost two miles, extending roughly one mile west and three-quarters of a mile east of the crossroads, generally conforming to White Oak Road. Five brigades of infantry, three of Pickett's Division and two from Dick Anderson's Corps, manned the line, supported by ten pieces of artillery dispersed throughout. Colonel Tom Munford with Fitz Lee's Cavalry Division held the refused left flank, maintaining a tenuous link with the main Petersburg works, while Rooney Lee's Division manned the extreme right—the literal end of the line. Rosser's two mounted brigades provided a mobile reserve. Although not as exposed as he had been only hours before, Pickett remained dangerously vulnerable, but he could do nothing about it. He had to hold Five Forks at all costs. The presence of a large Federal force on their far right reduced to a matter of days, if not hours, the length of time the Confederates might hope to hold Petersburg and Richmond—before Sheridan's cavalry cut the Southside Railroad. Robert E. Lee understood this, and without the Southside road up and running he could not bring supplies in or get his army out. The failure of Gordon's attack at Fort Stedman left Lee only one option: to pull his army out of its trenches and make a break for the interior and a rendezvous with Joe Johnston's small army before Grant's blue host surrounded him. Lee needed time to make his final preparations—time Pickett had to buy for him at Five Forks.[15]

Grant, of course, had hoped to prevent the union of Lee's and Johnston's forces by sending Sheridan to cut the Southside line; now he wished to keep Lee from getting away at all. Sheridan certainly believed that his

*Colonel Thomas Munford. Courtesy of the National Archives*

troopers, supported by a corps of infantry, could overrun Pickett's position and gain the Confederate rear, but he had no infantry corps at his disposal—the deliberate Warren still had not shown. Noon passed before Sheridan established contact with Warren. Although furious over the delay, Little Phil believed the combined force still possessed the ability to crush Pickett's command before reinforcements arrived. He explained to Warren that Merritt would engage the main Rebel line with his dismounted troopers, while Custer menaced Pickett's right and Warren's three divisions hit the refused line on Pickett's left; Mackenzie's cavalry would cover Warren's right flank. Sheridan then directed Merritt to begin his "demonstrations," which Merritt gladly did.

Troopers across Pickett's front blazed away with their carbines, waiting for the V Corps to strike. They had a long wait. Colonel Horace Porter of Grant's staff, who accompanied Sheridan this day, described the army commander as "chafing with impatience and consumed with anxiety," like a "caged tiger." Sheridan found the infantry moving methodically to the staging point as its commander sat beneath a tree sketching the area, evidencing no sense of urgency. Sheridan, whose "disappointment grew into disgust," emphasized the need for alacrity: the army was running out of daylight, the cavalry was running out of ammunition, and he was running out of patience. Earlier in the day, Grant had given Sheridan authority to relieve Warren if he saw fit, but the cavalry commander had resisted the impulse to this point. Warren did not behave like Sheridan; few people did. But the former engineer officer had confirmed his own hero status long before Sheridan came to the killing fields of Virginia. Back in July 1863, during the pivotal second day of the Battle of Gettysburg, Warren, from his perch atop Little Round Top, recognized the crisis developing on the Federal left flank and sent staff officers, including, incidentally, Ranald Mackenzie, to rush troops to the threatened area. The subsequent defense of Little Round Top, one of the most celebrated events of the war, contributed significantly to the dramatic Federal victory at Gettysburg (and years later earned Warren a handsome statue on the site). Unfortunately for Warren, past performances amounted to nothing on this day, under this commander.[16]

When, finally, he advanced with his corps at 4:00 P.M., the attack went badly awry. Ayres's division struck the angle in the Rebel line as intended, but Sam Crawford's and Brigadier General Charles Griffin's divisions veered north of the mark, leaving Ayres's men unsupported. Sheridan sent staff officers to correct this flaw but, noticing Ayres's attack faltering under strong Confederate resistance, he took matters into his own hands. Mounted on Rienzi, Sheridan grabbed his red and white battle standard and charged among the wavering ranks, "shaking his fist, encouraging, entreating, threatening, praying, swearing." Sheridan's performance represented, believed Porter, "the true personification of chivalry, the very incarnation of battle." To one soldier, blood spurting from a mortal neck wound, Sheridan yelled, "You're not hurt a bit. Pick up your gun, man, and move right to the front." The man did as he was told and "rushed forward a dozen paces before he fell, never to rise again." Ayres and his officers followed Sheridan's bold example, rallying the command, which soon pierced Pickett's works.[17]

Now Sheridan's plan came together in full fury. Little Phil cursed Warren's tardiness, but the delay might well have played into Federal hands. The Confederate leaders apparently never expected an attack. A resourceful Tom Rosser, who had caught a number of fish during an earlier diversion, invited Pickett and Fitz Lee to his camp in the Confederate rear for an afternoon shad

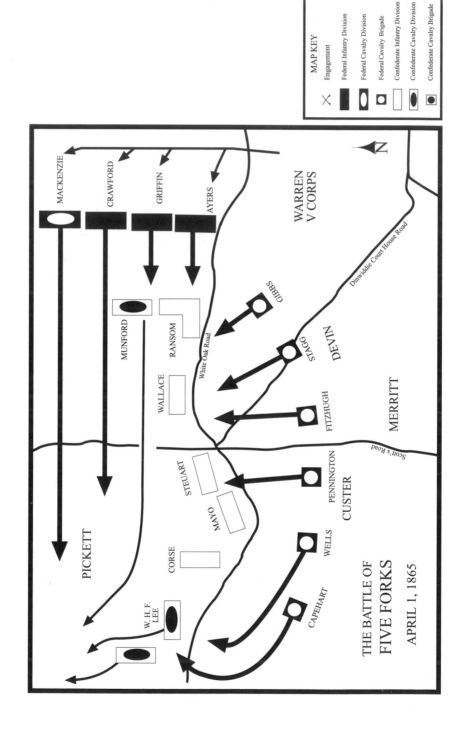

MAP KEY

× Engagement

Federal Infantry Division

Federal Cavalry Division

Federal Cavalry Brigade

Confederate Infantry Division

Confederate Cavalry Division

Confederate Cavalry Brigade

N

THE BATTLE OF
FIVE FORKS

APRIL 1, 1865

WARREN
V CORPS

MACKENZIE

CRAWFORD

GRIFFIN

AYERS

MUNFORD

RANSOM

WALLACE

WHITE Oak Road

GIBBS

STAGG

DEVIN

FITZHUGH

MERRITT

Dinwiddie Court House Road

Scott's Road

STEUART

MAYO

PENNINGTON

CUSTER

CORSE

WELLS

CAPEHART

W. H. F.
LEE

PICKETT

bake. Every soldier in the Army of Northern Virginia suffered from hunger, but these leaders accepted the invitation and left their commands to eat, incredibly, at a time when the Confederacy faced imminent extinction. So that afternoon, as blue columns formed on their front and flanks, Pickett and Lee could not be found. By the time they heard the roar of musketry from Ayres's attack, it was too late. Rebel officers and men on the line fought desperately, but without the coordinating influence of an overall commander, they could do nothing but mind their own positions, which many did with exceptional obstinacy. Once the Federal infantry overcame this initial resistance on the Rebel left, Pickett's command and Robert E. Lee's hopes for escape disintegrated.[18]

Ayres's men now swarmed over the earthwork, Sheridan in the thick of it, jumping Rienzi over the breastworks and joining the infantrymen inside the angle. Hapless defenders surrendered by the hundreds. Griffin's division came in on Ayres's right, led by another Gettysburg hero, Brigadier General Joshua Lawrence Chamberlain. "By God, that's what I want to see," Sheridan yelled, "general officers at the front." To the north, Crawford's wayward division, with Warren on hand, drove back Munford's troopers, gaining the Confederate rear. Mackenzie's cavalry, marching on Warren's right, confronted the brigade on the extreme left of Lee's main Petersburg line. Mackenzie personally led a mounted charge that bounded over the Rebel works, routing the stunned infantrymen and driving a wedge between Pickett's force and Robert E. Lee's army. Leaving a detachment to hold the position and round up prisoners, Mackenzie dashed off for Five Forks.[19]

In concert with the V Corps advance, Devin's dismounted troopers poured over the main line, joining the infantry inside the works, as Crawford and Mackenzie swept around the rear, cutting avenues of escape. The Confederate position dissolved, and hundreds of Rebel soldiers from the commands of Brigadier Generals George H. Steuart, Matt W. Ransom, and William Wallace dropped their weapons and raised their hands in surrender. On the western flank, Custer's men faced stiff resistance from Rooney Lee's cavalry and the infantry brigades of Brigadier General Montgomery Corse and Colonel Robert Mayo. Rooney Lee beat back a mounted charge led personally by Custer, but the hopelessness of the situation compelled him to withdraw. As his soldiers extinguished pockets of resistance and rounded up prisoners, Sheridan received reports from all parts of the field. One such message came from Warren, who proudly announced that he had gained the Confederate rear and grabbed up many prisoners. Sheridan growled to the befuddled aide, "By God, sir, tell General Warren he wasn't in the fight." He was in no mood for celebration yet. Not content with his present success, Sheridan wanted to cut the Southside rail before dark. To a group of V Corps officers, the frenzied general shouted, "I

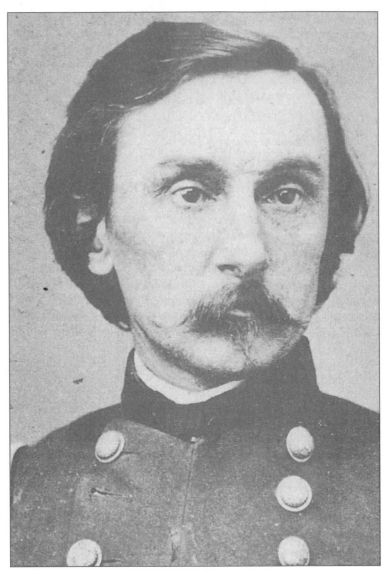

*General Gouverneur K. Warren. Courtesy of the National Archives*

want you men to understand we have a record to make, before that sun goes down, that will make hell tremble!"[20]

Nightfall and the need to consolidate his position, in case Lee tried to reclaim his flank, prevented Sheridan from reaching the railroad. He might not have been satisfied, but his men had delivered a fateful victory. As Custer's and Mackenzie's troopers sealed off the escape routes, the accounting began. The Yankees held almost 6,000 prisoners, six guns, 8,000 muskets, and thirteen battle flags among their trophies. Pickett, who dashed to the field as his line collapsed, managed to escape, as did most of the cavalry. The damage to the greater Confederate condition was irreparable. Sheridan's total losses for the day approached 1,000. The final blow of this battle, though, fell on General Warren. As he issued orders for the next day (and in anticipation of much fast-paced action ahead), Sheridan exercised his prerogative and relieved Warren, handing the V Corps to Griffin.

The relief of Warren at the close of fighting at Five Forks reflected poorly on Sheridan. For this day's action, perhaps, Warren deserved better, but his slowness of movement and lack of aggressiveness as a corps commander had long confounded his superiors. Sheridan's anger toward Warren, triggered initially by Grant's unreasonable timetable and exacerbated by that officer's deliberate approach to the battlefield, climaxed when Ayres's division wavered and Sheridan could not find the corps commander among the officers who rallied the command (because Warren had gone to redirect Crawford's wayward division). No one, not even Sheridan, could question Warren's courage or commitment, but in the frenetic atmosphere of this terminal campaign, Sheridan quite reasonably came to doubt his senior's ability to direct a corps under the present demands. Certainly, in light of the day's success, Sheridan could have displayed more magnanimity, but once disappointed he rarely showed such character, as Averell and Torbert understood all too well. In a scene described by Chamberlain, Warren approached Sheridan and asked him to reconsider, to which Sheridan exclaimed, "Reconsider. Hell! I don't reconsider my decisions. Obey the order!" This tragic episode came to define Sheridan as much as did his battlefield performances. Warren never recovered from this professional wound, but just now no one had time to worry about it.[21]

The fight at Five Forks revealed again the incredible battlefield presence that Sheridan possessed. He also displayed strong tactical awareness; he knew what he had to do to achieve victory and practically willed it to happen. His cavalry had seen it before, but the men of the V Corps, with many a reason to dislike this upstart army commander, now understood Sheridan's magic as well. General Chamberlain, who condemned Warren's removal, nonetheless recognized Sheridan's special value—and he knew a thing or two about inspirational leadership. Sheridan, he noted, "transfuses into his subordinates the vitality and energy of his purpose; transforms them into part of his own mind and will. He shows the power of a commander—inspiring both confidence and fear." Chamberlain and the men of the V Corps "reserved room for question whether [Sheridan] exhibited all the qualities essential to a chief commander" but, he admitted, "We had had a taste of his style of fighting . . . and we liked it."[22]

The Battle of Five Forks marked the beginning of the end for the Confederacy. The Southside Railroad into Petersburg and the Danville line that fed Richmond fell to the Federals the following day, rendering the two cities untenable. Lee labored to get his army and the Confederate government out before the trap closed. Grant wanted to end it here. That night, April 1, he ordered a general advance by four army corps all along the Petersburg front for 4:00 A.M., to be preceded by a massive artillery barrage that commenced right away. Grant also detached Brigadier General Nelson A. Miles's division of the II Corps to support Sheridan should Lee move on him in large force. Barring that, Sheridan's command prepared to march for the Confederate rear at Petersburg.

At 4:00 on April 2, 65,000 blue-jacketed soldiers of the II, VI, IX, and XXIV Corps assaulted Lee's lines at Petersburg, achieving significant breakthroughs southwest of the city. An ailing General Lee, with no other alternative, issued orders for his army to abandon the works of Petersburg and Richmond that night, if his troops could hold that long. He also advised recently appointed Secretary of War John C. Breckinridge, who had fought Sheridan in the Valley, and President Jefferson Davis that the time had come to evacuate the capital. As preparations for the evacuation proceeded, chaos erupted. Southwest of Petersburg, where Federal troops entered Confederate lines, Lieutenant General A. P. Hill died trying to rally his shattered command. Troops under Longstreet and Gordon managed to hold the inner works, but most of Hill's men were cut off by the VI Corps advance, as was Anderson's Corps, which attempted to march to Pickett's relief. At the western terminus of the Petersburg trenches, the II Corps drove Major General Henry Heth's Division from its works. Heth's men fell back to Sutherland Station on the Southside line, pursued by Miles's division, freed from its duty with Sheridan. After an intense fight of several hours, Miles finally broke the position, capturing hundreds of worn-out defenders and cutting the Southside line. The remnant of Heth's command raced for the Appomattox River. That night, President Davis and his cabinet, carrying the Confederate archives and what remained of the treasury, boarded one of the last trains out of Richmond, bound for Danville. Lee's army pulled out as well, leaving behind demolition teams to destroy government stores and public property and the bridges over the James and Appomattox Rivers. Richmond descended into anarchy as fire swept through the city. Early the next morning, elements of Major General Godfrey Weitzel's XXV Corps entered the Confederate capital. Ironically, this corps, composed of U.S. Colored Troops, restored order and fought fires, helping to save what remained of Richmond. On April 3, Grant and Lincoln visited Petersburg (Lincoln toured Richmond the following day).[23]

After releasing Miles's division on April 2, Sheridan's combined command turned away from Petersburg to pursue the Rebels moving westward

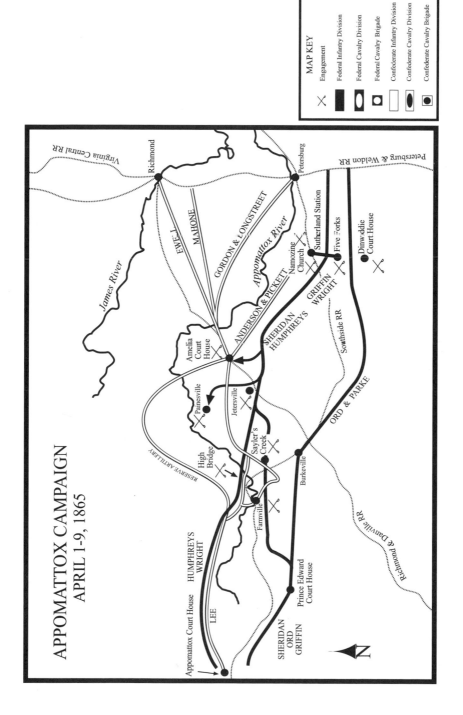

APPOMATTOX CAMPAIGN
APRIL 1-9, 1865

MAP KEY

Engagement
Federal Infantry Division
Federal Cavalry Division
Federal Cavalry Brigade
Confederate Infantry Division
Confederate Cavalry Division
Confederate Cavalry Brigade

Virginia Central RR
Richmond
Petersburg
Petersburg & Weldon RR
James River
EWELL
MAHONE
GORDON & LONGSTREET
Appomattox River
ANDERSON & PICKETT
Namozine Church
Sutherland Station
Five Forks
Dinwiddie Court House
GRIFFIN
WRIGHT
SHERIDAN
HUMPHREYS
Southside RR
Amelia Court House
Painesville
Jetersville
ORD & PARKE
Sayler's Creek
Burkeville
High Bridge
RESERVE ARTILLERY
Farmville
Prince Edward Court House
Richmond & Danville RR
HUMPHREYS
WRIGHT
Appomattox Court House
LEE
SHERIDAN
ORD
GRIFFIN

N

along the Appomattox River. The cavalry led the way, with the V Corps infantrymen keeping an admirable pace. Lee had designated Amelia Court House,
some thirty miles southwest of Richmond, as the rallying point for his various scattered commands and ordered rations to be sent there and to Danville.
Sheridan's cavalry pressed the pursuit, gathering up prisoners and discarded
equipment along the way. On April 3, Custer's division attacked a rear-guard
cavalry brigade at Namozine Church and, after a stiff fight, captured most of the
defenders. Custer's younger brother Tom earned the Medal of Honor for charging into the Confederate line and capturing a flag. By now, Sheridan believed
that Lee planned to concentrate his forces at Amelia Court House, preparatory
to a move along the Richmond & Danville line by way of Burkeville. This route
led Lee's starving soldiers toward much-needed food and carried them closer
to a rendezvous with Johnston's forces in North Carolina. Sheridan intended
to deny Lee this avenue by getting ahead of the Confederates and cutting the
Danville line.

Early on the morning of April 4, Crook's cavalry division rode for
Jetersville, followed by the fast-marching V Corps, which had indeed adapted
to Sheridan's style of warfare. Merritt with his two divisions basically paralleled
the retreating Confederates toward Amelia. Lee's columns began to arrive at
Amelia Court House the same day, but much to the great general's astonish-
ment, he found no rations waiting for his hungry and exhausted army. Sheridan
and a small escort arrived at Jetersville that afternoon, ahead of the V Corps.
Here Federal pickets captured a messenger who carried a note from Lee to the
commissary officers at Danville and Lynchburg requesting that 300,000 rations
be sent to Burkeville. Sheridan thus confirmed that Lee's forces had reached
Amelia, needed food, and were definitely headed for Danville. He also sent
scouts to transmit Lee's order, hoping to grab the provisions sent to Lee for his
own soldiers, who, having outdistanced their own supply trains, needed sustenance as well. Then, Sheridan turned his attention to blocking Lee's path to
Burkeville. As the V Corps filed in, he placed it astride the railroad and called
in Crook and Merritt, leaving Mackenzie to shadow the Rebels at Amelia
Court House. During the rest of the day and into the next, Union regiments
arrived near Jetersville. By afternoon on April 5 most of the Cavalry Corps, the
V Corps, and the II Corps held a strong blocking position, crushing whatever
hopes Lee nourished about getting to Danville via Burkeville. When a very
ill General Meade joined his troops at Jetersville, he dashed Sheridan's plans
to attack Lee at Amelia, wishing to wait until his VI Corps reached the field.
Typically (and appropriately in this case), Sheridan fumed.

Sheridan had ample reason to be annoyed by Meade's reluctance to
attack—he knew that Lee was moving again. Although Lee spent what
amounted to an extra day at Amelia in a futile attempt to gather food, by

noon on April 5, well aware of the Federal concentration at Jetersville, he ordered his army to march northwestward, around the Federals, and head for
Farmville, twenty-three miles to the west. Here Lee's weary command would
find the Southside Railroad and hoped-for provisions. Sheridan had a pretty
good idea of what Lee intended to do, because a reconnaissance by Davies's
brigade of Crook's Second Division struck a large wagon train at Painesville,
about seven miles northwest of Amelia. Davies' troopers captured 320 Confederates and an equal number of black teamsters, destroyed 200 supply and
headquarters wagons, and carried off five guns and eleven flags. Davies then
fought off a Rebel attack at Amelia Springs before reaching Sheridan with the
important information. Frustrated by Meade's intransigence and fearing that
Lee might elude him, Sheridan sent a message to Grant at 3:00 P.M. "I wish you
were here yourself," wrote Sheridan, "I feel confident of capturing the Army of
Northern Virginia if we exert ourselves. I see no escape for Lee." Grant, riding
with General Ord's Army of the James toward Burkeville, was fifteen miles away
when he received Sheridan's message at 6:30. No doubt recognizing a potential showdown between his two top subordinates, Grant headed for Jetersville
with only a small escort, arriving before midnight. During an early morning
conference, Meade voiced his plan to attack Lee at Amelia Court House on
the sixth, and Grant did not overrule him, but Sheridan would "not permit the
cavalry to participate in Meade's useless advance." He returned the V Corps to
Meade's control and issued orders for the cavalry to prepare to march. Sheridan
intended to race Lee westward and block his path for good.[24]

When Meade advanced on Amelia Court House on the morning of
April 6, he discovered, as Sheridan knew he would, that Lee was long gone and
resumed the chase. Sheridan meanwhile marched westward parallel to Lee's
column, slashing at its flanks at opportune moments. Lee got the jump on
the Federals, but during the bitter night march his army became badly strung
out over several miles. Broken vehicles and spent animals filled the road to
Farmville. Proud Southern men who had done more than anyone could have
expected of them now fell by the wayside by the dozens as Lee's ever-dwindling
force left in its wake a scene of wreckage, human and material, that signaled
the impending death of a truly great army. Miraculously, thousands of famished
soldiers kept marching, walking really, and when threatened these living scare-
crows still inflicted punishment. But straggling and the careless placement of
trains left dangerous gaps between the separate components of Lee's army—gaps
that Sheridan's cavalry now exploited with devastating effect.

That morning, April 6, Lee and Longstreet reached Rice's Station on
the Southside line a few miles short of Farmville and waited for the army to
close up. But five miles back, on Sayler's Creek, the diminished corps of Dick
Anderson and an ad hoc corps from the Richmond defenses commanded by

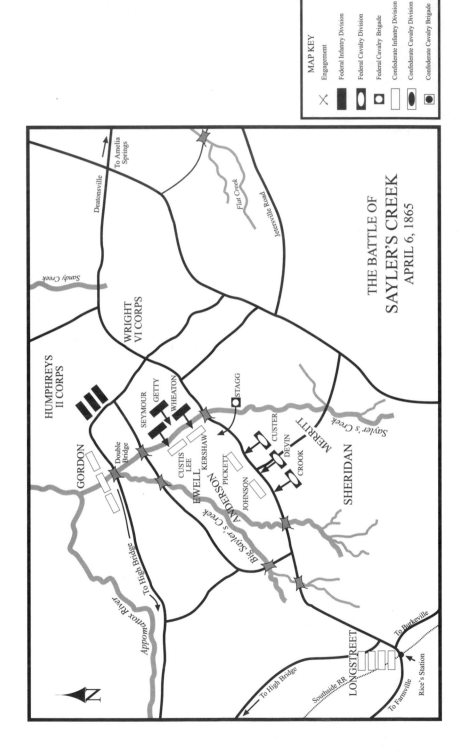

MAP KEY

×  Engagement

Federal Infantry Division

Federal Cavalry Division

Federal Cavalry Brigade

Confederate Infantry Division

Confederate Cavalry Division

Confederate Cavalry Brigade

THE BATTLE OF
SAYLER'S CREEK
APRIL 6, 1865

To Amelia Springs

Deatonsville

Flat Creek

Jetersville Road

Sandy Creek

WRIGHT
VI CORPS

HUMPHREYS
II CORPS

SEYMOUR  GETTY  WHEATON

STAGG

Sayler's Creek

CUSTER

MERRITT

DEVIN

CROOK

GORDON

Double Bridge

CUSTIS LEE  KERSHAW

EWELL

PICKETT

JOHNSON

ANDERSON

SHERIDAN

Big Sayler's Creek

To High Bridge

Appomattox River

LONGSTREET

To High Bridge

Southside RR

To Farmville

Rice's Station

To Burkeville

Lieutenant General Richard S. Ewell found their path blocked by Sheridan's cavalry, who assailed the preceding wagon train before noon. Custer's division charged into the train with sabers swinging, capturing hundreds of wagons and men and ten guns. Alert to the danger posed to his rearward trains, Ewell sent them northwestward on an alternate route. Gordon, whose rear-guard corps was fighting off pressure from Humphreys's pursuit, followed the trains, leaving Anderson and Ewell isolated. While he threatened Anderson's corps with his cavalry, Sheridan sent word for Wright's familiar VI Corps, which Grant had attached to Sheridan earlier in the day, to swing in behind Ewell. What followed was, Sheridan believed, "one of the severest conflicts of the war."

Ewell's Corps, comprised of Joseph Kershaw's reliable division and a division of home guards, convalescents, heavy artillerists (serving as infantry), and a naval battalion, all commanded by Major General George Washington Custis Lee, Robert E. Lee's eldest son, numbered perhaps 3,000 men. Most of these men had never been in a flight like this, and now they faced the battle-hardened VI Corps, 12,000 strong, supported by Stagg's cavalry brigade. When Wright's men attacked, they met a ferocious defense, but soon the weight of numbers told, and they overwhelmed Ewell's position, capturing Ewell, Kershaw, Custis Lee, and two brigadiers. Across the field, Anderson, with the remnants of Pickett's and Major General Bushrod Johnson's Divisions (maybe 6,000 men), held back the three cavalry divisions. Finally, mounted charges by Crook's men on the left and Custer's on the right obliterated the line. Anderson, Pickett, and Johnson escaped with parts of their commands, but two more brigadiers and hundreds of troops surrendered. In all, seven general officers and at least 6,000 men became prisoners. (During this battle, Tom Custer grabbed another flag, for which he received a second Medal of Honor, becoming one of few men to achieve the feat.) Sheridan and Wright counted about 1,100 total casualties at Sayler's Creek. To the north of this battle, Gordon fought a desperate rearguard action against the II Corps, losing 1,700 men, almost 300 wagons and ambulances, three guns, and thirteen battle flags before extricating his battered corps. Total Confederate losses on April 6 came to at least 8,000—roughly one-third of Lee's total force. The Battle of Sayler's Creek lacked the drama of Sheridan's previous victories, but in net results it ranked as one of his most decisive. Not only had he cut off and captured a huge portion of the Confederate army and much of its supply train but also he crushed any hope Lee still retained for reaching Danville. Had Sheridan convinced Meade to act sooner at Amelia Court House, he might well have finished Lee on this day. As it was, he continued to prove himself the indispensable factor in the campaign. More than anyone else, Sheridan had pushed the conflict closer to its conclusion.

That night, Sheridan reported to Grant on this day's success, closing with "if the thing is pressed I think Lee will surrender." Grant forwarded the report to

Lincoln, who replied simply, "Let the thing be pressed." Pressed it was. Having thwarted an effort by a detachment from the Army of the James to capture High Bridge—an impressive stone structure that rose more than 100 feet above a wide flood plain and carried the Southside line westward to Farmville—Lee managed to get his forces to Farmville. Gordon, with the fragments of three corps, crossed the Appomattox at High Bridge, while Longstreet with what remained of his own and A. P. Hill's Corps marched from Rice's Station. The continued presence of Sheridan's cavalry and the knowledge that the Army of the James already held Burkeville forced Lee to head for Lynchburg, at least, abandoning any real possibility of joining Johnston. Now, by crossing the Appomattox and destroying the bridges behind them, Lee's men could put some distance between themselves and the Federal wolf pack. At Farmville on the morning of April 7, for the first time in days, Lee issued rations as his army crossed the Appomattox. For a few precious moments some Confederates enjoyed breakfast and felt a sense of hope.[25]

Sheridan's troopers mounted up early on the seventh, feeling mighty hopeful themselves. Before sunrise, Crook's men rode out to develop the situation at Farmville, while Merritt, with Custer's, Devin's, and Mackenzie's divisions, marched to Prince Edward Court House in case Lee attempted an overland march to Danville. When word of Crook's approach reached Lee, he suspended food distribution and hurried the army across the river, much to the displeasure of many soldiers who had yet to receive rations. Safely across, the Confederates burned both bridges at Farmville. Lee now had his entire command north of the Appomattox, but his aspirations for a strong head start perished when the rear guard covering Gordon's retreat failed to destroy the double-tracked High Bridge. The trailing II Corps saved the bridge and stayed hot on Lee's tail. That afternoon, Crook reached Farmville. Finding the bridges demolished, the Second Division forded the Appomattox and attacked the Confederate wagons on the opposite bank. Like wounded lions the Rebel cavalry struck back, driving Irvin Gregg's brigade across the river and capturing Gregg and many of his men. It was a humiliating setback for Crook and his command, who found out, as had the II Corps when it had gotten close to Gordon's rear guard earlier in the day, that these Confederates still packed a punch. "There was as much gallantry displayed by some of the Confederates in these little engagements," General Grant noted, "as was displayed at any time during the war." Still, Sheridan found one positive aspect in Crook's foray (information later confirmed by his scouts)—Lee was heading to Lynchburg via Appomattox Station, where plentiful rations waited in boxcars.[26]

The Confederates clearly had some fight left in them, but by the evening of April 7, Grant judged Lee's chances of escape "utterly hopeless." He now opened communications with his still-defiant adversary: "GENERAL: the result of the

*Colonel John Irvin Gregg. Courtesy of the National Archives*

last week must convince you of the hopelessness of further resistance on the part of the Army of Northern Virginia in this struggle. I feel that it is so, and regard it as my duty to shift from myself the responsibility of any further effusion of blood, by asking of you the surrender of that portion of the C. S. Army known as the Army of Northern Virginia." Lee's response reached Grant the next morning. Although the old warrior refused to concede the hopelessness of his situation, he asked for Grant's terms. Grant, who earned his first fame of the war for offering the defenders of Fort Donelson no terms but immediate and unconditional surrender, replied with generous conditions in the interest of peace and proposed a meeting to discuss particulars. Lee, who had not expected such a conciliatory posture from "Unconditional Surrender" Grant, pondered his options during another grueling night march, as his army continued to melt away. Grant, not taking any chances with the wily Lee, ordered the vigorous pursuit maintained on April 8. Again, Sheridan and his lieutenants had the lead.[27]

# 8

# "Fragments Scattered in His Path"

On the morning of April 8, Sheridan gathered his cavalry at Prospect Station, on the Southside line between Farmville and Appomattox Station. This day's mission, a relatively easy one by recent standards, was to beat Lee's army to Appomattox Station. Once there, the Federals could deny Lee's men the accumulated rations and block their further progress until the infantry arrived to finish the job. It all depended on getting there first. Sheridan appeared ready to sacrifice his precious horsemen if it meant ending the thing. The four superb cavalry divisions—each led by a Sheridan favorite and each honed to a razor-sharp edge—started for Appomattox and their appointment with destiny. Each division seemed to mirror its commander: Mackenzie's, hard riding, efficient, and fiery; Devin's, hard hitting, reliable, seemingly always there at the right time; Crook's, solid and underappreciated; and Custer's, opportunistic, flashy, and impetuous. Merritt, like a martial puppet master, made it all work. As fate would have it at this pivotal juncture, Custer led the way. General Grant praised Sheridan's horsemen: "They were ready to move without rations and travel without rest until the end. Straggling had entirely ceased, and every man was now a rival for the front."[1]

The troopers made good time, marching south of the railroad on a beautiful spring day. Custer, riding ahead of the main column with his escort, reached Appomattox Station in the afternoon and found four trains laden with supplies for Lee's army. Without waiting for his division to catch up, the flamboyant general charged in and captured three trains, locomotives and cars intact, and immediately started them eastward, away from any threat of recapture, with his own troopers as engineers. A fourth train burned where it sat. But Custer soon discovered that his were not the only troops in the vicinity. A detachment guarding the reserve artillery and a large wagon train, which Lee had sent ahead of his main column by a northern route, attacked Custer, who deployed his arriving brigades and called upon Devin for assistance. After an initial shock, the Yankees drove their attackers toward Appomattox Court House, two miles distant. The fighting lasted well into the night before Sheridan's command gained control of the field, taking in the process twenty-four guns, numerous prisoners, and more than one hundred wagons and ambulances. More important, though, Sheridan had beaten Lee to his crucial supplies and now stood firmly across his line of march. Sheridan consolidated his position northeast of the station and waited for the infantry.

"I did not sleep at all, nor did anybody else," Sheridan wrote, "the entire command being up all night long; indeed there had been little rest in the cavalry for the past eight days." Sheridan sent messenger after messenger to hurry along Ord's divisions and Griffin's V Corps, both of which had followed the cavalry. Lee might try to push through the cavalry, but the cavalry plus two large corps of infantry rendered such a move impossible if not suicidal. Around cavalry headquarters, Sheridan recalled, "everybody was overjoyed at the prospect that our weary work was about to end so happily."[2]

Lee's men reached the fields around Appomattox Court House that evening after a long but relatively uneventful march, with the Federal II and VI Corps hot on their heels. Here Lee learned of the disaster at Appomattox

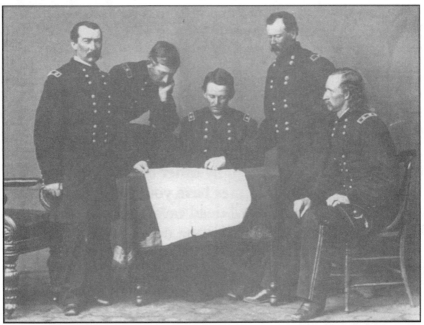

*Generals Sheridan, James Forsyth, Merritt, Devin, and Custer. Courtesy of the National Archives*

Station and of Sheridan's presence astride his path. He did not know, however, that to the south Ord kept marching toward Sheridan's position, trailing John Gibbon's XXIV Corps, Brigadier General William Birney's division of U.S. Colored Troops from the XXV Corps, and the V Corps. The sad remnant of the Army of Northern Virginia lay trapped between the two wings of Grant's force—and Grant's situation only stood to improve as his strung-out columns converged during the night. Even so, Lee met with Longstreet, Gordon, and Fitzhugh Lee to discuss their limited options. He broached the subject of surrender, but his corps commanders dismissed the idea in favor of the only other alternative. Not surprisingly, these dauntless warriors opted to fight. Gordon and Fitz Lee would attempt to rip open a gap in Sheridan's line, through which Longstreet and the army's wagons could then pass and resume the march to Lynchburg. They based this plan on the assumption that Sheridan had no infantry support. It was, in fact, an unrealistic design born of desperation and the sheer unwillingness to accept defeat, and it grew more hopeless with every mile Ord's divisions put behind them.

During this very long night the communication between Grant and Lee resumed. Lee, defiant to the last, responded to Grant's invitation to meet and discuss terms of surrender: "I do not think the emergency has arisen to call for the surrender of this army," he postured. But to promote the "restoration of peace," Lee proposed to meet Grant between the lines at 10:00 the following morning. Early on April 9, Grant replied that his terms were clear—unless Lee planned to surrender, a meeting "could lead to no good." Lee did not receive Grant's response until late the next morning, so he planned to meet Grant as he proposed even as his army readied for its breakout attempt.

Sheridan knew that Grant had entered negotiations with Lee. In fact, Grant had expected Lee's surrender the previous day. In reporting Custer's actions at Appomattox Station, Sheridan wrote prophetically, "If Gibbon and the Fifth Corps can get up to-night we will perhaps finish the job in the morning." But the cavalry chief did not share his commander's optimism about Lee's intentions: "I do not think Lee means to surrender until compelled to do so." Sheridan had done all he could do to achieve that end. Now he could only await the infantry and hope it got there soon. He understood, too, that an attack on his front offered the only chance Lee's army retained for escape, and he prepared accordingly. During this campaign, he had displayed growing maturity as a battlefield tactician, but this morning would test him. Until the infantry got up, his cavalry had to hold. Everything he had accomplished over the past several months led him to this moment. During the night, he deployed his four divisions across the Lynchburg road, with Mackenzie on the left, Crook in the center, Devin on the right, and Custer in reserve, and prepared to receive the anticipated Confederate attack. He did not have long to wait.[3]

At 5:00 A.M. on this Palm Sunday, Gordon led his command forward with the same tenacity he always summoned in battle, and his men responded as if they were charging into the Federal flank at Chancellorsville two years before. Sheridan coolly watched events unfold as he expected. He could afford to be cool, because Ord had reached the field ahead of his troops, who had completed an extraordinary all-night march. The V Corps, too, had come up. Now, Sheridan ordered Merritt to execute a fighting withdrawal, slowly pulling off to the right. Crook and Mackenzie, already hotly engaged, received word to pull back as well, giving ground grudgingly. These moves opened an apparent gap in the Federal line into which the Rebels charged with abandon. As Gordon's men rushed onto the ridge vacated by the cavalry, they discovered to their shock heavy lines of blue-clad infantry. Sheridan's beautifully realized battle plan, reminiscent of Wellington's at Waterloo, brought the attack to an abrupt halt—the trap had sprung. As Ord and Griffin advanced, the cavalry mounted up to deliver the final blow. Gordon's men continued to offer a bold front, while Longstreet hastily staked out a defensive position at Appomattox Court House. Fitz Lee and most of the Rebel cavalry took this opportunity to quit the field, riding hard for Lynchburg to avoid being subject to the surrender that must surely follow. Meanwhile, Sheridan joined Merritt as the cavalry prepared to charge the Confederate left flank. From Merritt's staging point, Sheridan could see the other wing of Lee's army contesting the II Corps advance northeast of the tiny village. There before him lay the ultimate prize, waiting to be swept away by his cavalry. Custer's men, as always, were ready to attack, Devin's almost so, when a courier from Custer dashed up to Sheridan with news that Lee had surrendered. Reportedly, Sheridan cursed in disappointment and shook his fist, as his chance to destroy Lee's army vanished under a white flag.[4]

Sheridan might have been disappointed, but General Lee was devastated. The Virginian had begun the day with faint hope, but by 8:00 he knew that Gordon's attack had failed and his army was trapped. He consulted his officers for the last time, but finding no profit in further sacrifice, accepted the inevitable. At 8:30, Lee, in a handsome new dress uniform, mounted his familiar gray horse Traveler and rode away with two aides and an orderly. Thirty minutes later, he passed through his lines northeast of Appomattox for his meeting with Grant, unaware that the Union commander had no intention of meeting him. Between the lines, II Corps pickets challenged Lee's party. At length, General Humpheys informed Lee that Grant had moved to Sheridan's front, where fighting continued. Lee, with no recourse, dictated a new message to Grant, requesting a meeting expressly to discuss the surrender of his army. He intended to wait where he was for Grant's reply and requested a suspension of hostilities until he could meet with Grant, but Humphreys was poised to attack, and neither he nor General Meade had the authority to suspend hostilities. Lee reluctantly returned to his lines, ordered his officers to hold their own fire if they could, and sent a courier to Gordon, instructing him to seek a truce on his front pending negotiations. He could only hope that Meade's attack did not commence before Grant called a truce.

Lee's message to Gordon reached the Georgian as he braced for Sheridan's attack. He sent the courier on into the Federal line under a flag of truce. Unable to find Grant or Sheridan, Captain Robert Sims delivered the message to Custer, who dispatched an aide to Sheridan. According to Southern accounts, Custer then took it upon himself to receive Gordon's surrender. Following the courier into Confederate lines, the brash Custer met Gordon and, in the name of Sheridan and under the threat of annihilation, demanded the immediate surrender of his forces. Gordon replied that he had not the authority to surrender anything, and if Sheridan chose to attack during a truce, the blood would be on his hands. Unrewarded, Custer next went to Longstreet and haughtily delivered the same ultimatum. Like Gordon, Longstreet was not impressed by the opulently attired twenty-five-year-old, nor did he intend to suffer his brash behavior. He exploded, informing Custer that he had entered Confederate lines without authorization, that he had no authority to demand anything—since Lee and Grant had entered negotiations—and that he was addressing a superior officer. If he or Sheridan wished to attack, Longstreet would happily oblige them. Suitably rebuffed, Custer withdrew. Regrettably, Custer's thirst for glory often involved behavior that justly soiled his image and made him many enemies, which tended to overshadow his spectacular battlefield performances. On a day when men on both sides of the lines displayed great magnanimity, Custer showed none.[5]

Sheridan almost yielded to similar impulses. He, too, rode into Gordon's lines only to be fired upon by a group of Rebel cavalry who had not been alerted to the truce. When he reached Gordon, he demanded an explanation. Gordon apologized, and Sheridan sent a staff officer under a white flag to inform the offenders, who continued to fire into Merritt's position, of the truce. Brigadier General Martin Gary, whose small South Carolina brigade was causing the trouble, seized the staff officer, exclaiming, "South Carolinians never surrender." Merritt soon charged the position, freed the officer, and put an end to Gary's "absurdity." In fact, firing had ceased across the field. Getting back to business, Gordon shook off Sheridan's snide references to the Valley Campaign and informed Little Phil that Lee had asked for the truce pending negotiations with Grant. Sheridan found the Confederates' actions disingenuous, perhaps a ruse to buy time. If Lee planned to surrender, why then had Gordon attacked? Sheridan proclaimed: "I will entertain no terms except that Lee shall surrender to General Grant on his arrival here. If these terms are not accepted we will renew hostilities." Gordon, long Lee's most valuable subordinate, assured Sheridan and Ord, who had joined the discussion, that Lee indeed intended to surrender. The generals parted company to brief their troops on the proceedings, agreeing to meet again in half an hour.[6]

Thirty minutes later the generals reconvened, with Longstreet joining the talks. Longstreet produced a copy of Lee's message to Grant, which satisfied Sheridan. Since Grant, still en route to Sheridan's position, remained unaware of the developing events, Sheridan dispatched a staff officer to bring in the commander. Longstreet also voiced concern about Meade's impending attack northeast of Appomattox Court House, so Sheridan sent his own chief of staff, James Forsyth, with one of Longstreet's aides through the Confederate lines to Meade's position—a small errand that likely saved hundreds of lives. During the lull, officers from both sides gathered between the lines, many renewing old friendships. Some, perhaps hundreds, of the Confederates quietly slipped away rather than face surrender.[7]

Grant received Lee's message at 11:50. He had suffered from a terrible headache all day but, as he recalled, "the instant I saw the contents of the note I was cured." He sent Lieutenant Colonel Orville Babcock of his staff with a reply, agreeing to meet General Lee at a place of his choosing. Babcock dashed off to find Lee, while Grant headed for Sheridan's lines. When Babcock reached Sheridan's lines Forsyth conducted him to Lee. Although ready to meet his fate, Lee wanted to make sure the temporary truce on Meade's front held, so Babcock drafted an order in Grant's name to suspend hostilities indefinitely, which Forsyth managed to get to Meade just as Humphreys geared up for an attack. Meanwhile, Lee sent his aide, Colonel Charles Marshall, ahead to select a suitable meeting place. Marshall settled on the residence of Wilmer McLean, who in one of the great coincidences of the war had moved his family from Manassas to Appomattox Court House to escape the fighting after the First Battle of Bull Run. McLean had witnessed the beginning; now he hosted the beginning of the end.

Lee arrived at the McLean house at 1:00, before Grant, who appeared about thirty minutes later. Lee looked every bit of the almost mythical figure he had become. In his new dress uniform with a beautiful sword at his side, Lee, erect and dignified, offered a stark contrast to Grant, who wore a mud-spattered private's coat with lieutenant general's bars sewn on the shoulders. Grant wore no sword. They greeted each other cordially and spoke briefly, surrounded by members of Grant's staff and Generals Ord and Sheridan. Most of the onlookers left the room while Lee and Grant discussed the details of the surrender. Grant proved even more generous than Lee could have imagined, taking the first great step toward reuniting the nation. The other officers reentered the parlor when the agreements were signed. At 3:00, Lee left the McLean house to return to his men. Like Grant, he set an example for others to follow and thus did his part to heal America's deepest wound. Union officers then bought up the contents of the McLean parlor as souvenirs. Sheridan reportedly gave $20 in gold for the table upon which Grant wrote out his terms and presented it to Custer as a gift for his wife.

Just as Sheridan wanted, just as he willed it—to the point of insubordination—his cavalry played the decisive role in the crowning event of the war. No one could deny it. He had pushed his cavalry and the supporting infantry divisions well past the point of reasonable expectation and often beyond the normal extent of human endurance. His use of cavalry was simply revolutionary in American military history. His personal leadership on the field positively turned the tide of battle. Grant's ubiquitous aide Colonel Horace Porter wrote of Sheridan: "In this campaign, as in the others, he had shown himself possessed of military traits of the highest order." Sheridan refused to allow Grant's orders, the perceived weaknesses of subordinate commanders, or the tenacious fighting of his enemy to deter him. As Porter noted, Sheridan left "nothing of those who barred his way except the fragments scattered in his path." Unfortunately, those fragments included friend and foe alike. Like Grant, Sheridan understood that war required sacrifice, and he seemed prepared to sacrifice it all, putting himself into the heaviest fighting when the situation demanded. But while equally daring soldiers fell around him, Sheridan received not a scratch. During the Appomattox Campaign, the cavalry, including Mackenzie's division, suffered almost 200 men killed and 1,500 wounded and missing, or some 15 percent of Grant's total casualties. Such was the price of glory.[8]

Sheridan's role at Appomattox ended the next day when the Cavalry Corps marched back to Burkeville, but his presence was felt in the form of men who contributed to his glory. Grant designated Wesley Merritt and Sheridan's collaborators John Gibbon and Charles Griffin as his commissioners to work out the details of the surrender. Mackenzie's command stayed behind, along with Griffin's V Corps and Gibbon's XXIV Corps, as the official detail assigned to receive the surrender of Lee's army. On April 12, General Chamberlain's brigade of the V Corps was among the first to receive the Confederates as they filed by to stack arms, led by Sheridan's worthy adversary John Brown Gordon. Mackenzie's cavalry remained active in the area, occupying Lynchburg and capturing a large cache of war materiel on April 14. While in Lynchburg, Mackenzie visited and paroled Confederate Brigadier General James Dearing, a West Point classmate who lay in a local hospital, dying of wounds he had received defending High Bridge. On April 26, Mackenzie's command moved on to Richmond, where it remained until August.

Merritt rejoined the Cavalry Corps as it marched to Petersburg, where it arrived on April 18. En route the corps learned the sad news of Lincoln's assassination. At Petersburg, Sheridan received orders, no more welcomed now than they were a month before, to join Sherman's army in North Carolina. Sheridan took his time readying the corps for the march, no doubt hoping that events would intervene. With no such luck, the cavalry and the VI Corps infantry headed for North Carolina on April 24 and got as far as South Boston, Virginia, before Sheridan learned of Joseph Johnston's surrender to Sherman. The troopers and foot soldiers happily retraced their steps to Petersburg. Sheridan went on to Washington by steamer, while Merritt conducted the corps overland to camps outside the capital, where it would march in the Grand Review of the Army of the Potomac on May 23. But when that day arrived, Sheridan, who as much as anyone in the Union deserved a prominent place in the parade of honor, would not be riding at the head of the Cavalry Corps.

On May 17, Grant ordered Sheridan to take charge of the situation west of the Mississippi and "restore Texas, and that part of Louisiana held by the enemy, to the Union in the shortest practicable time." In this region of the Confederacy—the Trans-Mississippi Department—command by General Edmund Kirby Smith had yet to surrender. But Grant had a broader mission in mind when he assigned Sheridan to the West. Under the guise of debt collection, in 1862, French troops invaded and occupied Mexico, replacing the legitimate republican government of Benito Juárez with the puppet monarchy of Emperor Maximilian, an idealistic young Austrian archduke—a clear violation of the Monroe Doctrine. Preoccupied with its own war, the United States could do little to contest the European incursion, and imperial Mexico and the Confederacy developed a cozy relationship, which they maintained throughout the war. Now, with thousands of battle-hardened men still in the ranks, Grant found the opportunity to apply some considerable intimidation. In dispatching Sheridan, his most aggressive general, and some 50,000 Federal troops to South Texas, Grant would be sending a most compelling message to Maximilian and France's Napoleon III.

Clearly, this assignment represented Grant's confidence in Sheridan's ability, but Sheridan balked at Grant's insistence that he leave immediately for his new post. He asked that his departure be delayed until after the Grand Review, but this time Grant held firm. Perhaps excluding Sheridan from the review served some larger political purpose, such as giving the neglected Meade a place of unchallenged prominence. Sheridan, after all, had been showered with adulation, while Meade had toiled in obscurity. Still, Sheridan always regretted that he missed the review he had so obviously earned. "I left Washington," he wrote, "without an opportunity of seeing again in a body the men who, while under my command, had gone through so many trials and unremittingly pursued and assailed the enemy, from the beginning of the campaign of 1864 till the white flag came into their hands at Appomattox Court House." A deeply disappointed Sheridan boarded a train for St. Louis even as his men polished their spurs for the coming festivities.[9]

With Sheridan's departure and the absence of Crook (the senior officer in the corps, away on leave), the honor of leading the cavalry in the review fell appropriately to Wesley Merritt, who, like Meade, had been overshadowed by a more conspicuous comrade. "The weather was superb" on the morning of May 23, and thousands of cheering citizens packed the stands and crowded the sidewalks of Pennsylvania Avenue as George Gordon Meade led the Army of the Potomac in the Grand Review before the appreciative eyes of Grant, Sherman, President Andrew Johnson and his cabinet, senators and congressmen, Supreme Court justices, and foreign representatives. Following Meade and his staff, in a place befitting its contribution rode the Cavalry Corps, with Major General Merritt at the front. Custer followed and once again stole the show. "His long golden locks floating in the wind, his low-cut collar, his crimson necktie, and his buckskin breeches, presented a combination which made him look half general and half scout, and gave him a daredevil appearance which singled him out for general remark and applause." Whether by design or by accident (since he was known to be an excellent rider), Custer's horse bolted before the president's box, sending the "Boy General" bounding past the assembled dignitaries "like a tornado." Custer got to display his marvelous horsemanship in regaining control of the spirited mount and resumed his place in line. Merritt was not amused.[10]

The Third Division, Custer's men, who all sported bright red neckties like their chief's, filed past the grandstand. Next came the Second Division, commanded fittingly by Henry Davies in Crook's absence. Finally, grizzled Tom Devin, the old man of the Cavalry Corps, brought up his First Division. The admiring crowd showered the troopers in flowers and cheered wildly as the long column passed—a fine tribute to these men, who rode so far and fought so well for Little Phil Sheridan. Merritt, Custer, and Devin had experienced it all, as had hundreds of the officers and men. Later in the day, the V Corps, which also bore Sheridan's brand, marched past the stands behind Charles Griffin. Doubtless a few hearts went out to aggrieved General Warren, who perhaps as much as Sheridan deserved to be there. But Sheridan and Warren were not the only ones missing.

As the Cavalry Corps passed into history, not one of its division or brigade commanders had held that position when the fighting commenced in May 1864, and the Army of the Shenandoah no longer existed. David Gregg retired before the final campaign, tired of the killing. James Harrison Wilson, out from under Sheridan's shadow, became a major hero in his own right in the Western Theater, leading a devastating cavalry raid across Alabama and Georgia that culminated in the capture of Jefferson Davis. Brilliant young Emory Upton, recovered from his Winchester wound, commanded one of Wilson's divisions.

Alfred Torbert, left behind in the Valley, never regained his stature. Steadfast David Russell and promising Charles Lowell were dead and John McIntosh crippled. Old William Emory and George Chapman, like Torbert stranded in the Valley, spent the rest of the war in obscurity. Cuvier Grover was in Savannah. Rutherford B. Hayes was in Congress. Even Horatio Wright's rock-solid VI Corps and Mackenzie's cavalry, both still on duty in Virginia, missed the parade.

During the weeks and months following the Grand Review, the men of the great volunteer army were mustered out of service or were reassigned, much to their displeasure, to trouble spots in the South and West. Sheridan was already in Texas, assembling a giant army of occupation. En route to New Orleans, he learned that Lieutenant General Simon Bolivar Buckner had surrendered the Trans-Mississippi Department, and Sheridan quickly turned his attention to Texas and Mexico. In addition to Major General Gordon Granger's XIII Corps, Sheridan received Major General David Stanley's IV Corps and Godfrey Weitzel's black soldiers of the XXV Corps. He also summoned his favorite lieutenants, Merritt and Custer, to organize and lead two new cavalry divisions. This last bit of Civil War business held none of the glory these men had come to expect. Merritt and Custer, now full major generals of U.S. Volunteers, spent much of their time in thankless and frustrating duties in South Texas and along the troublesome Rio Grande. These soldiers proved ill suited to the demands of Reconstruction politics.

Sheridan meanwhile got caught up in the business of Mexico, scheming with filibusters and Mexican liberals to destabilize the Maximilian regime and hinting overtly at imminent U.S. intervention, all while parading his large, well-equipped army along the Rio Grande. On Sheridan's watch, tons of surplus U.S. materiel found its way into the grateful hands of Juárez's republican armies. Although Sheridan's intimidation tactics and Secretary of State William Henry Seward's measured but insistent diplomacy often worked at odds, the combination did the job. Napoleon III in early 1866 ordered his soldiers out of Mexico, leaving a criminally manipulated Maximilian essentially undefended. In May 1867, Division General Mariano Escobedo's Juarista troops, many carrying U.S. Springfield muskets and wearing Yankee blue jackets, cornered Maximilian's inadequate imperial forces at Querétaro. Tragic Maximilian went before a Mexican firing squad a month later.[11]

Earlier that year, Congress had ushered in military Reconstruction in ten of the former Confederate states and, in so doing, redefined Sheridan's role as commander of the Fifth Military District, which included Texas and Louisiana. It was a job for which Sheridan lacked the requisite talents of tact and patience, as well as a host of other essential political and diplomatic nuances. He was a warrior with a conqueror's mentality, and soon his heavy-handed approach— a problem since his arrival in Texas—ran him afoul of President Johnson. In

August 1868, Johnson removed Sheridan as commander of the Fifth Military District and ordered him to take charge of the Department of the Missouri. The time had come to turn away from the South and look to the West.

By the time Sheridan steamed out of New Orleans, the great volunteer army had vanished, replaced by regulars. The demobilization of the U.S. Volunteers meant that officers who held lofty grades in that organization during the war returned to their regular ranks and regiments or to civilian life. For Sheridan's lieutenants, younger men without much seniority in the regulars, the impact was demoralizing. Merritt, Custer, and Crook, all full-rank major generals of Volunteers, held the regular rank of captain. Men such as Tom Devin and Nelson Miles, who entered the war from civilian life and rose to general officer rank in the Volunteer establishment, had no regular rank to fall back on. The seriously flawed brevet system complicated matters further. Brevets were issued liberally throughout the war as a reward for outstanding performances, but the practice rarely stopped there. Officers could receive brevets for being part of an operation or a unit without having performed daring deeds on the field of battle. Brevets had been issued for excellent staff work, for wounds received, and, at the end, for war service. Brevet ranks could be used to elevate a better-performing junior officer over a senior. The government dispensed brevets, in the case of regular officers, in both the regular and volunteer organizations. At the end of the war, Ranald Mackenzie held the full rank of brigadier general of Volunteers; he was also a major general of Volunteers and brigadier general in the regular army by brevet, but his substantive rank remained captain of engineers. When the government folded the Volunteer establishment in 1866, it kicked off a race for position and promotion that lasted into the twentieth century. Men who had been generals, who had commanded divisions or brigades through the greatest war in American history, now faced life as captains and majors at some far-flung Western post or at the head of a detachment of occupation troops in the Deep South, charged with upholding the newly granted civil rights of freed slaves. Most of these men understandably wanted to be generals again.

Clearly, the American military had to change to confront the new challenges of the postwar era. Grant and others perceived that a return to what had been essentially a frontier constabulary could no longer meet the manifold responsibilities presented by Reconstruction and Western expansion. The "Old Army" had to expand, and with this expansion America could find suitable positions for the heroes of the Civil War. But things did not quite work out that way. Congress, confronted by the staggering debt generated during the war, was in no mood to fund a large standing army. In something of a compromise, Congress passed a bill to establish the size and configuration of the postwar army. Reflecting the various constituencies of war making in a democracy,

Congress tried to accommodate everyone but succeeded in pleasing very few. First, the government tripled the authorized strength of the army, to a total of 54,000, adding twenty-six infantry regiments and four cavalry regiments (the more professional artillery remained at five regiments). To reward the citizen soldiers—the nonprofessionals—who contrary to popular belief had performed exceptionally well as a whole, and in deference to the many political generals now sitting in the Capitol who harbored great disdain for West Point–trained officers, half of the new officers' commissions went to these accomplished amateurs, the other half to worthy professionals. Of the new regiments, six—four infantry and two cavalry—were to be comprised of black soldiers, in recognition of the considerable contribution of some 200,000 African Americans who had served the Union during the war. Regrettably, Congress provided no system for the selection process, so politics and preference reigned. Crook, Custer, Merritt, and Mackenzie could expect Sheridan's forceful endorsement, but he was preoccupied during much of the selection process. And Sheridan faced competition from other Union chiefs; Grant had his favorites, as did Sherman, Halleck, Meade, and George Thomas—the other regular major generals. When the government issued new commissions, Sheridan's lieutenants came away disappointed.

Custer became lieutenant colonel of the new 7th Cavalry and Tom Devin, one of the nonprofessionals, accepted the same grade in the 8th Cavalry. But Merritt, Custer's senior—and his equal or superior in all but flamboyance—and Devin's commander, took a lieutenant colonelcy in the 9th Cavalry, one of the freshly constituted black regiments (many officers accepted lower rank to serve in white regiments, believing service in a "colored" regiment beneath them). Ranald Mackenzie, the junior among Sheridan's favorites, with Grant's advocacy became colonel of the 41st Infantry, another "colored" regiment, which later was consolidated into the 24th Infantry, with Mackenzie as colonel. Crook received perhaps the unkindest cut of all. He managed only a lieutenant colonel's appointment in the new 23rd Infantry, while two of his nonprofessional subordinates, J. Irvin Gregg (8th Cavalry) and Charles H. Smith (28th Infantry), became full colonels. Crook lamented that "it was not what a person did, but it was what he got credit of doing that gave him a reputation and at the close of the war gave him position." This process was a clear slap at Sheridan, who, as one of the five major generals of the line, had his place in the postwar army locked up. But it appeared that neither service under Sheridan in the late war nor his subsequent influence in Washington counted for much in his lieutenants' quest for rank and privilege in the new regular army.[12]

The army reorganization of 1866 certainly dealt a blow to the career aspirations of Sheridan's favorite subordinates. But things moved more slowly in the politically charged postwar years; Sheridan still had time to reward his favorites.

In 1866, Congress, in the name of a grateful nation, awarded Grant a fourth star, making him the first full general in the U.S. Army. Predictably, Sherman moved up to lieutenant general. When Grant won the presidency in 1868, he vacated the position of commanding general, which went to Sherman. President Grant then made one of his many controversial moves as chief executive, promoting Sheridan to lieutenant general over senior major generals Halleck and Meade, and Thomas. With the three stars, Sheridan also inherited the vast Military Division of the Missouri, which embraced the Great Plains—the hotbed of the nation's continuing struggle with the American Indians. As always, when time came for action, Sheridan turned to his old lieutenants, who brought to Indian fighting the same zeal and determination that marked their Civil War campaigns. And they became heroes all over again.

# Epilogue: "A Hold upon an Army"

$\mathscr{B}$ack during that anxious and hopeful spring of 1864, few Americans outside the army, and not all that many within the service, knew of Phil Sheridan or Wesley Merritt or George Crook or Ranald Mackenzie or Tom Devin. Custer, by then, had attracted some notoriety as the "Boy General," more for his outlandish appearance and scene-stealing antics than for his martial prowess. Certainly, no one could have predicted the impact that Sheridan, his lieutenants, and the men they led would have on the outcome of the Civil War. In one remarkable year, Sheridan changed the way the war was fought and with Wiliam T. Sherman redefined the limits of warfare in America—they ushered in total war on a grand scale. Sheridan's employment of cavalry as a main battle component anticipated armored warfare in the twentieth century. The success of aggressive young generals—most famously associated with Sheridan's command—helped to facilitate more rapid advancement for gifted young officers of the future.

The most immediate and obvious impact of Sheridan's Civil War influence came in the contributions of his lieutenants to the prosecution of the Indian Wars. Under Sheridan's direction, Custer struck the first meaningful blows against the Plains Indians with his campaign against the Southern Cheyennes in 1868, and two years after Sheridan's death, his former chief of staff, James Forsyth, commanding the 7th Cavalry, presided over the sad final act of the Indian Wars—the 1890 incident at Wounded Knee. Excepting Tom Devin, who, plagued by poor health, died in 1878 as colonel of the 3rd Cavalry, Sheridan's division commanders and other Civil War subordinates figured prominently in the Indian Wars and in the evolution of the American military establishment. Custer, of course, maintained a high profile, fueled increasingly by controversy rather than accomplishment, while Crook, Merritt, and Mackenzie, along with Nelson A. Miles, whose Civil War experience came in the II Corps, emerged as the army's premier Indian-fighting commanders.[1]

Sheridan's influence, however, stretched far beyond the prairies and deserts of the American West. Wesley Merritt and James Harrison Wilson became agents of expansion and empire during the 1898 Spanish–American War. Merritt led the U.S. troops who took Manila, while Wilson saw duty in the Caribbean and later participated in the suppression of the Boxer Rebellion in China. The war with Spain also united former adversaries, as Merritt, Wilson, Miles, and many other former Union generals fought under the same banner with Fitz Lee, Tom Rosser, and Matthew C. Butler in something of a symbolic reconciliation. In 1903, Lieutenant General Samuel B. M. Young initiated a new era in the evolution of the U.S. Army when he became its first chief of the general staff, having already served as the first president of the Army War College. In 1865, as the colonel of the 4th Pennsylvania Cavalry, Young commanded the captured Irvin Gregg's brigade during the Appomattox Campaign. Merritt and Young came to represent at the turn of the century the truly remarkable nexus of Sherman's quest for modernization and professionalism and Sheridan's brilliant cultivation of talent—something for which Sheridan never received due credit. Sherman understood Sheridan's value early on.

In his letter to Sheridan following his 1864 victory at Cedar Creek, Sherman observed that Sheridan's success had given him "a hold upon an army" and "a future better than older men can hope for." Indeed, Sheridan had a hold on the army, and he lived to realize much of the bright future Sherman predicted. As commander of the Division of the Missouri for sixteen years, Sheridan became the chief prosecutor of the war against the great tribes of the plains. In this role, he proved every bit as successful as he had been during the Civil War. By the time he succeeded Sherman as commanding general in 1884, the Arapahos, Cheyennes, Comanches, Kiowas, and Sioux had been subjugated, and within the next two years the last of the defiant Apaches had surrendered. In the meantime, Little Phil represented his nation as an official observer of the Franco-Prussian War and found time to start a family. Later, he continued the pursuit of modernization and professionalism in the army begun under Sherman, but his robust lifestyle took a heavy toll. In 1888, Congress, moved by Sheridan's rapidly failing heath, voted to revive the four-star grade and promoted him to full general, only the third man in the history of the U.S. Army to hold that rank.[2]

Only weeks after receiving his fourth star, the pinnacle of his career, Sheridan died of a massive heart attack in his vacation home at Nonquitt, Massachusetts. Hard living, and a renowned fondness for food and drink, had wrecked the once-vigorous general. He was only fifty-seven years old. A bitter George Crook, who never forgave his old friend's assumption of credit for Crook's exploits in the victories at Winchester and Fisher's Hill, wrote caustically (and pretty accurately) of Sheridan: "the adulations heaped upon him by a grateful nation for his supposed genius turned his head, which, added to his natural disposition, caused him to bloat his little carcass with debauchery and dissipation, which carried him off prematurely." Among the 1,500 mourners who attended Sheridan's spectacular funeral in Washington were Generals Merritt and Sherman, as well as longtime staffers Sandy Forsyth and James Forsyth. At the time of his death, Sheridan ranked among the nation's greatest military heroes. His many flaws notwithstanding, in terms of battlefield success and the influence he wielded in the evolution of the U.S. Army, Sheridan had earned the distinction.[3]

Of Sheridan's lieutenants, George Armstrong Custer eventually achieved the greatest prominence, even surpassing Little Phil in the public imagination as time went by. Custer, who never matched his less-celebrated colleagues in the quantity or quality of postwar service, nonetheless became one of the most famous soldiers in American history. He made headlines in 1867 with his nasty court-martial for leaving his command to visit his wife during an active campaign on the South Plains. The court returned a guilty verdict and suspended Custer, without rank or pay, for one year. Fortunately for the golden cavalier, about this time Sheridan took charge of the vast Military Division of the Missouri and wanted his old striker back in the fold for a winter campaign against the Southern Plains tribes. On a frigid November morning in 1868, with his regimental band attempting to play "Garry Owen" on frozen instruments, Custer led the 7th Cavalry in an attack on the village of Cheyenne chief Black Kettle, a long-standing peace advocate. These people had suffered a similar wanton attack by Colorado militia on Sand Creek in 1864. Although the village on the Washita River in the western part of the Indian Territory presented a legitimate military target, dozens of women and children died in the attack, as did Black Kettle. The "Washita Massacre" prompted outrage in some quarters, but to most Americans, Custer remained a hero.

A lightning rod for controversy, Custer helped to precipitate a massive Indian uprising on the Northern Plains when his expedition into the sacred Black Hills of the Dakota Territory discovered gold, which triggered a white invasion of reservation land. Meanwhile, Custer's various business interests, his flirtation with Democrats, and his testimony before Congress regarding corruption in the Grant administration landed him in hot water with the chief executive. On the eve of a great campaign to quiet the Northern Plains, which Custer was to lead, Grant removed him from command. For all his personal flaws, and they were many, Custer was a fighter, so his department commander Brigadier General Alfred Terry, division commander and mentor Sheridan, and Army commander Sherman interceded to have Custer restored. Grant relented, allowing the troublesome cavalry commander to lead only his regiment, under Terry's overall direction, in a three-pronged campaign set for spring 1876— which also featured columns under Crook and John Gibbon. In May, three separate commands converged on defiant Sioux, Cheyenne, and Arapaho bands camped along the Little Bighorn River in southern Montana Territory.

On June 25, Custer's column located a large village on the Little Bighorn where thousands of Indians congregated under the leadership of Sitting Bull. Without waiting for the other commands to converge (Crook's already had been defeated and turned back), Custer divided the 7th Cavalry into three battalions and, in typical Custer fashion, attacked. One battalion, under Major Marcus Reno, a veteran of the Valley Campaign, struck the village and suffered heavy casualties before retreating to a nearby ridge, where the survivors linked up with the battalion commanded by Captain Frederick Benteen and managed to hold out until help arrived. Custer's own battalion, 225 strong, approached the giant village from the opposite direction, unaware that they were impossibly outnumbered. Perhaps 2,000 (and possibly many more) highly motivated, well-armed Sioux, Cheyenne, and Arapaho warriors under the inspired leadership of Crazy Horse and Gall overran Custer's command, killing every man. Custer's heroic demise assured for him the glory he so craved and bought him a place in history that his stellar Civil War career could never touch. Although his reputation as a soldier eventually declined, at least among historians, Custer became one of the most recognizable and studied soldiers in American history.[4]

While Custer passed larger than life into the popular imagination, the remarkable careers and excellent service of his Civil War comrades—Crook, Merritt, and Mackenzie—went comparatively unnoticed. The brilliant but erratic Ranald Slidell Mackenzie quietly built the kind of record Custer never approached. In a military case study of style over substance, beginning in the Civil War, Custer received five brevets for gallantry and suffered one slight wound, while Mackenzie, with a year's less service, earned seven brevets and suffered six wounds, three of which were serious and left him in constant pain. When he accepted command of a black regiment in the postwar reorganization, Mackenzie quickly turned it into a top-notch outfit. In 1870 the Army rewarded him with a transfer to command of the 4th Cavalry, which under his hard-driving leadership became the finest combat regiment in the service. In 1873, on nothing but Sheridan's verbal instructions, Mackenzie led a raid across the Rio Grande, in clear violation of Mexican sovereignty, to root out bands of Lipans and Kickapoos who preyed upon South Texas. A year later, in a stunning demonstration of total war, Mackenzie and the elite 4th Cavalry brought final defeat to the dreaded Comanches and Kiowas on the Texas frontier. Following the disaster at the Little Bighorn, Mackenzie led one of the columns that avenged Custer in a winter campaign that practically ended Sioux and Cheyenne resistance. His very presence and decisive leadership ended a Ute uprising in Colorado without firing a shot, and he repeated the feat in Arizona by thwarting a Navajo and Apache threat in a similarly bloodless fashion. As

Sheridan's frontier troubleshooter, in fifteen years Mackenzie never lost a fight, and his commands suffered and inflicted relatively few casualties. He tended to treat his Indian adversaries with respect and dignity, gaining a reputation as a benevolent conqueror. Sadly, by the time he received the coveted promotion to brigadier general in 1882, his health had collapsed, and within two years his mind had given way to insanity. Forcibly retired by an examining board convened at New York's Bloomingdale Asylum, Mackenzie died a forgotten hero five years later at the age of forty-eight. In his memoir, U. S. Grant wrote: "I regarded Mackenzie as the most promising young officer in the army. Graduating at West Point, as he did, during the second year of the war, he had won his way up to the command of a corps before its close. This he did upon his own merit and without influence."[5]

While Custer, Merritt, and Mackenzie remained devoted to Sheridan during the postwar years, George Crook grew increasingly embittered toward his close friend from the academy. Perhaps because he was jealous of the attention Sheridan received, but more likely because he believed Sheridan took credit for Crook's own planning and execution during the Battles of Winchester and Fisher's Hill, Crook distanced himself from his former chief. But the eccentric Crook, who preferred a civilian suit to a uniform and a mule to a horse, distinguished himself as a different type of frontier officer. Imaginative, inventive, and energetic, he became an able campaigner in the West, but his genuine concern for the plight of American Indians attracted criticism from many in the army and the government. He championed the use of pack mules instead of bulky wagon trains for the rugged Western frontier, and his extensive employment of Indian scouts and auxiliaries was revolutionary and generally successful. After brokering a tenuous peace with the Apaches of Arizona, Crook won promotion, over many senior officers, directly from lieutenant colonel to brigadier general. As commander of the Department of the Platte, Crook participated, with much less success, in the Sioux Wars. In June 1876, he led one of three columns sent to subdue hostile Sioux and Cheyenne bands camped in the Yellowstone region and drew further criticism for his defeat by Crazy Horse's warriors on the Rosebud River, which contributed to Custer's demise on the Little Bighorn. Crook then directed troops from his department, including the regiments of Mackenzie and Merritt, in the campaign that essentially ended hostilities on the Northern Plains.

Returning to Arizona, where renegade Apaches shattered the peace he had helped to establish a decade before, Crook devoted great energy and much personal credibility to quieting the situation. His efforts to treat with recalcitrant leaders such as Geronimo appeared to bear fruit, but when violence erupted again in 1885, Crook's benevolent methods and his reliance on Indian auxiliaries attracted new indictments. In 1886, Sheridan, now commanding general, relieved Crook of command in Arizona, replacing him with the ambitious and aggressive Nelson Miles, to whom Geronimo eventually surrendered. What remained of the friendship between Crook and Sheridan vanished. Crook returned to the Department of the Platte and committed himself to the campaign for Indian rights. In 1888, the year of Sheridan's death, Crook assumed command of the Military Division of the Missouri and once again became a major general. He died two years later, having never forgiven Sheridan for his perceived injustices.[6]

Perhaps Sheridan's least-heralded lieutenant was his best. During the postwar years, Wesley Merritt continued to display the quiet competence that had made him one of the finest cavalry commanders of the Civil War. Although just as ambitious as Custer, he found Custer's grandstanding disgusting. In fact, Custer's Civil War glory grabbing had soured their relationship. And although he could have expected a better postwar assignment, Merritt toiled thanklessly for almost ten years with the 9th Cavalry, working to build that regiment of "Buffalo Soldiers" into an excellent command, despite the discrimination it faced. The "colored" regiments routinely received the worst postings, equipment, and horseflesh the government had to offer. In 1876, Merritt received overdue promotion to colonel, when he took charge of the excellent 5th Cavalry, with which he campaigned in the Sioux War. He avoided the career peaks and valleys experienced by Crook and Custer and never matched the dramatic victories of Mackenzie, and therefore went mostly unnoticed. But Sheridan remained a forceful advocate, and in 1882, Merritt became superintendent of the United States Military Academy at West Point, in which capacity he thrived for five years. In 1887, Merritt, with Sheridan's hearty endorsement, finally regained the rank of brigadier general. He was only fifty years old.

At a time when most of his Civil War colleagues were passing from the scene, Merritt remained quite active, exercising important commands (the Department of the Missouri and the Department of Dakota). During this interesting time of transition, he oversaw the 1889 Oklahoma land rush and enthusiastically supported modernization, conducting the army's first war games. When violent railroad strikes erupted in the 1890s, troops from Merritt's Department of Dakota, through which ran the Northern Pacific and Great Northern roads, displayed marked restraint and professionalism in protecting the cargoes, equipment, and passengers of the troubled rail companies. This was unpleasant work, with plenty of potential for disaster, but Merritt possessed a keen awareness of the situation and maintained control of his forces, avoiding much of the bloodshed that symbolized the labor strife of the decade.[7]

In 1895, Merritt became a major general—again, thirty years after he first held that grade in the U.S. Volunteers. No officer in the army deserved it more. He turned sixty-two in June 1898, and should have been contemplating retirement, but a new war beckoned. The United States had declared war on Spain over Cuba, and American expansionists saw an opportunity to grab an overseas empire at the expense of a decrepit Old World monarchy. While most of the nation's excitement focused on Cuba, Commodore George Dewey and his Asiatic Squadron destroyed the Spanish fleet in Manila Bay, the Philippines, where, as in Cuba, insurrectionists fought for independence. Merritt took charge of ground forces sent to "liberate" the Philippines. In sharp contrast to the bungled operations in the Caribbean Theater, where mismanagement and poor leadership ruled and thousands of U.S. troops died of disease, Merritt's Philippines campaign offered a study of efficiency and military administration. He managed an almost bloodless surrender of Manila while keeping the insurrectionists at bay. And as he had done throughout his long career, he took care of his men, making sure they had adequate food, water, shelter, and clothing, and thus avoided the catastrophe that befell troops in Cuba and Puerto Rico. And, as usual, his efforts went largely unnoticed by an American public enthralled by the romance of Teddy Roosevelt's Rough Riders.

After serving briefly as military governor, Merritt left Manila to advise the peace commission meeting in Paris to work out the dismemberment of the Spanish Empire and thus had no hand in the ugly Filipino-American war that followed. Merritt was retired by law on his sixty-fourth birthday in 1900, having contributed significantly to victory in three major wars during a truly remarkable forty years of active service. He devoted his remaining years to travel and writing and continued to champion military reform, testifying before Congress in support of a proposed new general staff system, which went into effect in 1903, with his Civil War colleague S. B. M. Young as chief of the general staff. General Merritt died in 1910.

William T. Sherman, often credited with being America's first modern soldier, indeed mandated reforms that facilitated the modernization of an army that during much of the nineteenth century served as little more than a frontier constabulary. He also fostered the professionalism embraced by Merritt and others. Sheridan lacked Sherman's vision, and he could never match his own successor John M. Schofield's martial intellect, but it can be argued, certainly, that no other Civil War general surpassed Sheridan's impact on who led the postwar army and how it fought. Four of the five most conspicuous campaigners—Crook, Custer, Mackenzie, and Merritt—earned their postwar positions by contributing to Sheridan's Civil War success. In a very real sense, the genesis of the modern army can be traced to the day Sheridan took charge of the Cavalry Corps, Army of the Potomac, in 1864. Few if any soldiers so connected had a greater impact on American military history over such a span of time than did Sheridan and his lieutenants.

# Notes

## PREFACE

1. Bruce Catton, *Reflections on the Civil War*, ed. John Leekley (Garden City, NY: Doubleday, 1981), 142.

2. T. Harry Williams, *Lincoln and His Generals* (New York: Alfred A. Knopf, 1952), 86. This popular quote touches on the intangible attribute needed to succeed as an army commander during the Civil War. Grant, a West Pointer and Mexican War veteran, had, like Lee, the will to fight. His success stemmed not from training or experience but from the incredible ability to order death and risk destruction on the battlefield.

## INTRODUCTION

1. There are several good works on Grant. See William S. McFeely, *Grant: A Biography* (New York: W. W. Norton, 1981). See also Grant's remarkable autobiography, *Personal Memoirs of U. S. Grant*, 2 vols. (New York: Charles L. Webster, 1885). Winfield Scott was a lieutenant general by brevet but never held the substantive rank.

2. Grant, *Memoirs*, 2:133; Roy Morris Jr., *Sheridan: The Life and Wars of General Phil Sheridan* (New York: Crown, 1992), 153. United States War Department, *The War of the Rebellion: A Compilation of the Official Records of the Union and Confederate Armies*, 128 vols. (Washington, DC: Government Printing Office, 1880–1901), hereafter cited as *OR*, volume 33, part 3, 122. All references to the *Official Records* apply to series 1, unless otherwise noted. According to Morris, Major General William B. Franklin was Grant's first choice. Sheridan has received surprisingly little scholarly attention. See also Richard O'Connor, *Sheridan the Inevitable* (Indianapolis: Bobbs-Merrill, 1953); and Sheridan's autobiography, *Personal Memoirs of P. H. Sheridan*, 2 vols. (New York: Charles L. Webster, 1888).

3. For Sheridan's early life and career, see Morris, *Sheridan*, and Sheridan, *Memoirs*.

4. Morris, *Sheridan*, 16–23.

5. Grant, *Memoirs*, 2:105.

# CHAPTER 1

1. Horace Porter, *Campaigning with Grant* (reprint ed.; New York: Konecky and Konecky, 1992), 23–24; originally published in 1897.

2. Sheridan, *Memoirs*, 1:344–48; *OR*, volume 32, part 3, 258–59; volume 33, 798, 806.

3. *OR*, volume 33, 721, 806; Stephen Z. Starr, *The Union Cavalry in the Civil War: The War in the East from Gettysburg to Appomattox, 1863–1865*, vol. 2 (Baton Rouge: Louisiana State University Press, 1981), 72–75. This second volume in Starr's definitive three-volume history of the Federal cavalry is essential to any study of Sheridan's role in the closing stages of the war and provides much of the basic information for this work. See also Edward G. Longacre, *Lincoln's Cavalrymen: A History of the Mounted Forces of the Army of the Potomac* (Mechanicsburg, PA: Stackpole Books, 2000).

4. For the events of 1863, see Stephen Z. Starr, *The Union Cavalry in the Civil War: From Fort Sumter to Gettysburg, 1861–1863*, vol. 1 (Baton Rouge: Louisiana State University Press, 1979).

5. Starr, *Union Cavalry*, 1:4–8, 68–71.

6. Starr, *Union Cavalry*, 1:57–67.

7. Starr, *Union Cavalry*, 1:75–78; Sheridan, *Memoirs*, 1:348–52. Sheridan claimed to have asked for Wilson's appointment, but according to Starr, Grant made the call.

8. Theodore Lyman, *Meade's Headquarters 1863–1865, Letters of Colonel Theodore Lyman from the Wilderness to Appomattox* (Boston: Atlantic Monthly Press, 1922), 82.

9. For details of Merritt's life and career, see Don E. Alberts, *General Wesley Merritt: Brandy Station to Manila Bay* (Columbus, OH: The General's Books, 2001). For biographical sketches of all Federal generals, see Ezra J. Warner, *Generals in Blue: Lives of the Union Commanders* (Baton Rouge: Louisiana State University Press, 1964). There is controversy over Merritt's date of birth. Alberts gives June 16, 1836, while Warner claims that the year was 1834 and that the discrepancy arose when Merritt accepted his brother's appointment to West Point, thereafter carrying the incorrect date on army records for the remainder of his career.

10. Custer is among the most chronicled military men in American history. Most works focus on his post–Civil War career. For an extended study of his Civil War activities, see Gregory J. W. Urwin, *Custer Victorious: The Civil War Career of General George Armstrong Custer* (reprint ed.; Lincoln: University of Nebraska Press, 1990).

11. Robert Underwood Johnson and Clarence Clough Buel, *Battles and Leaders of the Civil War*, 4 vols. (New York: Century, 1887–1888), 4:188.

12. Starr, *Union Cavalry*, 1:76–77.

13. Sheridan, *Memoirs*, 1:354–57.

## CHAPTER 2

1. *OR*, volume 32, part 3, 246–47.
2. Starr, *Union Cavalry*, 2:86–88.
3. For the Battle of the Wilderness, see Gordon C. Rhea, *The Battle of the Wilderness, May 5–6, 1864* (Baton Rouge: Louisiana State University Press, 1994); and Noah Andre Trudeau, *Bloody Roads South: The Wilderness to Cold Harbor, May–June, 1864* (Boston: Little, Brown, 1989). The cavalry actions during the battle are covered in Starr, *Union Cavalry*, 2:86–93. See also Sheridan's report in *OR*, volume 36, part 1, 773–75, 787–88.
4. *OR*, volume 36, part 1, 815–17, 853.
5. *OR*, volume 36, part 1, 787–88, 803, 812, 853.
6. Porter, *Campaigning with Grant*, 83–84.
7. *OR*, volume 36, part 2, 552. For details of the raid see Starr, *Union Cavalry*, 2:95–126.
8. *OR*, volume 36, part 1, 790–91, 813, 817–18. Private Huff was killed at Haw's Shop on May 28. For an excellent version of events from the Confederate perspective, see Douglas Southall Freeman, *Lee's Lieutenants: A Study in Command*, 3 vols. (New York: Charles Scribner's Sons, 1942–1944), 3:420–25.
9. *OR*, volume 36, part 1, 791, 813–14, 819.
10. *OR*, volume 36, part 1, 793, 854.
11. *OR*, volume 36, part 1, 794, 822.
12. *OR*, volume 36, part 1, 794, 805–6.
13. *OR*, volume 36, part 1, 794.
14. *OR*, volume 36, part 3, 629.
15. *OR*, volume 36, part 1, 795–96. Estimates of Sheridan's troops' strength vary widely from a low of 6,000 (Sheridan, *Memoirs*, 1:417) to a high of more than 10,000. Estimates of Confederate strength range from 4,700 to 6,700. Sheridan likely had an advantage of roughly 2,500 men. For a discussion of this matter and other details of the Battle of Trevilian Station, see Eric J. Wittenberg, *Glory Enough for All: Sheridan's Second Raid and the Battle of Trevilian Station* (Washington, DC: Brassey's, 2001), 25.
16. *OR*, volume 36, part 1, 795–96, 807.
17. *OR*, volume 36, part 1, 808.
18. *OR*, volume 36, part 1, 798.
19. *OR*, volume 36, part 1, 799.

## CHAPTER 3

1. *OR*, volume 37, part 2, 558, 572, 573.
2. *OR*, volume 37, part 2, 719.
3. *OR*, volume 37, part 2, 301, 329.
4. *OR*, volume 36, part 1, 801.

5. *OR*, volume 43, part 1, 501–3, 744. See also Starr, *Union Cavalry*, 2:246–51.

6. Sheridan, *Memoirs*, 1:463–64.

7. Sheridan, *Memoirs*, 1:467–68.

8. Starr, *Union Cavalry*, 2:246–52.

9. Starr, *Union Cavalry*, 2:256–57; *OR*, volume 43, part 1, 46; Sheridan, *Memoirs*, 2:9.

## CHAPTER 4

1. Johnson and Buel, *Battles and Leaders*, 4:506, 507, 522. In his essay on the Valley Campaign, Merritt made an interesting comment: "In light of the criticisms, then, it is curious that the world is now inclined to call Sheridan reckless and foolhardy."

2. For details of the 1864 Valley Campaign, see Jeffry D. Wert, *From Winchester to Cedar Creek: The Shenandoah Campaign of 1864*, new edition (Mechanicsburg, PA: Stackpole Books, 1997).

3. For a study of the extraordinary Upton, see Stephen E. Ambrose, *Upton and the Army* (Baton Rouge: Louisiana State University Press, 1964).

4. Theodore Vaill, *History of the Second Connecticut Volunteer Heavy Artillery* (Winsted, CT: Winsted Printing Company, 1868), 95–96; Sheridan, *Memoirs*, 2:23. The best of many fairly recent biographies of Mackenzie is Michael D. Pierce, *The Most Promising Young Officer: A Life of Ranald Slidell Mackenzie* (Norman: University of Oklahoma Press, 1993).

5. Sheridan, *Memoirs*, 2:24.

6. *OR*, volume 43, part 1, 443–44.

7. *OR*, volume 43, part 1, 456.

8. *OR*, volume 43, part 1, 444.

9. Vaill, *Second Connecticut*, 95; Ambrose, *Upton*, 41.

10. *OR*, volume 43, part 1, 445, 458.

11. *OR*, volume 43, part 2, 110.

12. *OR*, volume 43, part 1, 117–18.

13. Johnson and Buel, *Battles and Leaders*, 4:523–24.

14. Both Sheridan and Crook claimed credit for orchestrating the flank attacks at Winchester and Fisher's Hill. Most authorities side with Crook. The controversy eventually wrecked the friendship between the former West Point roommates. See Sheridan, *Memoirs*, 2:35, and Martin F. Schmitt, ed., *General George Crook: His Autobiography* (Norman: University of Oklahoma Press, 1946), 129–31. See also Wert, *From Winchester to Cedar Creek*, 81–82, 111–12.

15. *OR*, volume 43, part 1, 26–27.

16. Sheridan, *Memoirs*, 2:42.

17. Sheridan, *Memoirs*, 2:43–44; *OR*, volume 43, part 2, 170, 218, 249.

# CHAPTER 5

1. *OR*, volume 43, part 2, 208.

2. *OR*, volume 43, part 2, 249.

3. *OR*, volume 43, part 2, 202.

4. J. H. Kidd, *Personal Recollections of a Cavalryman: With Custer's Michigan Cavalry Brigade in the Civil War* (reprint ed.; Grand Rapids, MI: Black Letter Press, 1969), 398–99; originally published in 1908.

5. *OR*, volume 43, part 1, 443; volume 43, part 2, 308. See also Michael G. Mahon, *The Shenandoah Valley, 1861–1865: The Destruction of the Granary of the Confederacy* (Mechanicsburg, PA: Stackpole Books, 1999). In this study of the Valley during the war, Mahon, while acknowledging the immense destruction carried out by the Federal army, discounts the volume claimed by Sheridan and his officers and also refutes the long-held notion that the devastation of the Valley substantially impacted food supplies to Lee's army, which, the author maintains, by this stage in the war came mostly from the Deep South.

6. Wert, *From Winchester to Cedar Creek*, 151–53.

7. Wert, *From Winchester to Cedar Creek*, 145; Sheridan, *Memoirs*, 2:51–52; Johnson and Buel, *Battles and Leaders*, 4:525.

8. Edward W. Emerson, ed., *Life and Letters of Charles Russell Lowell* (reprint ed.; Port Washington, NY: Kennikat Press, 1971), 353.

9. *OR*, volume 43, part 2, 327.

10. Sheridan, *Memoirs*, 2:57–59. For details of the battle, see Wert, *From Winchester to Cedar Creek*, 160–64.

11. *OR*, volume 43, part 1, 447–48.

12. *OR*, volume 43, part 1, 31–32, 448; Sheridan, *Memoirs*, 2:56–57.

13. *OR*, volume 43, part 2, 346.

14. *OR*, volume 43, part 2, 355.

15. *OR*, volume 43, part 2, 386, 390; part 1, 52.

16. Sheridan, *Memoirs*, 2:65–67.

17. Emerson, *Life and Letters of Charles Russell Lowell*, 364.

18. John Brown Gordon, *Reminiscences of the Civil War* (New York: Charles Scribner's Sons, 1904), 333–36; Johnson and Buel, *Battles and Leaders*, 4:526.

19. Gordon, *Reminiscences*, 336.

20. For details of the Battle of Cedar Creek, see Wert, *From Winchester to Cedar Creek*, and Thomas A. Lewis, *The Guns of Cedar Creek* (New York: Harper and Row, 1988). Also useful are Early's account in Johnson and Buel, *Battles and Leaders*, 4:526–29; and Gordon, *Reminiscences*, 336–51.

21. Schmitt, *General George Crook*, 134.

22. Vaill, *Second Connecticut*, 122–29.

23. *OR*, volume 43, part 1, 435, 450, 478, 523. Lomax, with Early's largest mounted division, had been sent via Front Royal to seal off the federal escape route but was nowhere near close enough to render service at this juncture.

24. Gordon, *Reminiscences*, 341–44; Johnson and Buel, *Battles and Leaders*, 4:528.

## CHAPTER 6

1. Morris, *Sheridan*, 211–16; Sheridan, *Memoirs*, 2:67–76.
2. Sheridan, *Memoirs*, 2:76–84; *OR*, volume 43, part 1, 53.
3. Sheridan, *Memoirs*, 2:84–86.
4. Kidd, *Personal Recollections*, 416.
5. Johnson and Buel, *Battles and Leaders*, 4:528.
6. Sheridan, *Memoirs*, 2:87–88.
7. Sheridan, *Memoirs*, 2:87–88, 89; Vaill, *Second Connecticut*, 122–29; *OR*, volume 43, part 1, 159, 424.
8. *OR*, volume 43, part 1, 434, 450.
9. *OR*, volume 43, part 1, 524, 525.
10. *OR*, volume 43, part 1, 435, 451–55, 479–80, 525–27, 581–82. A considerable controversy developed over who got credit for what captures. Custer claimed that his men took almost all the prizes, while Devin and Merritt maintained the First Division had in fact taken some twenty-two of the artillery pieces and much of the other captured equipment. The controversy soured the relationship between Merritt and Custer.
11. *OR*, volume 43, part 1, 564; volume 43, part 2, 901.
12. *OR*, volume 43, part 2, 423, 458.
13. *OR*, volume 43, part 2, 437, 725, 785, 804; Sheridan, *Memoirs*, 2:96. Both Sheridan and Grant requested Emory's promotion to major general of Volunteers, the normal rank for a Federal corps commander. The promotion finally came after the war had ended.
14. *OR*, volume 43, part 2, 436.
15. Morris, *Sheridan*, 228.
16. *OR*, volume 43, part 2, 645, 649, 653, 671, 683.
17. *OR*, volume 43, part 2, 672, 679, 730; Sheridan, *Memoirs*, 2:99–100.
18. *OR*, volume 43, part 2, 683, 740, 743, 765, 778, 780, 800.
19. Johnson and Buel, *Battles and Leaders*, 4:520–21; Sheridan, *Memoirs*, 2:102, 104.
20. Sheridan, *Memoirs*, 2:107–8; *OR*, volume 43, part 2, 823–24.
21. *OR*, volume 46, part 2, 495, 605–6, 701.
22. *OR*, volume 46, part 2, 712; Sheridan, *Memoirs*, 2:112. Torbert returned from leave to command the remnant of the army left in the Valley and remained there for the duration of the war.
23. Sheridan, *Memoirs*, 2:112–16; *OR*, volume 46, part 2, 702–3. Early reported to Lee's headquarters two weeks later, but Lee had no command to offer him. Early was relieved of duty and sent home to await orders that never came. Freeman, *Lee's Lieutenants*, 3:635–36.
24. Sheridan, *Memoirs*, 2:118–19.
25. Sheridan, *Memoirs*, 2:120–23; Morris, *Sheridan*, 239–40.

## CHAPTER 7

1. Sheridan, *Memoirs*, 2:124–25; *OR*, volume 46, part 3, 58, 68, 80.

2. *OR*, volume 46, part 3, 46, 47, 80.

3. Sheridan, *Memoirs*, 2:125–31; Grant, *Memoirs*, 2:437–38; Porter, *Campaigning with Grant*, 410–15.

4. Sheridan, *Memoirs*, 2:131–33.

5. *OR*, volume 46, part 2, 494, 630; part 3, 28, 29, 59, 61. If Sheridan had a hand in Crook's selection the record does not show it, nor did Sheridan mention it in his writings. The date of Crook's appointment, however, coincides with the time when Sheridan reestablished contact with Grant after his march from the Valley. It is also likely that Sheridan had recommended Mackenzie back in February. General Wheaton suffered "from piles" and felt he was not up to cavalry service.

6. *OR*, volume 46, part 1, 148; part 2, 947, 950, 977. Kautz received command of an infantry division of U.S. Colored Troops in the XXV Corps. As with Crook's case, there is nothing in the record to indicate that Sheridan advanced Mackenzie for the cavalry position, but he clearly admired the officer's performance.

7. The actual strength of Sheridan's command is open to question. Sheridan estimated it at 10,000, counting Mackenzie's division, but organizational returns of March 31 place the number of effectives at more than 15,000, again counting Mackenzie's division. For a discussion of this discrepancy, see Starr, *Union Cavalry*, 2:427–29.

8. *OR*, volume 46, part 3, 234.

9. *OR*, volume 46, part 3, 266.

10. *OR*, volume 46, part 3, 325, 380; Sheridan, *Memoirs*, 2:141–47; Porter, *Campaigning with Grant*, 428–29.

11. For details of the Battles of Dinwiddie Court House and Five Forks, see Starr, *Union Cavalry*, 2:437–43, and Sheridan, *Memoirs*, 2:149–54.

12. Sheridan, *Memoirs*, 2:149–54.

13. *OR*, volume 46, part 3, 339–42, 365, 380, 381.

14. *OR*, volume 46, part 3, 419–20.

15. For the Confederate perspective, see Freeman, *Lee's Lieutenants*, 3:655–71.

16. Porter, *Campaigning with Grant*, 434–36; Sheridan, *Memoirs*, 2:159–61.

17. Porter, *Campaigning with Grant*, 436–38.

18. For a discussion of the generals' shad bake, see Freeman, *Lee's Lieutenants*, 3:665–70.

19. Joshua Lawrence Chamberlain, *The Passing of the Armies* (reprint ed.; Dayton, OH: Morningside, 1982), 127–31; originally published in 1915.

20. Chamberlain, *The Passing of the Armies*, 142–44.

21. Chamberlain, *The Passing of the Armies*, 144–51; Sheridan, *Memoirs*, 2:165–70. It should be noted that Grant and later Sherman sustained Sheridan. After briefly commanding the District of Vicksburg, Warren resigned his volunteer commission but continued in the regular army as major of engineers. He devoted much of his energy to having a court of inquiry review his dismissal by Sheridan. The court, convened in 1879, sat for three years and finally ruled in Warren's favor, but he died before the verdict was rendered.

22. Chamberlain, *The Passing of the Armies*, 153–54.

23. For details of the Appomattox Campaign, see Noah Andre Trudeau, *Out of the Storm: The End of the Civil War, April–June 1865* (Boston: Little, Brown, 1994), and William Marvel, *Lee's Last Retreat: The Flight to Appomattox* (Chapel Hill: University of North Carolina Press, 2002). See also Sheridan, *Memoirs*, 2:172–204, and Freeman, *Lee's Lieutenants*, 3:675–740.

24. *OR*, volume 46, part 3, 582; Sheridan, *Memoirs*, 2:179.

25. Sheridan, *Memoirs*, 2:187; *OR*, volume 46, part 3, 610.

26. Grant, *Memoirs*, 2:472.

27. *OR*, volume 46, part 1, 55–57.

## CHAPTER 8

1. Grant, *Memoirs*, 2:461.

2. Sheridan, *Memoirs*, 2:191.

3. *OR*, volume 46, part 3, 652–53.

4. Morris, *Sheridan*, 255–56.

5. Gordon, *Reminiscences*, 438–40; Freeman, *Lee's Lieutenants*, 3:733–36; Marvel, *Lee's Last Retreat*, 175.

6. Sheridan, *Memoirs*, 2:194, 196–98.

7. Sheridan, *Memoirs*, 2:198–99.

8. Porter, *Campaigning with Grant*, 469; Starr, *Union Cavalry*, 2:488.

9. Sheridan, *Memoirs*, 2:206, 208–10.

10. Quotations from Porter, *Campaigning with Grant*, 506–7; details from Alberts, *General Wesley Merritt*, 174.

11. For a brief discussion of events in Mexico, see David Coffey, *Soldier Princess: The Life and Legend of Agnes Salm-Salm in North America, 1861–1867* (College Station: Texas A&M University Press, 2002).

12. Robert M. Utley, *Frontier Regulars: The United States Army and the Indian, 1866–1891* (New York: Macmillan, 1973), 10–36; Schmitt, *General George Crook*, 141. For issues of rank and assignment during the Civil War and postwar years, see Francis B. Heitman, *Historical Register and Dictionary of the United States Army, from Its Organization, September 29, 1789, to March 2, 1903*, 2 vols. (Washington, DC: Government Printing Office, 1903).

## EPILOGUE

1. For an excellent overview of the Indian Wars and the postwar military, see Utley, *Frontier Regulars*.

2. *OR*, volume 43, part 1, 553. For Sheridan's postwar career, see Paul Andrew Hutton, *Phil Sheridan and His Army* (Lincoln: University of Nebraska Press, 1985).

3. Schmitt, *General George Crook*, 134; Morris, *Sheridan*, 388–92.

4. There are dozens of biographical treatments of Custer. For his postwar career, see Robert M. Utley, *Cavalier in Buckskin: George Armstrong Custer and the Western Military Frontier* (Norman: University of Oklahoma Press, 1989), and Jeffry D. Wert, *Custer: The Controversial Life of George Armstrong Custer* (New York: Simon and Schuster, 1996).

5. Grant, *Memoirs*, 2:541. For Mackenzie's life and career, see Pierce, *The Most Promising Young Officer*. Grant, by the way, was mistaken in one regard: Mackenzie never commanded a corps.

6. For Crook's postwar career, see Schmitt, *General George Crook*, and John G. Bourke, *On the Border with Crook* (New York: Charles Scribner's Sons, 1891).

7. For Merritt's postwar life and career, see Alberts, *General Wesley Merritt*.

# Bibliographical Essay

$\mathcal{T}$he men and events covered in this work appear in hundreds of monographs, biographies, campaign studies, unit histories, and memoirs. I pulled heavily from each of these varieties but cannot hope to represent all that has been written over 140 years. No doubt, I have missed important points of view, which is not to say that I avoided them intentionally. Phil Sheridan remains a controversial figure. And while I find his contribution to American military history significant (and generally praiseworthy), this view is by no means a consensus. It is not my intention to represent Sheridan or his lieutenants as pillars of enlightenment or virtue but as soldiers doing what their nation expected of them and doing it very well. Clearly, Sheridan, Custer, and the other officers featured in this work must ultimately be considered within the larger framework of American history. But for this study, I endeavored to focus on military aspects of their careers—on their impact and influence during the Civil War—and how they impacted and influenced events over a forty-five-year period.

Sheridan has received comparatively little scholarly attention. For this study, I relied upon two modern biographies: Roy Morris Jr., *Sheridan: The Life and Wars of General Phil Sheridan* (New York: Crown, 1992), and Richard O'Connor, *Sheridan the Inevitable* (Indianapolis: Bobbs-Merrill, 1953). Also useful, especially for Sheridan's postwar career, was Paul Andrew Hutton, *Phil Sheridan and His Army* (Lincoln: University of Nebraska Press, 1985). Hutton's title essentially underscores my thesis. For a more negative treatment of Sheridan, see Eric J. Wittenberg's study, *Little Phil: A Reassessment of the Civil War Leadership of Gen. Philip H. Sheridan* (Washington, DC: Brassey's, 2002). Wittenberg has done extensive work on Sheridan and his campaigns during the last year of the Civil War. While he makes some excellent observations, with many of which I agree, he rather ignores the essential truth of Sheridan's success and importance within the context of his time, which, as unpleasant as it may be to admit, was enormous.

Sheridan, *Personal Memoirs of P. H. Sheridan* (New York: Charles L. Webster, 1888), as with any memoir, is far from objective. Still, it provided some valuable material and nice quotes. I pulled from numerous other important memoirs and letter collections, including U. S. Grant, *Personal Memoirs of U. S. Grant* (New York: Charles L. Webster, 1885); Horace Porter, *Campaigning with Grant* (reprint, New York: Konecky and Konecky, 1992, originally published in 1897); George A. Forsyth, *Thrilling Days in Army Life* (New York: Harper and Brothers, 1900); Theodore Lyman, *Meade's Headquarters*

*1863–1865, Letters of Colonel Theodore Lyman from the Wilderness to Appomattox* (Boston: Atlantic Monthly Press, 1922); Martin F. Schmitt, ed., *General George Crook: His Autobiography* (Norman: University of Oklahoma Press, 1946); J. H. Kidd, *Personal Recollections of a Cavalryman: With Custer's Michigan Cavalry Brigade in the Civil War* (reprint, Grand Rapids, MI: Black Letter Press, 1969, originally published in 1908); Edward W. Emerson, ed., *Life and Letters of Charles Russell Lowell* (reprint, Port Washington, NY: Kennikat Press, 1971, originally published in 1907); and Joshua Lawrence Chamberlain, *The Passing of the Armies* (reprint, Dayton, OH: Morningside, 1982, originally published in 1915).

Confederate memoirs consulted or cited here include Edward Porter Alexander, *Fighting for the Confederacy: The Personal Recollections of General Edward Porter Alexander,* ed. Gary W. Gallagher (Chapel Hill: University of North Carolina Press, 1989); John Brown Gordon, *Reminiscences of the Civil War* (New York: Charles Scribner's Sons, 1904); and James Longstreet, *From Manassas to Appomattox: Memoirs of the Civil War in America* (Philadelphia: J. B. Lippincott, 1896).

Robert Underwood Johnson and Clarence Clough Buel, eds., *Battles and Leaders of the Civil War,* 4 vols. (New York: Century, 1887–1888), offers useful contributions from participants on both sides of the conflict, particularly those cited herein by Theophilus F. Rodenbough, Jedediah Hotchkiss, Wesley Merritt, Jubal Early, and Horace Porter.

Much of my information on Union cavalry organization and operations came from Stephen Z. Starr's excellent cavalry trilogy, particularly the second volume, *The Union Cavalry in the Civil War: The War in the East from Gettysburg to Appomattox, 1863–1865* (Baton Rouge: Louisiana State University Press, 1981). Also extremely useful was Edward G. Longacre's voluminous work on Federal cavalry, *Lincoln's Cavalrymen: A History of the Mounted Forces of the Army of the Potomac* (Mechanicsburg, PA: Stackpole Books, 2000); *Custer and His Wolverines: The Michigan Cavalry Brigade, 1861–1865* (New York: Da Capo, 1997); and his recent *The Cavalry at Appomattox: A Tactical Study of the Mounted Operations during the Civil War's Climactic Campaign, March 27–April 9, 1865* (Mechanicsburg, PA: Stackpole Books, 2003). For the contributions of African American soldiers, see Noah Andre Trudeau's wonderful *Like Men of War: Black Troops in the Civil War, 1862–1865* (Boston: Little, Brown, 1998). A fine example of postwar unit histories is Theodore Vaill, *History of the Second Connecticut Volunteer Heavy Artillery* (Winsted, CT: Winsted Printing Company, 1868), from which I drew valuable observations on Mackenzie and the Battles of Winchester and Cedar Creek. The classic study of the Army of the Potomac during the final year of the Civil War is Bruce Catton, *A Stillness at Appomattox* (Garden City, NY: Doubleday, 1953), the third volume of his popular Army of the Potomac trilogy.

There are a number of good biographies available on the leading figures in this study, many of which I consulted extensively. Among several good recent treatments of Grant, Brooks D. Simpson, *Ulysses S. Grant: Triumph over Adversity, 1822–1865* (Boston: Houghton Mifflin, 2000), stands out. A more critical study is William S. McFeely, *Grant: A Biography* (New York: W. W. Norton, 1981). Most of the works on Sheridan's Civil War lieutenants focus on their postwar careers but generally offer useful details on their Civil War years. Don E. Alberts, *General Wesley Merritt: Brandy Station to Manila Bay* (Columbus, OH: The General's Books, 2001), remains the only full biography of this remarkable soldier. Mackenzie has enjoyed a rash of fairly recent attention, including Michael D. Pierce, *The Most Promising Young Officer: A Life of Ranald Slidell Mackenzie* (Norman: University of Oklahoma Press, 1993), and Charles M. Robinson III, *Bad Hand: A Biography of General Ranald S. Mackenzie* (Austin, TX: State House Press, 1993). Edward Longacre, *Grant's Cavalryman: The Life and Wars of General James H. Wilson* (Mechanicsburg, PA: Stackpole Books, 1996), is one of the few biographical treatments of Wilson. For George Crook, the only recent biographical work is Charles M. Robinson III, *General Crook and the Western Frontier* (Norman: University of Oklahoma Press, 2001). Also of note is Stephen E. Ambrose, *Upton and the Army* (Baton Rouge: Louisiana State University Press, 1964), which not only deals with the enigmatic Emory Upton but also addresses military modernization and professionalism during the postwar era.

Of all the figures featured in this study, Custer has received and will continue to receive by far the most attention, both popular and scholarly. A few of the more useful works are Gregory J. W. Urwin, *Custer Victorious: The Civil War Career of General George Armstrong Custer* (reprint, Lincoln: University of Nebraska Press, 1990); Robert M. Utley, *Cavalier in Buckskin: George Armstrong Custer and the Western Military Frontier* (Norman: University of Oklahoma Press, 1989); Jeffry D. Wert, *Custer: The Controversial Life of George Armstrong Custer* (New York: Simon and Schuster, 1996); and Evan S. Connell, *Son of the Morning Star: Custer and the Little Bighorn* (San Francisco: North Point Press, 1984).

Recent campaign studies consulted for this book include Gordon C. Rhea's four-volume (to date) treatment of the Overland Campaign, *The Battle of the Wilderness, May 5–6, 1864* (Baton Rouge: Louisiana State University Press, 1994); *The Battles for Spotsylvania Court House and the Road to Yellow Tavern, May 7–12, 1864* (Baton Rouge: Louisiana State University Press, 1997); *To the North Anna: Grant and Lee, May 13–25, 1864* (Baton Rouge: Louisiana State University Press, 2000); and *Cold Harbor: Grant and Lee, May 26–June 3, 1864* (Baton Rouge: Louisiana State University Press, 2002). Noah Andre Trudeau's well-rendered trilogy—*Bloody Roads South: The Wilderness to Cold Harbor, May–June 1864* (Boston: Little, Brown, 1989); *The Last Citadel: Petersburg, Virginia, June 1864–April 1865* (Boston: Little, Brown, 1991); and *Out of the Storm: The End of the Civil War, April–June 1865* (Boston: Little, Brown, 1994)—was also quite useful. For the Trevilian raid, I consulted Eric J. Wittenberg, *Glory Enough for All: Sheridan's Second Raid and the Battle of Trevilian Station* (Washington, DC: Brassey's, 2001). Jeffry D. Wert, *From Winchester to Cedar Creek: The Shenandoah Campaign of 1864* (Mechanicsburg, PA: Stackpole Books, 1997), provided essential information on the Valley Campaign, as did Thomas A. Lewis, *The Guns of Cedar Creek* (New York: Harper and Row, 1988). Edwin C. Bearss and Chris M. Calkins, *The Battles of Five Forks* (Lynchburg, VA: H. E. Howard, 1985), contains some useful information. I relied on William Marvel, *Lee's Last Retreat: The Flight to Appomattox* (Chapel Hill: University of North Carolina Press, 2002), for details of the Appomattox Campaign. I found Jay Winik, *April 1865: The Month That Saved America* (New York: HarperCollins, 2001), helpful as well.

For the Confederate perspective, I looked to Douglas Southall Freeman's still-amazing *Lee's Lieutenants: A Study in Command*, 3 vols. (New York: Charles Scribner's

Sons, 1942–1944). In fact, Freeman's approach provided the conceptual framework for this study and many before it. J. Tracy Power, *Lee's Miserables: Life in the Army of Northern Virginia from the Wilderness to Appomattox* (Chapel Hill: University of North Carolina Press, 1998), deserves mention for its compelling look at Lee's army during the last year of the war.

Finally, no Civil War study is possible without the 128 volumes of the *OR*, otherwise known as *The War of the Rebellion: A Compilation of the Official Records of the Union and Confederate Armies* (Washington, DC: Government Printing Office, 1880–1901). Francis B. Heitman's remarkable *Historical Register and Dictionary of the United States Army, from Its Organization, September 29, 1789, to March 2, 1903*, 2 vols. (Washington, DC: Government Printing Office, 1903), proved immensely valuable for issues of appointments and promotions. I am heavily indebted to these and numerous other great reference works on the Civil War that make my job much easier.

# Index

# About the Author

David Coffey holds a Ph.D. from Texas Christian University and is chair of the Department of History and Philosophy at the University of Tennessee at Martin, where he teaches U.S. and Latin American history. His books include *John Bell Hood and the Struggle for Atlanta* and *Soldier Princess: The Life and Legend of Agnes Salm-Salm in North America, 1861–1867*. He has contributed to seven major historical reference works and is an associate editor of the award-winning *Encyclopedia of the Vietnam War* and *Encyclopedia of American Military History*.